Black Texans

A History of African Americans In Texas

1528–1995

Second Edition

By
Alwyn Barr

RedRiver books

University of Oklahoma Press
Norman

Library of Congress Cataloging-in-Publication Data

Barr, Alwyn.
   Black Texans : a history of African Americans in
Texas, 1528–1995 / by Alwyn Barr. — 2nd ed.
      p.   cm.
   Originally published : Austin, Tex. : Jenkins Pub.
Co., 1973. Includes bibliographical references and
index.
   ISBN 0-8061-2878-X (alk. paper)
      1. Afro-Americans—Texas—History. 2. Texas—
History. I. Title.
E185.93.T4B37   1996
976.400496'073—dc20   96-23097
                                                  CIP

The paper in this book meets the guidelines for
permanence and durability of the Committee on
Production Guidelines for Book Longevity of the
Council on Library Resources, Inc. ⊗

2 3 4 5 6 7 8 9 10

Contents

Illustrations

Preface
to the
Second Edition

Black people have lived in Texas, though not continuously, for more than four hundred years—longer than in any other section of the United States—considerably longer than the dominant Anglo population of the state, as long as the Spanish ancestors of its Mexican Americans, and preceded only by the forebears of its few remaining American Indian citizens. The African-American population in Texas declined in percentage from a peak of about 30 percent, between 1860 and 1870, to 12 percent in 1990, but increased in actual numbers to more than two million. Thus the longer span of black history and the greater variety of African-American experiences under several flags, as well as the large number of individuals involved, suggest the value of a separate volume on black Texans.

This book is intended primarily to provide general readers with a summary of information about African Americans in Texas—much of it previously tucked away in scholarly journals and in relatively inaccessible unpublished theses and dissertations. Yet the book is more than a narrative of events, for I have sought to reinterpret some experiences of black Texans in the light of recent studies by scholars who specialize in black history or the history of race relations in the United States.

High school and college instructors in Texas history should find this volume of value because, in both factual material and interpretation, it supplements existing textbook treatments of African Americans in Texas. Recent texts are definite improvements over previous volumes and editions in their coverage of the role of black people in Texas. For lack of space, however, textbooks may not be able to include the kinds of detail and analysis that help clarify the complex African-American experience and why it differs from the general flow of Texas and United States history.

In the first edition of *Black Texans,* published in 1973, I used the terms "black" and "Negro," which were widely accepted at that time. The six original chapters are reprinted in this edition with that terminology. In this second edition the title, the preface, the new chapter on events from 1970 to 1995, and the supplement to the bibliography employ "black" and "African American," the most widely accepted terms in the 1990s.

Since the first edition of this book appeared, new studies have been published on several pre-1970 aspects of black history in Texas. General volumes that span the period include Ruthe Winegarten, *Black Texas Women: 150 Years of Trial and Triumph* (Austin, 1995); Alwyn Barr and Robert A. Calvert, eds., *Black Leaders: Texans for Their Times* (Austin, 1980); and Howard Beeth and Cary D. Wintz, eds., *Black Dixie: Afro-Texan History and Culture in Houston* (College Station, 1993). For more detailed discussions of both books and articles, see the chapters by Alwyn Barr in Light Townsend Cummins and Alvin R. Bailey Jr., eds., *A Guide to the History of Texas* (New York, 1988), and in Walter Buenger and Robert A. Calvert, eds., *Texas Through Time: Evolving Interpretations* (College Station, 1991).

For new studies of slaves and free blacks before the Civil War, see Randolph B. Campbell, *An Empire for Slavery: The Peculiar Institution in Texas* (Baton Rouge, 1989); Ron Tyler and Lawrence R. Murphy, eds., *The Slave Narratives of Texas* (Austin, 1974); and George R. Woolfolk, *The Free Negro in Texas, 1800–1860: A Study in Cultural Compromise* (Ann Arbor, 1976).

Recent accounts of events in the late nineteenth century are by James M. Smallwood, *Time of Hope, Time of Despair: Black Texans during Reconstruction* (Port Washington, 1981); Barry A. Crouch, *The Freedmen's Bureau and Black Texans* (Austin, 1992); Vernon McDaniel, *History of the Teachers State Association of Texas* (Washington, 1977); Michael R. Heintze, *Private Black Colleges in Texas, 1865–1954* (College Station, 1985); Merline Pitre, *Through Many Dangers, Toils and Snares: The Black Leadership of Texas, 1868–1900* (Austin, 1983); Gregg Cantrell, *Kenneth and John B. Rayner and the Limits of Southern Dissent* (Urbana, 1993); Patricia Smith Prather and Jane Clements Monday, *From Slave to Statesman: The Legacy of Joshua Houston, Servant to*

Sam Houston (Denton, 1993); and Kevin Mulroy, *Freedom on the Border: The Seminole Maroons in Florida, the Indian Territory, Coahuila, and Texas* (Lubbock, 1993).

On the early to mid-twentieth century, see William Brophy, "The Black Texan, 1900–1950: A Quantitative History" (Ph.D. dissertation: Vanderbilt University, 1974). Problems for African Americans in the military service are considered in Garna L. Christian, *Black Soldiers in Jim Crow Texas, 1899–1917* (College Station, 1995); and Robert V. Haynes, *A Night of Violence: The Houston Riot of 1917* (Baton Rouge, 1976).

For politics and civil rights in the twentieth century, see Darlene Clark Hine, *Black Victory: The Rise and Fall of the White Primary in Texas* (Millwood, 1979); James Farmer, *Lay Bare the Heart: An Autobiography of the Civil Rights Movement* (New York, 1985); Chandler Davidson, *Biracial Politics: Conflict and Coalition in the Metropolitan South* (Baton Rouge, 1972), for Houston; Joyce E. Williams, *Black Community Control: A Study of Transition in a Texas Ghetto* (New York, 1973); Jim Schutze, *The Accommodation: The Politics of Race in an American City* (Secaucus, 1986), for Dallas; Ira B. Bryant, *Barbara Charline Jordan: From the Ghetto to the Capitol* (Houston, 1977); and Barbara Jordan and Shelby Hearon, *Barbara Jordan: A Self Portrait* (Garden City, 1979). For economic and social events, see Eddie Stimpson Jr., *My Remembers: A Black Sharecropper's Recollections of the Depression* (Denton, 1995).

For education and sports in the twentieth century, see Randy Roberts, *Papa Jack: Jack Johnson and the Era of White Hopes* (New York, 1983); Richard Pennington, *Breaking the Ice: The Racial Integration of Southwest Conference Football* (Jefferson, N.C.,

1987); and Almetrius Marsh Duren and Louise Iscoe, *Overcoming: A History of Black Integration at the University of Texas at Austin* (Austin, 1979). Aspects of culture are discussed by Peter Gammond, *Scott Joplin and the Ragtime Era* (London, 1975); James Haskins and Kathleen Benson, *Scott Joplin* (Garden City, 1975); Alan Govenar and Benny Joseph, *The Early Years of Rhythm and Blues: Focus on Houston* (Houston, 1990); Robert M. Farnsworth, *Melvin B. Tolson, 1898–1961: Plain Talk and Poetic Prophecy* (Columbia, 1984); John Edward Weems, John Thomas Biggers, and Carroll Sims, *Black Art in Houston: The Texas Southern University Experience* (College Station, 1978); Lynne Adele, *Black History/Black Vision: The Visionary Image in Texas* (Austin, 1989); Gyen Alyn, *I Say Me for a Parable: The Oral Autobiography of Mance Lipscomb, Texas Bluesman* (New York, 1993); Doris L. Rich, *Queen Bess: Daredevil Aviator* (Washington, 1993); and Elizabeth A. H. Freydberg, *Bessie Coleman: The Brownskin Lady Bird* (Hamden, 1994).

This volume is based to some extent upon my own research, but primarily it rests on the works of other scholars that are discussed in the bibliographical essay, including a new section related to the new chapter. James Reese of Stephen F. Austin State University graciously read the first six chapters. Paul Lack of McMurry University, James Renberg of North Carolina, Lawrence Rice of the University of Southwestern Louisiana, Bruce Glasrud of California State University at Hayward, Neil Sapper of Amarillo College, and Robert A. Calvert of Texas A & M University each read and commented on specific chapters. Other historians, librarians, and interested persons too numerous to mention—for fear of forgetting someone—have assisted my efforts and enlightened me on various aspects of black history in

Texas. I wish to express appreciation to them and to absolve them of any blame for errors that may remain or for interpretations with which they may not agree. I gratefully acknowledge permission from the University of Chicago Press for several quotations from B. A. Botkin, ed., *Lay My Burden Down: A Folk History of Slavery* (Chicago, 1945); and from Alfred A. Knopf, Inc., for the quotation of a portion of a poem in Witter Bynner, *Take Away the Darkness* (New York, 1947).

Alwyn Barr
March 1996

1

Explorers and Settlers

A storm churned across the Gulf of Mexico in November, 1528, and thrust ashore on an island along the Texas coast two makeshift boats full of exhausted men. Among those survivors of a Spanish expedition to Florida under Pánfilo de Narváez one stood in marked contrast physically and historically. Estevan, a black Moor of Azamor in Morocco and the slave of another survivor, Captain Andres Dorantes, had become the first Negro to land in what would be Texas or the United States.

Winter and disease reduced the survivors to

sixteen by April, 1529, when most of them including Estevan crossed to the mainland. Indians soon captured and enslaved them for the next five years as ill-treated laborers. In September, 1534, the remaining four, Estevan, Dorantes, Alonzo de Castillo, and Cabeza de Vaca, escaped from the coastal Indians. They made their way inland where other Indians accepted them as medicine men and came in great numbers to exchange gifts for treatment. Estevan in the course of their hardships had become more a partner than a slave, especially because of his ability to learn Indian languages and signs. As the survivors continued westward in search of Spanish settlements he frequently acted as an emissary and diplomat with new groups of Indians. The four men eventually crossed the Rio Grande and passed through modern Chihuahua before locating Spanish settlements in Sonora during March, 1536.

From Sonora they traveled to Mexico City where Estevan joined his Spanish companions in at least one audience with the Viceroy, who sought unsuccessfully to buy him from Dorantes. Estevan agreed to remain in Mexico, however, and to guide an expedition north in search of the rich Indian cities of which he and his companions had heard during their wanderings. Estevan wisely chose greater freedom in a semi-independent status similar to his relationship with the other survivors, rather than a return to slave restrictions in the settled sections of Mexico or in Spain. As the guide for Fray Marcos de Niza in 1539 he ranged well ahead collecting an Indian retinue which irritated the austere priest. Yet he regularly sent back news and prepared the way until he reached the Zuni Indians in Arizona. Because he carried a foreign religious gourd rattle acquired from the Indians to the south and because he might lead invaders into their land the Zuni killed him. The priest immediately turned back, but Estevan had marked a route that Coronado would soon follow with an expedition composed partially of black men.

Later Spanish expeditions found people of African ancestry among the Indians at the mouth of the Rio Grande. They apparently had descended either from blacks in short-lived Spanish settlements there or from survivors of other shipwrecks along the Gulf Coast.

In 1691 a black bugler accompanied Domingo Teran on the second Spanish missionary expedition to the Indians of East Texas. When the Spanish established permanent settlements in Texas in the eighteenth century Negroes or men of mixed Afro-Spanish-Indian background formed part of the garrisons. Gil Antonio Ybarbo took a black weaver along to teach his trade to other settlers when Ybarbo established Bucareli on the Trinity River in 1776. San Antonio counted 151 "colored" people among its population of 2,060 a year later. By 1792 the province of Texas numbered 34 Negroes and 414 mulattoes in a total population of 2,992. They formed 15 per cent of the population, compared to 20 to 30 per cent in California. Some owned land and cattle. Others, such as Pedro Ramirez, worked on ranches near San Antonio. Most black people in Spanish Texas had been born in Texas or Mexico, but after 1803 an increasing number came from the United States. Felipe Elua, a black Louisiana Creole, bought his freedom and moved in 1807 to San Antonio where he owned houses and town lots and raised sugar, cotton, and vegetables outside the settlement. Others had escaped from slavery in Louisiana.

The flow of free Negroes into Texas

3

continued after Mexican independence. Several interracial couples moved to Texas to avoid the social pressure of more settled areas. John F. Webber, who founded Webberville near Austin, freed his slave wife and several children whose difficulty in acquiring an education caused him to move to Mexico in 1851. William Goyens came from North Carolina to settle near Nacogdoches about 1820, married a white woman from Georgia in 1832, and became a prominent blacksmith, freighter, innkeeper, and land speculator. Several mixed couples named Ashworth moved across the Sabine River into Texas from Louisiana. David Towns freed his slave wife Sophia and their children after they settled near Nacogdoches in the 1830's. Harriet Newell Sands came from Michigan in 1834 with her white common-law husband. Some free Negroes moved to Texas to be with their slave wives and children taken there by migrant slaveholders. Nelson Kavanaugh, a barber from Richmond, Kentucky, and others moved to avoid the restrictions on free blacks and possible reenslavement in the United States. A few like Thomas Morgan bought their freedom after arriving in Texas as slaves. Goyens and many others sought a better material life through the acquisition of land and wealth.

Most free black immigrants came as farmers like Emanuel J. Hardin of Brazoria County and Jean Baptiste Maturia of Nacogdoches in the 1820's. Others followed a variety of occupations. Robert Thompson became a rancher in Montgomery County during 1831. James Richardson sold oysters and refreshments between Velasco and San Luis on the coast. Greenbury Logan, a blacksmith from Missouri, reached Texas in 1831.

Some mulattoes sought with considerable success to pass the color line in frontier Texas. A slave pointed out two well dressed men among the whites at a dance in Bastrop as persons of African descent. Others felt no need to disguise their racial heritage. Both church and state under Spanish rule had taken official positions which restrained harsh treatment and promoted manumission of black slaves, though such laws frequently were ignored. Intermarriage among whites, blacks, and Indians in Mexico proved fairly common, since Spanish immigrants remained rather limited, and virtually eliminated Negroes as a separate ethnic group by the late eighteenth century. Thus Mexicans generally accepted black people, especially mulattoes, more readily than did the predominantly Anglo population across the Sabine. Clearly sparse frontier population and the greater acceptance by Mexicans, created more freedom of movement and opportunity for free Negroes in Texas than in the United States. Goyens paid a bribe to avoid enslavement in the 1820's before he officially established his free status. Thereafter he attended Mexican social events, acted as an arbitrator and attorney in the Mexican courts, and voted in a local election.

Because of the favorable legal and social conditions Benjamin Lundy, a white abolitionist, and Nicholas Drouett, a mulatto who had retired as an officer in the Mexican army, sought permission to establish a colony of free blacks from the United States in Texas during the 1830's. The Mexican government reacted favorably, but most whites in the United States and Texas opposed the project as an impediment to their westward movement. Most free Negroes in the United States also opposed it because of the cost of travel or

5

because they preferred to fight for their rights as citizens rather than emigrate. The idea died with the outbreak of fighting which led to the Texas Revolution.

Despite their advantages under Mexican laws and customs, several free blacks and a few slaves served in the Texas Revolution. Some probably supported the revolt because they shared Anglo-Texan feelings toward the Mexican government; others hoped to improve their status in Anglo eyes or feared retaliation if they failed to serve. Samuel McCullough may have been the first casualty of the revolution when he received an incapacitating shoulder wound during the Texas capture of the Mexican fort at Goliad in October, 1835. Texan commanders would not begin their attack on San Antonio in December, 1835, until Hendrick Arnold arrived to act as one of the three guides. In the assault Greenbury Logan suffered a disabling arm wound. Thomas Stephens, a slave, also served in the Texas army at San Antonio. Peter Allen, a musician in a Pennsylvania company died with James W. Fannin's command at Goliad in early 1836. John, a slave boy, died in the Alamo, though the Mexicans allowed Joe, the slave of William B. Travis, and Sam, the slave of James Bowie, to go free after the battle. James Richardson served with the Velasco garrison. Cary, the slave of Thomas F. McKinney, acted as a messenger during the revolution. Peter, the slave of Wyly Martin, won his freedom by freighting military supplies in his own wagon. Hendrick Arnold and Dick, a drummer, helped win Texas independence at San Jacinto in April, 1836, along with slaves James Robinson and Mark Smith. Some older black settlers with closer ties to Mexican society offered less active aid and avoided direct

6

military service against Mexican troops. William Goyens acted as an interpreter for Sam Houston in his negotiations with the East Texas Indians from 1835 to 1838. Robert Thompson and the Ashworths provided funds and supplies to the Texas cause. After the revolution Joe Griffin died in the defeat and capture of William Dawson's command by Mexican troops near San Antonio in September, 1842.

Despite the services of such men in the Texas cause, the end of Mexican rule quickly resulted in the first limitations on further immigration by free blacks to Texas and on the legal status of those already residing in the new republic. A few had been accused of threats against whites, which aroused fears they might instigate a slave revolt. But Anglo-Texan attitudes toward Negroes had been well developed long before the Texas Revolution. They represented the cumulative results of racial contacts for a period of over two hundred years. Englishmen and other Europeans employed Renaissance technological advances to thrust themselves ahead of Asian and African nations and to explore and lay claim to the Americas. Unlike southern Europeans such as the Spanish and Portuguese, the English came into contact with Africans without prior relations on a more equal technological basis. Englishmen then translated cultural differences in dress, manners, religion, and architecture, as well as the literary concepts of "black" as a synonym for evil and filth, into assumptions of African racial inferiority. Such views combined with demands for a large but cheap labor force in the British colonies of the seventeenth century to produce the rapid development of slavery as an institution for white economic advancement and control of race

7

relations. Black slavery continued to serve both functions in southern states in the early nineteenth century, which resulted in a restrictive environment for slaves that reinforced white stereotypes about Negroes. White Texans, overwhelmingly southern in background, brought with them favorable views of slavery and unfavorable views of black people.

Under republic laws free persons of one-eighth Negro blood could not vote, own property, testify in court against whites, or intermarry with them. The 1836 constitution required an appeal to Congress by free blacks who wished to reside in Texas. In 1837 Congress voted to allow all free Negroes in Texas at independence to remain if they continued to abide by the laws of the republic. Several pre-war black settlers then petitioned Congress for property rights and post-war immigrants requested approval of residence. Despite white supporting signatures on many of the petitions, Congress refused to pass any of the requests in 1838 and 1839. Yet the republic made little effort to enforce all its restrictions on free blacks who continued to hold their pre-war property. A trickle of immigration also continued, though knowledge of Texas laws in the United States apparently discouraged most potential migrants.

The Houston city council sought to act against free Negroes in 1839, however, through a temporary wartime act of 1836 and by adoption of a restrictive city ordinance. The local grand jury charged free blacks with being criminals, lazy, abolitionists, and bad influences on slaves, though little or no evidence could be produced to support the individual accusations. The next year Houston denied free Negroes and slaves the right to hold dances without the permission of the mayor. In 1840 Congress stiffened its views by adopting a law which required all free Negroes to leave Texas by January 1, 1842. President Sam Houston postponed the effective date, however, first to 1843 and then to 1845.

In December, 1840, Congress again granted pre-revolutionary free black residents the right to remain in Texas along with some relatives who came after the war. Finally in 1843 Congress conferred property rights on several black petitioners. It continued to refuse similar petitions from others, but most seem to have continued in control of their property despite local disputes and harassment. Some free Negroes avoided legal problems by having white friends appointed guardians of their persons and property. A few others legally indentured or sold themselves to whites to avoid deportation or imprisonment for debt, but continued to act as free men.

After annexation the state of Texas adopted even more elaborate restrictions on the life of free Negroes. For crimes they faced branding, whipping, pilloring, and forced labor on public works—punishments generally reserved for slaves rather than free men. Free Negroes could expect from twenty-five to a hundred lashes for insulting, abusive, or threatening language to whites. They could not have firearms, gamble, hire slaves, or dispense medicine, nor could they preach without two slaveholders as witnesses. Because of these limitations and continued opposition to their immigration, the free black population decreased from 397 in 1850 to 355 in 1860, though the census returns list as white a few free persons known to have been black. Manumission of slaves increased the free Negro population little. In populous Galveston County only nine slaves received their freedom between 1840 and 1860.

Most free Negroes sought a livelihood as farmers and agricultural laborers in East Texas from Nacogdoches to the Gulf Coast. Goyens held 12,423 acres and an estate of $11,917.60 when he died in 1856. Several stock raisers also lived along the coast from Sabine Pass south to Jackson County. The Ashworths of Jefferson County included several moderately wealthy landowners—one widow owned $11,444 in 1860—some of whom brought with them white wives from Louisiana and employed tutors for their children. Goyens and some of the Ashworths also bought and sold slaves, though they had reputations for kind treatment and may have purchased relatives or friends to improve their condition. Aaron Ashworth owned 2,570 cattle in 1850, the largest herd in the county. Despite their achievements the Ashworths faced random miscegenation suits and a vigilante order to leave the county in 1856 as part of a bloody local feud. Some members of the family moved temporarily to Louisiana but returned by 1860.

Free Negro artisans and servants settled more often in San Antonio, Brownsville, and Austin away from the plantation section, though some also lived in Galveston and Houston. They found employment as barbers, such as Henry Sigler of Galveston and Nelson Kavanaugh, Henry Tucker, and Peter Allen of Houston. Sigler also invented a simplified fish hook and sold the patent for $625. Peter Martin sold liquor and dabbled in town lots at Richmond. Mary Madison of Galveston acted as a nurse. Cary McKinney operated a livery stable in the same town. Another free black served as a dancing master and musician who played at many

10

Galveston social events. The free Negro wife of a white merchant kept a boarding house in Eagle Pass. Andrew Bell labored as a mason in San Antonio. Others worked as painters, tailors, seamstresses, engineers, dairymen, carpenters, blacksmiths, and teamsters.

Despite intermittent complaints against them only a few free blacks faced conviction for the rather mild crimes of selling liquor without a license, larceny, fighting, and interracial sex. At least two sued in court and won freedom from being held illegally as slaves. The British consuls in Galveston intervened on at least three occasions to keep black sailors from British colonies from being sold into slavery by unscrupulous sea captains. One consul aided the escape of a boy who had been frightened into signing a sixty-year indenture after being left in port. Four Negro sailors from Boston tried unsuccessfully to hide a runaway slave in Galveston in 1852 and faced sale into slavery, but abolitionists succeeded in buying and freeing them. In 1860 a local doctor judged as part Negro a Portuguese singer with a minstrel group. Authorities then hired out the singer for six months for illegal entry. The Houston city council became disturbed again in 1864 because Confederate officers employed thirty free black sailors captured at the battle of Galveston and allowed them considerable freedom in the town.

In the Spanish and Mexican periods Texas had been a haven of greater opportunity and better treatment for free Negroes. Especially for those years Frederick Jackson Turner's concept of the frontier as a "safety-valve" for persons who wished to escape the problems of the settled sections of the United States seems accurate when applied to free black pioneers in Texas. The dominant

11

attitude toward free Negroes changed, however, when the Texas Revolution brought to power Anglo-Americans who adopted restrictions on free black immigration. As a result, in 1850, five years after annexation, Texas ranked twenty-seventh of thirty-one states in white population, twelfth of fifteen slaveholding states in slave population, but thirtieth of thirty-one states in free black population. By 1860 Texas had advanced to twenty-first of thirty-four states in white population, to tenth in slave population, but had fallen to thirty-first in free Negro population, ahead of only Arkansas and the new states of Minnesota and Oregon.

White Texans also developed restrictions on free Negro participation in society. Yet frontier communities usually needed any skilled artisans available and the few free Negroes represented little threat to white labor; therefore whites made no apparent effort to restrict free black occupations. Nor did Texas deny them liquor as did some slave states. Texas had few public schools from which to exclude free blacks, but 60 to 70 per cent of the state's free Negroes achieved literacy although only twenty students in 1850 and eleven in 1860 could find teachers willing to educate them. Thus Texas laws did not extend as broadly as those of some slave states with larger free black population, but compared closely to those of other slave states and the free states along the Ohio River. They remained harsher than such laws in New England. Ironically the restrictions on free black immigration probably reduced Anglo pressure for greater discrimination and control and made life somewhat better for the few free Negroes already in Texas. Yet the haven of pre-revolutionary Texas clearly had disappeared.

2

Slaves

Negro slavery existed rather tenuously in Spanish Texas and never developed into a basic institution of the society. Three Frenchmen with two black slaves settled on the Trinity River to trade with Indians in 1751 but Spanish authorities arrested them and ended their venture. In 1783 the Spanish census of Texas listed thirty-six bondsmen in the entire territory. Slaves accompanied Philip Nolan on his horse hunting expeditions in the 1790's into Texas where Spanish troops killed him and captured his followers in 1801. When Spain returned Louisiana to France which then sold the healthy arrival of their bondsmen in Texas. Domestic slave traders used both water and land routes to further increase the slave population of Texas, though they operated illegally until the Texas revolution and did not become numerous until the late 1850's.

Anglo Texans brought in a few slaves illegally from the West Indies or directly from Africa. James Fannin smuggled in 153 from Cuba in 1833. Monroe Edwards landed 171 from the *Shenandoah* in 1836. As smaller numbers continued to arrive, the British consul estimated about 500 had been illegally imported during the 1830's. Some arrived "so enfeebled from close confinement that they could not travel," nearly destitute of clothes, with no knowledge of English, and fearful of their future. Although smugglers landed small groups as late as 1858, efforts in Texas and the South to re-open the external slave trade in the 1850's met opposition and produced no results.

Traders brought slaves to markets in Galveston, Houston, and lesser towns where auctioneers sold them to factors, planters, farmers, and some urban dwellers for prices ranging from $300 to $2,000, depending on the age, sex, and abilities of the slave and general economic conditions. Slaveholders put bondsmen on the block to pay off debts. While some owners sought to keep slave families together, others did not. Some sought to disguise the health and age of slaves, which resulted in intimate physical exams by prospective purchasers and left many slaves angered and frustrated by treatment similar to that awarded horses. High bids might bring a certain sense of pride to unattached young slaves. But many never forgot the moment when their masters separated them from parents, brothers, and sisters. Jeff Hamilton, who was thirteen at the time, recalled: "I stood on the slaveblock in the blazing sun for at least two hours. . . . my legs ached. My hunger had become almost unbearable. . . . I was filled with terror, and did not know what was to become of me. I had been crying for a long time."

Through these processes the slave population of Texas grew steadily from 443 owned by sixty-nine slaveholders in Austin's colony by 1825 to approximately 5,000 in 1836. In the rapid influx of settlers which followed the Texas Revolution, slaves increased to 11,323 in 1840, 58,161 owned by 7,747 slaveholders in 1850, and 182,566 owned by 21,878 slaveholders—about one out of four white families—in 1860. Texas ranked tenth in total slave population and ninth in percentage of slave population—30 per cent—on the eve of the Civil War. The average tax evaluation of Texas bondsmen rose from $326 in 1846 to $672 in 1860.

About 40 per cent of Texas slaves lived along the coast and in the East Texas river valleys where they labored in groups of from twenty up to 313 primarily as field hands on plantations to produce cotton, corn, and a limited amount of sugar in coastal counties below Houston. Arising early for breakfast they worked generally from 7:00 a.m. to 6:00 p.m. or sundown, with an hour off for lunch, Monday through Friday and Saturday morning. Field hands, both men and women, cultivated and harvested crops, cut wood, built fences, shelled corn, killed hogs and cattle, constructed roads, cleared land, and dug wells. An exceptional cotton picker might bring in 600 pounds in a day, though the average fell considerably lower. On plantations they labored in large gangs under the eye of the

17

planter, an overseer, or a slave foreman. Some planters preferred slave carpenters and blacksmiths over free labor because they could be more easily controlled. Other planters often employed white craftsmen to relieve most slaves for work in the fields. Planters who held more slaves than they personally could use hired out the remainder at $50 to $480 a year. A great demand existed for those skilled in sugar production. Feeble old slaves who could no longer labor in the fields received the duty of caring for slave children under the age of ten or twelve who were still too young for field tasks. From five or six years of age they might be called on to care for gardens, gather firewood, or tend cows, horses, and hogs.

Planters selected a few slaves to act as house servants—cooks, butlers, coachmen, nurses, and seamstresses. These individuals had some opportunity to develop personal relationships with their owners. Mariah Robinson recalled: "They's good to me and likes to make me the best-looking and neatest slave in that place. I had such as pretty starched dresses, and they help me fix the hair nice." Yet other house servants did their tasks without inspiration or care for, as one slaveholder admitted with insight, "Their time isn't any value to themselves," since they had little chance of freedom or advancement.

Slave quarters generally consisted of one or two room log cabins clustered near the house of the slaveholder. Planters spent from $20 a year up to $8.00 in some months on food for their slaves, whose diet included bread, molasses, beef, chicken, pork, sweet potatoes, hominy, and on occasion turkey, possum, and deer meat. Each spring and fall most field hands received two shirts, two pairs of pants, and a hat with a coat for winter weather, while women usually acquired two dresses at the same intervals. Slave women made clothes on some plantations; other planters paid $10 a year per person to clothe their bondsmen. House servants also received old clothes of their owners.

Slaves suffered from the same diseases and health problems that attacked white Texans—pneumonia, rheumatism, cramps, whooping cough, measles, smallpox, yellow fever, cholera, venereal diseases, and colds. Infants died at a high rate. Field hands collapsed of heat strokes. Some planters brought their slaves out of the river bottoms during the summer or in from the fields when the weather turned cold or rainy. Owners, overseers, and slave nurses treated illnesses, unless they became critical, with herbs, quinine, calomel, Epsom salts, castor oil, and a variety of pills. Medical costs varied, according to general health conditions, from $1.00 to $8.00 a year for each bondsman.

Half the slaves in Texas labored singly or in groups of less than twenty on smaller farms scattered from the Nueces River to the Red River and from the Louisiana border to the edge of settlement west of San Antonio, Austin, Waco, and Fort Worth. Their lives generally resembled those of plantation slaves. They probably faced a greater variety of daily tasks, but few acquired the skills of any particular craft or the status of domestic servants and slave foremen. Their clothes, living quarters, food, and medical care compared closely with those of plantation field hands. Yet some barriers of caste and class may have broken down at times to allow varying degrees of individual rapport with owners who sweated in the furrow alongside them.

Early Texas cattlemen along the Gulf coast

employed slaves as cowboys to herd cattle, sheep, and hogs, and to break horses. Some preferred white bronc riders, however, because of the potential monetary loss if a slave were killed at the dangerous task. Francis R. Lubbock, a Civil War governor of Texas, allowed Willis, one of his black cowboys, to acquire cattle and horses of his own while still a slave and later to buy freedom for himself and his family.

Before the Civil War slavery did not expand beyond the areas already described because of hostile Indians on the western frontier and the competition of cheap Mexican labor between the Nueces River and the Rio Grande. Yet the postwar use of black cowboys and seasonal farm laborers in West Texas raises serious doubts about the theory that slavery had reached its natural limits by 1860.

Neither labor, housing, diet, clothing, or medical problems set slaves wholly apart from white Texans of the period, for some slaveholders and many nonslaveholders lived similar lives especially when they first settled in the state. Yet the whites could hope to improve their own condition and create a brighter future for their children. Slaves with very few exceptions could only expect to repeat the same routine of hard work under limited living conditions throughout life and pass it on to their sons and daughters.

To produce the labor, the degree of control, and the subservient attitude they desired from slaves, all slaveholders resorted to various forms of discipline and punishment. One planter advised his overseer that "Negroes lack the motive of self-interest to make them careful and diligent, hence the necessity of great patience in the management of them." Yet most resorted to whipping. Even pregnant women at times felt the lash. One slave received 300 lashes in three days for assault. An overseer cut another slave with a knife in addition to whipping him. Even most slaveholders who prided themselves on kind treatment employed whips and irons, handcuffs, or jails at times to punish escape attempts and "impudence." Owners used dogs to hunt runaways and one let a dog attack a slave accused of stealing plums. Another slaveholder branded a slave boy for an attempted assault. Bondsmen who killed whites faced swift hanging. Whites who attacked or mistreated slaves generally went free since slaves could not testify against them in court. The courts did convict at least four non-slaveholders for mistreatment of slaves owned by other whites. But for slaveholders the only restraint was the limited fear that brutal treatment of bondsmen might become widely known and reduce the owner's social standing. For the death of a slave one judge did require the slaveholder to post a $5,000 bond.

To help control slaves the state or local communities adopted laws which forbade them to have liquor or weapons, to sell agricultural products, and to hire their own time or be hired by free Negroes. Counties created patrols to restrict to their plantations slaves without passes from their owners and to break up any secret slave assemblies.

Slaveholders also sought through time off and limited concessions to promote hard work and greater acceptance by slaves of their status. Saturday afternoon, Sunday, and holidays at the end of harvest time, Christmas, New Year's day, after planting, and on July 4 served that purpose. On such occasions and at night slaves might be allowed to dance, sing, rest, fish, and hunt. Some planters offered rewards for the best cotton picker, allowed bondsmen to raise vegetables, tobacco, cotton, chickens, hogs, and corn, and let them sell their products to purchase clothes or tobacco. Mothers with small babies generally received lighter tasks for the first month after giving birth.

Slaveholders read the Bible to their slaves, brought them to sit in a segregated section of the white church, or in a few cases organized separate meetings or churches on some large plantations. Methodists, Baptists, Catholics, Episcopalians, Presbyterians, and Disciples of Christ all accepted slave members. Baptists and Methodists appointed missionaries to the slaves. By 1860 Methodists claimed 7,451 bondsmen as members in Texas. Slaves assisted in the construction of some churches. Some slaveholders felt an honest concern for the souls of their bondsmen. Most hoped that an emphasis on the afterlife would ease slaves' concern over their present conditions, or the emotional release of participatory religion would ease the day-to-day frustrations of slavery. Both white and black ministers preached to slave congregations under the watchful eyes of owners. Methodist Homer Thrall spoke for most white preachers when he said, "Slavery is not only innocent but scriptural and right and...it is our imperative duty to protect and perpetuate this institution as a blessing to both races" because "a state of bondage is the normal state of the African race." Anderson Edwards, a slave preacher, followed the advice of his master to "tell them niggers iffen they obeys the master they goes to Heaven; but I knowed there's something better for them but daren't tell them 'cept on the sly. That I done lots. I tells 'em iffen they keeps praying, the Lord will set 'em free." Slave ministers such as Edwards often held secret services in the woods at night, despite slaveholder opposition, and exercised considerable influence among bondsmen.

On some occasions slave owners provided the religious formality of marriage for their bondsmen, though it had no legal basis. Slave couples who did not face separation by their owner remained together or parted on the basis of their practical interests and personal feelings. Owners looked favorably on female slaves who had large families and frowned on unattached young slave women. Not all female slaves readily accepted their master's views. Rose Williams held out with a fire poker for two days before accepting the man her master expected her to take as a husband. A few slaveholders required young men to live with more than one woman in the hope of producing more children. The freedom exercised by some slaveholders and overseers to have sexual relations with female slaves produced tremendous bitterness, humiliation, and frustration for many slave women and their husbands because of their helplessness to resist. Family life remained tenuous at best for slaves whose husband or wife lived on another plantation. All faced the possibility of separation by sale. Yet many developed deep affections and strong marital and family ties.

Although Texas had no law against the education of slaves as did most southern states, opposition to their instruction produced a black population over 95 per cent illiterate at the end of the Civil War. Some planters did educate personal servants or craftsmen who in turn taught others. But only 2 per cent of the newspaper advertisements for runaway slaves attributed to them the ability to read and write.

White Texans drew sharp lines between themselves and black slaves by subjecting the bondsmen to different and harsher punishments, and by limiting their freedom of movement and assembly, their means of self defense, the nature of their religion, the stability of their family life, and their opportunity for education. The impact of these restrictions varied from one slaveholder to another. Some planters and farmers showed a paternalistic concern for the basic physical comfort of their slaves and some flexibility and restraint in exercising their authority over bondsmen, but only within the general bounds of the caste system. Such limitations produced black reactions which ranged from bitterness and frustration to self doubt and resignation as slaves watched whites enjoy the opportunities and control over their individual lives which were denied bondsmen.

The vast majority of slaves in Texas lived in rural areas, but over a thousand resided in both Galveston and Houston by 1860 with several hundred in Austin, San Antonio, and other large towns. The number of urban slaves in Texas continued to grow in the 1850's, unlike the situation in major southern cities to the east. Business and professional men held most town bondsmen, though some craftsmen also owned slaves. Many urban slaves labored as house servants. Others worked on farms at the edge of town. Lesser numbers acted as cooks and waiters in hotels, teamsters, coachmen, blacksmiths, carpenters, bricklayers, barbers, and boatmen on steamers. A few labored in flour mills, sawmills, brickyards, implement and utensil factories, and in the construction crews for railroads and buildings. Some slaveholders hired out their bondsmen or allowed them to hire out their own services, though most towns passed laws against self-hiring. At times their presence stirred white laborers to protest "being put in competition with Negro Mechanicks."

City laws, which also called for patrols and ruled assemblies, the possession of liquor or weapons, and separate housing illegal for slaves, received only sporadic enforcement. Urban slaves frequently lived apart from their owners, held separate dances and meetings attended by some nonslaveholding whites and Mexicans, moved about towns rather freely, and kept guns and knives. On weekends and at night they hunted, drank, attended minstrel shows and circuses, and gambled like their white counterparts. Some refused to remove their hats and talked back to whites on the streets. While the life of urban slaves compared generally to that of rural bondsmen in diet, clothing, housing, and forms of punishment, they clearly enjoyed greater freedoms, variety, and opportunity than the far more numerous agricultural slaves. Yet their reactions remained mixed, for while most sought to protect their advantages and avoid being sent to the country, some became more restive and frustrated as their status approached but still did not approximate freedom.

Though most urban slaveholders did not overly concern themselves with loose enforcement of slave codes and the greater activities of their bondsmen, some newspaper editors and other citizens exhibited reoccurring worries over the issue. They criticized slave owners, law enforcement and town officials, and the public in general for failures to act more vigorously in controlling the situation. Yet only rumors of slave revolt aroused support for their demands for action. Then city councils readily adopted new laws and official and unofficial groups enforced old

purposes. Others stretched grape vines across roads at night to throw white slave patrols from their horses. More than one slave attacked or poisoned slaveholders, despite the assurance of hanging if caught.

Large numbers of slaves ran away. Some sought to avoid punishment, excessive labor, or the withdrawal of special privileges such as hiring their own time by escaping into nearby woods or swamps. There they hid for days, weeks, or even months, showing themselves at times to enhance their status among the remaining slaves who often smuggled them food and other necessities. Some eventually returned, but if they met harsh punishment many left a second time. Others remained in hiding until emancipation. One young mulatto woman escaped and registered at a hotel in Brenham before her owner discovered her. Still other runaways sought husbands, wives, or families from whom they had been separated. A few left cruel masters to seek out old owners who had treated them better. Occasionally a slave enhanced his own status by guiding whites to the hiding place of a runaway.

Many slaves aimed at complete escape from slaveholding territory into the North, among Indians, or into Mexico. Because of the distance involved less followed the North Star than other routes to freedom. A few secretly boarded ships along the coast bound for northern or foreign ports.

Some runaway slaves in the 1820's and 1830's lived with the East Texas Indian tribes, who generally treated them better than whites did though not as complete equals. Escaped slaves fought with the Cherokees against the Texan army which drove that tribe from East Texas in 1838.

Most slaves fought with their owners against the Comanches, who usually killed or captured slaves along with whites in raids and later sold the Negroes to Cherokees and Creeks in the Indian Territory. A few joined the plains Indians and rose to positions of prominence because their knowledge of white society made them useful as translators in planning and directing raids. In 1850 John and Rye, armed with a musket and a rifle, led an escape from Smith County into the Indian Territory. With them went Rachael, though several months pregnant, and five children ranging in age from twelve to two and a half years.

Mexico became the most attractive goal for Texas runaways after the Texas Revolution. Several escaped to Matamoros during the fighting in 1836. A band of slaves killed the sheriff of Gonzales when he tried to stop them near Victoria and continued on toward the Rio Grande. Over thirty reached Matamoros in 1844. The next year twenty-five slaves left Bastrop armed and on horseback, though pursuers captured seventeen on the Guadalupe River. Six more headed for Mexico from near Waco in 1845 with a herd of twenty-five horses. Some slaves from the lower South also sought freedom in Mexico by crossing Texas while it remained sparsely settled up to 1845. Wild Cat, a Seminole Indian chief, led a band of over one hundred and fifty Indians and Negroes from the Indian Territory into Mexico in 1849. The Mexican government accepted them as a possible barrier to raids by plains Indians and allowed them to settle along the Rio Grande near Eagle Pass. There Wild Cat welcomed black recruits from Texas and the Indian Territory. Some died trying to cross the rather barren region between the Nueces and the Rio Grande, inhabited by Indians, panthers, wolves, and snakes. Yet by 1851 an estimated 3,000 slaves had made good their escape into Mexico. Another 1,000 reached that haven from the "peculiar institution" between 1851 and 1855.

Most runaways went in groups of two to five persons, though many escaped alone. They fled from all parts of the state—counties on the Red River and on the Nueces, on the coast and on the frontier. Men formed 90 per cent of the runaways, since they had greater opportunities and chances of success. Escaped slaves ranged in age from five months to sixty years, but the vast majority fell in the twenty to forty age group who could best stand the physical and psychological strain of making lengthy night marches, hiding in woods or thickets during the day, and worrying over possible recapture. Field hands constituted an overwhelming majority of the runaways, though domestic servants, artisans, and preachers also joined the flight from slavery. Some took advantage of temporary passes to begin their escape undetected. Others posed as free Negroes or as white men. Several escaped armed and mounted. One wore a silk cap and carried an umbrella and overcoat, though most were not well dressed. Escapes took place in all seasons of the year, with winter slightly more popular and spring somewhat less attractive. Those facts suggest that the spring and fall periods of hard labor may have deadened thoughts of freedom to some extent, while less arduous summer and winter months left a little more opportunity to consider flight. Slaveholders described the runaways in terms ranging from impudent, surly, and cunning to affable, polite, and resolute, which suggests that escape depended more on opportunity and external motivation than on personality or outward adjustment to slavery. A few received limited assistance in their escapes from poor Mexicans and a minute number of Anglos or Germans.

In Mexico ex-slaves faced difficulties until they learned Spanish. A settlement of poor English-speaking Negroes developed on the Rio Grande near Eagle Pass. Others mastered the language and became a part of Mexican society as servants, artisans, teamsters, and laborers. Some married into Mexican families.

Texas slaveholders expressed concern over the flight of their bondsmen as early as 1836 when they sent representatives to Matamoros in an unsuccessful effort to reclaim runaways. From 1849 to 1860 Texans urged the United States government to negotiate an extradition treaty with Mexico which would apply to slaves. The United States army did receive orders to halt escaped slaves. Texas officials and private groups offered rewards which averaged $127, although they ranged from $10 to $1,200 according to the value of the bondsman or the threat he might pose to white society. They also commissioned slave hunters who in some cases crossed into Mexico illegally to recapture ex-bondsmen. Four hundred Texans joined the revolt of José María Jesus Carvajal in northern Mexico during 1851 because he promised them any runaways they captured and assured them his Republic of Sierra Madre would return escaped slaves. Negroes with Wild Cat helped Mexico defeat the revolt.

An increased flow of escaped slaves into Mexico during the early 1850's stirred the slaveholders of San Antonio and neighboring towns to hold several meetings, in 1854 and 1855, where they collected $20,000 for an expedition to recapture runaways. After attempts at private negotiations with Mexican officials failed, slave-holders sent James H. Callahan with 130 men to attack Wild Cat and his followers. In October, 1855, they crossed the Rio Grande near Eagle Pass, but a combined Mexican-Indian-Negro force drove them back into Piedras Negras which they partially burned to cover their retreat. Though the expedition failed, the citizens of Piedras Negras returned at least one escaped slave to avoid similar invasions. In the late 1850's Sam Houston and other Texans suggested a United States protectorate over Mexico, which in part would relieve their continuing problem of runaway slaves.

White Texans feared more than individual violence or escapes the threat of a slave revolt, which the legislature defined as "an assemblage of three or more, with arms, with intent to obtain their liberty by force." When the Texas Revolution began in the fall of 1835 whites defeated and severely punished almost a hundred slaves who participated in an uprising along the Brazos, stimulated by rumors of approaching Mexican troops. A few runaways served with the Mexican forces. Two escaped slaves died fighting with Vicente Cordova, who led Negroes, Mexicans, and Indians in an abortive counter revolt against the Texas republic in 1838. Texas troops executed one black prisoner and resold another into slavery. Other runaways served under Antonio Canales in his unsuccessful effort to establish the Republic of the Rio Grande in 1840.

White settlers around San Augustine became extremely uneasy about a possible revolt when numerous signs of discontent appeared in 1841. Two slaves poisoned their owner. Others rode horses and held dances at night without permission. In September, 1856, Anglos in

Colorado County announced the discovery of an insurrection plan which involved over two hundred slaves armed with pistols and knives. They apparently intended to kill anyone who opposed them, seize supplies, and escape into Mexico. One slave leader escaped, but two were hanged and the other participants whipped. Anglos drove out of the county several Mexicans and one Anglo accused of aiding the would-be rebels. Whites in Lavaca, De Witt, and Victoria counties believed they uncovered during November a similar plan in which killing all dogs in the area represented the first step. A man from Ohio named Davidson received a hundred lashes as one of three whites accused of being abolitionists connected with the revolt.

In July and August, 1860, a series of fires swept North, Central, and East Texas towns. Amidst high tension following John Brown's raid in 1859, white Texans imprisoned and questioned hundreds of suspected slaves. Several confessed to various forms of a plot supposedly led by white abolitionists who sought to avenge Brown's execution. The plan as described in Texas newspapers aimed at control of Texas trade, religion, and education by northerners who would arrange for the escape of slaves to the North. The abolitionists presumably would rise to power after slaves poisoned their owners and burned existing arms and food supplies. Whites discovered some weapons, powder, and poison in the possession of slaves. They seized white ministers of the northern Methodist church, "tavern keepers," druggists, a wagonmaker, a blacksmith, and two salesmen as possible instigators of the revolt. Before fears and tension subsided as many as eighty slaves and thirty-seven whites may have met execution.

declaration of causes repeatedly proclaimed, white Texans seceded in 1861, primarily to defend "the servitude of the African to the white race."

Slavery in Texas continued through the Civil War in much the same form it had existed prior to the conflict. Slave prices remained high until the last months when defeat became inevitable for the Confederacy. As Federal armies occupied portions of Arkansas and Louisiana many slaveholders from those states moved their bondsmen into Texas to avoid individual runaways or the possible loss of their entire slave force. Probably 250,000 slaves lived in Texas by 1865.

A few personal servants went to war with their owners. To construct earthworks for defense of the Texas coast and to drive military supply wagons Confederate officers called on slaveholders for slave labor. When many owners refused or delayed, the army temporarily impressed one-fourth the slaves on each plantation. Some slaveholders hid their slaves from the army and urged those already impressed to return home. Several did escape, though most probably did not go back to their owners.

The Texas legislature, local governments, and private groups tightened laws and local practices to restrict slave escapes, revolts, or assistance to the Union. Slaves could not operate farms or ranches without white supervision or own and sell property, though more received overseers' responsibilities. Patrols rode more often and any man convicted of providing arms to slaves faced two to five years in the penitentiary at hard labor. Preaching to bondsmen stopped in many areas to avoid large meetings of slaves. Runaways from owners continued, however, with a few more heading north as Federal troops advanced into

Arkansas and the Indian Territory. Unlike slaves in states partially occupied by northern armies, Texas bondsmen could not easily reach Federal lines and only forty-seven enlisted in the Union army. But they followed the course of the war as best they could with at least a general understanding of its importance for them. When a white minister asked one group to raise their hands if they wanted to pray for a southern victory, William Adams recalled: "We all raised our hands 'cause we was scared not to, but we sure didn't want the South to win."

In later years some ex-slaves such as James Smith remembered that: "My folks always said the best time of they lives was on the old plantation." But Martin Johnson, another former bondsmen cautioned:

> Lots of old slaves closes the door before they tell the truth about their days of slavery. When the door is open, they tell how kind their masters was and how rosy it all was. You can't blame them for this, because they had plenty of early discipline making them cautious about saying anything uncomplimentary about their masters. . . . However, I can tell you the life of the average slave was not rosy. They were dealt out plenty of cruel suffering.

H. C. Smith probably spoke for a majority in 1867 when he said: "Freedom, in poverty and in trials and tribulations, even amidst the most cruel prejudices, is sweeter than the best fed or the best clothed slavery in the world." Margrett Nillin agreed sixty years later:

37

What I likes best, to be slave or free?
Well, it's this way. In slavery I owns
nothing and never owns nothing. In
freedom I's own the home and raise the
family. All that cause me worriment, and
in slavery I has no worriment, but I takes
the freedom.

3

Freedmen

Freedom arrived officially for black Texans on June 19, 1865, when Federal troops landed at Galveston. Emancipation actually came as Union troops spread out over the state or as individual slaveholders accepted the results of the war and freed their bondsmen. Some East Texas newspaper editors in the summer of 1865 urged slaveholders to maintain control over their slaves and opposed ratification of the Thirteenth Amendment, which abolished slavery, because the editors hoped for gradual emancipation and compulsory labor. Some slaveholders continued to hold their slaves well into the fall of 1865.

When the word finally came, black reactions varied widely depending on the slave and his personal background. On some plantations the immediate departure of most freedmen reflected their negative views of slavery under that particular owner. Over half the slaves left before Harriett Robinson's former master even finished his offer of continued labor for wages. Austin Grant believed, "There wasn't but one family left with" his ex-slaveholder, "the rest was just like birds, they just flew." "Everybody went wild," recalled Felix Haywood. "We was free. Just like that, we was free. . . . Nobody took our homes away, but right off colored folks started on the move. They seemed to want to get closer to freedom, so they'd know what it was." Certainly freedom seemed unreal for many until they left the farm or plantation where they had labored and found that no one forced them to return. Some sought better employers or land of their own to farm. Others satisfied their curiosity about towns and stayed to enjoy the greater religious, social, and educational opportunities of urban life. An ex-Confederate officer explained: "The freedmen are more willing to work in cities, because they can there secure better protection to their persons. . ." Still others sought husbands, wives, children, and other relatives who had been separated from them under slavery. Some ex-slaves from Arkansas and Louisiana returned to the areas of those states where they had friends and relatives. Since few slaves had been able to acquire any possessions while in bondage, many like Anna Miller left with "nothing on 'cept old rags."

Better treated slaves and those with less knowledge of the world, felt more tentative about freedom, " 'cause they don't know where to go," as Andrew Goodman explained; therefore on some plantations, many "just stay on for hands on the old place." At least a few former slaveholders gave their ex-bondsmen small plots of land or helped them find farms to purchase with savings or on time.

After the initial moments of joy, fear, searching, and confusion as slavery ended, came a longer period of groping to establish a new status for black people. The "reconstruction" of politics, economics, education, and social life for black Texans lasted about eight years.

Politics, Violence, and Legal Status

If white Texans reluctantly accepted the end of slavery, they generally did not change their view of black people as inferior. Newspapers used the term "nigger," compared freedmen to apes, and published articles emphasizing "white" as a synonym for purity and innocence and "black" as a substitute for wickedness and death. The ex-Confederate majority constantly opposed the extension of social or political rights and equality to Negroes, though some former Unionists at least considered the possibility. Confusion existed in the fall of 1865 over what General Gordon Granger, the commander of federal troops in Texas, meant when he proclaimed "equality of personal rights and right of property" for freedmen. Some Texas courts allowed Negroes to testify in cases which involved them or their property, though most whites, because of their racial views, regarded black testimony as unreliable. Other judges accepted Negro testimony only against other freedmen. "It seem like the white people can't git over us being free," recalled Allen Manning, "and they do

41

everything to hold us down all the time."

When an all white state constitutional convention met in early 1866 to write a new constitution which would define the new status of black men, one delegate conceded "them nothing but the station of 'hewers of wood and drawers of water.'" Another urged "that the permanent preservation of the white race being the paramount object of the people of Texas," the legislature should be allowed to remove all Negroes in the state. The convention ignored that idea and showed some further restraint because of northern criticism directed at other southern state constitutions already completed. It accepted the end of slavery and granted property rights to freedmen. Yet the delegates allowed black testimony only in court cases involving Negroes and required separate cars on railroads. The convention also refused to extend the suffrage to even literate Negroes, despite varying appeals from German Unionist Edward Degener, Provisional Governor A. J. Hamilton, and John H. Reagan, former postmaster general of the Confederacy who became aware of northern opinion while in a federal prison. The first legislature elected under the new constitution prohibited intermarriage, voting, officeholding, and jury service by freedmen. Local custom followed the same general pattern in 1866, as hotels and theaters segregated their customers or refused admission to black people.

With no means of presenting testimony in court or voting on local officials to ensure equal legal protection, Negroes faced a constant threat of violence. Orange Bray defended himself with an ax when his former master tried to whip him for protesting the lashes given his wife for insolence.

The ex-slaveholder shot Bray and a Lamar County jury then sentenced the freedman to several years in the penitentiary while his former owner went free. Lucy Grimes refused to whip her small child for playing with money her employer left lying about the house. Two white men then beat her to death in a nearby woods. The United States army fined another white man $100 for shooting a black woman he considered impudent. John Wesley Hardin and other Texas gunfighters made their early reputations as "nigger killers." When armed Negroes gathered at Millican in July, 1868, because of rumors that a black man had been lynched, the white sheriff led two attacks on the group and may have killed as many as twenty-five freedmen before the army arrived to restore order. Similar events erupted at Hempstead and at Cedar Creek in Bastrop County.

Between 1865 and 1868, 468 freedmen met violent deaths — 90 per cent at the hands of white men. Negroes killed only about 1 per cent of the 509 whites murdered during the same period. Certainly some of the violence resulted from the frontier nature of Texas society. But the figures indicate strong racial overtones in many of the deaths. White intimidation of black people for social and economic reasons proved quite effective under such circumstances. But it also strengthened the cause of northern Republicans who sought to wrest control of Reconstruction from President Andrew Johnson in part to guarantee greater legal protection to freedmen.

The Freedmen's Bureau, a federal agency, and the army intervened in some cases to arrest white criminals ignored by civil courts for lack of white testimony and to seek the release of Negroes such as Bray who had been convicted on questionable charges or evidence. At times bureau and military officers became over zealous in their efforts by transferring cases to military courts before civil courts had a chance to administer justice or show bias. Negro troops in one cased lynched the accused murderer of a black man because they had little faith in white civil courts. Yet white Democrats protested most bureau and army actions, regardless of their merits, because they reduced white control over freedmen. Racial prejudice made freedmen's trials in the civil courts "worse than a farce" in the judgement of the Freedmen's Bureau commander who most planters respected as generally fair in his efforts.

In March, 1867, the Republican majority in Congress began to pass, over President Johnson's veto, a series of acts which divided the ten former Confederate states that refused to ratify the Fourteenth Amendment into five districts with military commanders. The acts also called for the enfranchisement of black men and the creation of new state constitutions which would accept the Fourteenth Amendment protection of equal civil rights. Despite some federal restrictions on voting and officeholding by ex-Confederates and charges of registration irregularities, the Galveston *News* estimated that four out of five white men in Texas could qualify. Black Texans began to develop political awareness and to seek political rights that spring with the organization in Austin, San Antonio, and Galveston of the Loyal Union League. G. T. Ruby, a northern Negro newspaper reporter and educator who had come to Texas from Louisiana to work with freedmen's schools, helped establish and guide the league. "An educated man" with "a very neat and genteel appearance" who proved "a ready debater," Ruby quickly became one of the most prominent black politicians in Texas. Final figures showed that 56,678 whites and 47,581 Negroes had registered.

Upset by the new course of events, white Democratic newspapers complained that freedmen had become "insolent and swaggering, puffed up with new and indigestible theories of equality, the most intolerable of created beings." Yet Republican papers criticized the continued difficulty of convicting any white men for crimes against Negroes. General Charles Griffin, the first military commander of Texas under the Reconstruction Acts, tried to correct the court situation by removing from the jury lists persons who could not take the loyalty oath and by adding black people. James W. Throckmorton, the Democratic governor of Texas, objected to both acts. Because the governor also differed with Griffin and his superior, Philip Sheridan, on other interpretations of the first Reconstruction act concerning the operation of the courts and the registration of voters, General Sheridan replaced Throckmorton in July, 1867, with E. M. Pease. A pre-Civil War governor and Unionist, Pease had been defeated for governor in 1866 by Throckmorton and in 1867 presided at the first Republican convention in Texas. President Johnson in August replaced Sheridan with General W. S. Hancock, whose sympathy for white Democratic views brought him into sharp conflict with Pease over lawlessness and law enforcement in Texas.

The Loyal League actively sought to develop black support for the Republican party in the February, 1868, election to decide if a new constitutional convention should be called and to elect delegates. To disarm and intimidate freedmen away from the polls or into the Democratic camp, and in a few cases to kill black and white Republican leaders, white Texans created autonomous chapters of the Ku Klux Klan. Though both organizations remained secret to some extent, they differed markedly in methods. The League generally informed freedmen of Republican views and voting procedures, while the Klan used threats and violence to accomplish its ends. The vast majority of Negro voters logically chose the Republican party because it had fought for emancipation and for civil and political rights for black people with the Democratic party generally in opposition. Negroes formed a majority of the delegates at the first Republican state convention in Houston during July, 1867, where Ruby served as a vice-president. A few freedmen voted or spoke for the Democrats who promised them jobs, food, and "protection."

Texans called a new constitutional convention by a vote of 44,689 to 11,440, and elected delegates including nine Negroes in February, 1868. Most white voters refused to vote in protest against military rule and in the hope that the convention would be ruled illegal if it did not receive support from a majority of registered voters.

In the Republican dominated convention some black delegates favored restrictions on voting by ex-Confederates. Others opposed any limitations on suffrage and the convention ultimately wrote voting provisions similar to the Fourteenth Amendment. Ruby, the leading Negro spokesman, offered resolutions against voter intimidation and bribery, but the convention tabled them. Another black delegate B. F. Williams presented a resolution that public places with state licenses be open to all citizens. It too failed. When the Republicans split in 1868 between "conservative" A. J. Hamilton and "radical" E. J. Davis, an ex-Unionist and federal general, most black delegates backed Davis, who gave stronger support to equal rights. In debates over a proposal to divide Texas into two or three states some "conservatives" argued that "radicals" hoped to create at least one black state with integrated schools. Yet the Negro delegates favored division by a narrow five to four margin. Tension among the delegates generated several verbal and physical conflicts including a fight between Ruby and a white Republican also from Galveston. Later Ruby and two other Negro delegates resigned in protest over confusion and conflict in the convention. But Ruby and C. W. Bryant, another young black delegate to the convention, joined eight white "radicals" in Washington during the spring of 1869 to lobby unsuccessfully for postponement of a ratification vote on the final draft of the state constitution. Although the new constitution did not include all provisions black leaders favored, it did reject legal discrimination and ensure free public schools for all students.

In the spring and summer of 1869 Ruby and Richard Allen, an ex-slave and Houston contractor, played prominent roles in two "radical" conventions which nominated Davis for governor in the fall election. Ruby also chaired the "radical" convention in his congressional district. Scipio McKee, a Negro sergeant-at-arms of the 1868-1869 convention, who had fought with Ruby while holding that office, became one of the few black speakers for Hamilton in the gubernatorial race. Davis, supported by the vast majority of Texas freedmen, won a narrow victory. The "radicals" also elected a majority to the Twelfth Legislature which included Ruby and Matt Gaines, a minister and former slave with a powerful oratorical style, in the senate and nine other Negroes in the house. Most black representatives came from counties with a high percentage of Negro population along the coast, the Brazos and Colorado rivers, and in Northeast Texas. Negroes also won election to some county and town offices across the state.

Ruby served on several senate committees and exerted considerable influence within the party in the distribution of patronage. He introduced a number of bills important to his Galveston constituents, to state economic development, and to the creation of a state militia. During some absences of the lieutenant governor, he presided over the senate. Gaines offered bills relating to education, aid to the insane, and restraints on bribery and fraud. Both men supported an education bill which allowed local districts to choose between integrated or segregated schools, though Gaines expressed personal opposition to separate facilities. Black members of the house offered resolutions in support of public schools and equal rights for all citizens. They generally showed themselves attentive to the broad interests of their districts and the specific hopes of freedmen for equal treatment.

Among its several acts the Twelfth Legislature in 1870 passed bills creating the State Police and a state militia to control the violence and crime prevalent in Texas. The acceptance of Negro members by both organizations aroused great hostility among white Democrats. Probably black men formed 40 percent of the State Police and a majority of the militia. State policemen made over 7,000 arrests and recovered $200,000 in property in four years. But most white Texans, raised amidst fears of slave revolts, saw these organizations only as armed Negroes who also opposed Klan activity and guarded voting places during elections. Some individual policemen, black and white, proved unfit and lost their positions on the force, but a number of others proved themselves good officers and some died while trying to enforce the law. Most Republicans and even some Democrats did appreciate the efforts of the State Police.

Davis called out the militia only under crisis conditions. Militia came to the support of state policemen who met armed white resistence while seeking the murderers of Negroes in Hill and Walker counties in 1871. Militiamen restored order after white riots against the State Police in Madisonville in 1870 and Limestone and Freestone counties in 1871. When Democrats gained control of the legislature in 1873 they reduced the governor's control over the militia and replaced the State Police with the Texas Rangers. Since the Rangers included several white former State Police but no Negroes, racial bias clearly helped stimulate opposition toward the integrated State Police and militia.

Black federal troops also served in Texas during Reconstruction as part of the forces attempting to protect and pacify the border and frontier regions. When Indians killed Negro frontiersman Brit Johnson while he was hauling supplies from Weatherford to Fort Griffin, as well as many white settlers, their deaths provided proof of the need for government action. The 9th United States Cavalry garrisoned the border forts along the Rio Grande from 1867 into the 1870's, supported after 1868 by the 24th and 25th United States Infantry—all three composed of Negroes whom the

Indians called "buffalo soldiers," a term of respect. The infantry built roads and forts, strung telegraph lines, escorted wagon trains, and guarded army posts. Cavalrymen patrolled for Indian raiders and for Mexican and Anglo border bandits. They also protected mail riders, stage routes, and cattle drives. Though spread too thin to stop all raids, they defeated Indians at Fort Lancaster in 1867, in the Santiago Mountains in 1868, on the Brazos River twice in 1869, and in the Guadalupe Mountains in 1870. In the early 1870's they captured Mexican revolutionaries and drove border bandits into Mexico on several occasions. Sergeant Emanuel Stance won the Congressional Medal of Honor for leading a small detachment which recaptured stolen horses and defended a wagon train against Indians in 1870. The 10th United States Cavalry, also Negro, in 1871 captured the Kiowa chiefs who had led raids from the Indian Territory into Texas. In 1873 several companies garrisoned forts on the Northwest Texas frontier where they recovered 1,200 stolen horses and cattle in four months.

Despite their service, the black soldiers met a variety of prejudices from white soldiers and settlers near their posts. They often faced harsher punishment than white troops for minor offenses and received poorer food and other supplies. Seldom did they get justice in local courts, where juries frequently allowed white murderers of Negro troopers to go free while imposing stiff penalties for any transgressions by the 'Buffalo soldiers." The black regiments maintained the lowest desertion rate in the army in spite of such treatment, because military service provided a steady income and a sense of respect often difficult to retain in civilian life.

While black troops defended the frontier some Negro politicians fought for greater influence in the Republican party which relied primarily on black votes for its success. "The white men here say that if we put a colored man in the field the Radicals will lose the race. That is just as good as to say that they will not go with us," charged Matt Gaines, who believed the party should nominate a Negro for the United States Senate or House, or for lieutenant governor. He also noted the failure of some "radicals" to put up bond money for freedmen elected to local offices. At the Republican state convention in June, 1872, Gaines urged that delegates who supported the civil rights bill then under debate in Congress be selected to the national Republican convention. Ruby, Allen, and Williams won three of the sixteen places in that delegation. In the 1872 state elections the number of black representatives fell to six. Democratic control of both houses in the new legislature reduced the influence and effectiveness of Negro legislators including Ruby and Gaines who continued in the senate.

A Colored Men's Convention met in Brenham on July 3 and 4, 1873, presided over by Norris Wright Cuney, an educated black politician and protégé of Ruby. The delegates hoped to promote "good feelings between ourselves and our white fellowcitizens" by agreeing "that a man's social relations cannot be made by legislative enactments. . . But we do demand our Civil Rights Bill of the Hon. Charles Sumner," which guaranteed equal access to public accommodations, transportation, and recreation facilities such as hotels, railroads, theaters, schools, and cemeteries. The convention then endorsed the Grant administration and the national Republican party for their efforts to protect civil rights.

At the Republican state convention in August black delegates pressed for nomination of a Negro as lieutenant governor. Ruby and Cuney received votes for the honor but lost. The convention then selected Ruby as chairman of the state executive committee during the upcoming campaign for state offices. In the election that followed most freedmen voted Republican in spite of physical intimidation from the Klan, economic coercion from Democratic employers and landowners, and threats of legal suits for delinquent taxes in some counties with Democratic officials. Democrats charged intimidation by the Loyal League against Negro Democrats. But heavy white immigration from other southern states in the early 1870's had created a clear white majority which defeated E. J. Davis in his bid for reelection 85,548 votes to 42,663. Davis with support of a black militia company held a portion of the state capitol in January, 1874, after the state supreme court ruled the election invalid. They left peacefully, however, when Grant refused to sustain their action. Political Reconstruction, the first period of black participation as voters, office holders, and public servants, had come to an end. A former Democratic governor hailed the Republican defeat as "the restoration of white supremacy and Democratic rule."

Labor and Economic Status

Throughout the Civil War in Texas there had been little disruption of the economy from Federal invasion. For economic reasons most white planters and farmers sought to maintain as nearly as possible the control they exercised over black laborers under slavery. Many refused to hire ex-slaves without favorable certificates from former owners—a policy aimed at reducing movement from one location to another. Some also felt a paternalistic concern for the freedmen based on an assumption that Negroes could not care for themselves. Few understood the numerous and varied causes which stirred their ex-slaves to leave the plantations either permanently or temporarily. Whites blamed such movement on racial traits or evil designs of northern troops and demanded army assistance to control laborers. Yet many black people, in addition to numerous personal reasons, left because they could not get acceptable contracts from planters. Others departed only after harvest time in the fall.

Freedmen met less than warm receptions in most towns, despite some demand for domestic servants. City officials designated any freedmen without jobs as vagrants and required them to repair streets or railroads, though many came seeking work or relatives. Federal troops often cooperated by driving Negro migrants away from Galveston and other military posts or by forcing them to cut wood or perform other jobs for the army. Provisional Governor Hamilton urged planters and freedmen to make one year contracts to establish a wage labor system. Military commanders generally took similar positions, required that black people have passes from their employers to travel, and informed planters if their ex-slaves appeared at military posts. General C. C. Andrews at Houston ordered in July, 1865, that "holidays must be put off until the crops are gathered," and insisted that freedmen "remain on the plantations with their former masters." Despite proclamations of emancipation it seemed to many Negroes that the army primarily served the interests of white employers and enforced a condition little different than slavery.

The Freedmen's Bureau began operations in Texas during September, 1865, under General E. M. Gregory. In the fall he toured the state and ordered his agents to see that black people received justice in their legal dealings with whites. He also directed the agents to require Negroes to work and to register contracts with the bureau. Many freedmen hoped to acquire farms from the government because the bureau controlled abandoned lands in some southern states. Thousands of acres along the Atlantic coast and in the Mississippi River valley had been sold or leased to ex-slaves during the war. Some Republicans in Congress hoped to confiscate or purchase additional acres in the South and make it as well as the remaining public lands available to Negroes. But the bureau held no abandoned property in Texas, because federal forces had occupied little of the state during the Civil War. The federal government owned no other land in the state since Texas had retained its public lands upon admission to the Union in 1845. Congress failed to acquire new land for distribution to freedmen. The *Harrison County Flag* denounced even the sale of land to black people as treason to the white race. Since rumors placed the land transfer at Christmas, despite announcements to the contrary by military and civil authorities, Negro hopes of homesteads from government land died only with the new year. Thereafter some black agricultural workers asked for their wages in the form of land.

In November the Freedmen's Bureau issued model contracts which called for a ten hour day, Monday through Friday, and labor on Saturday morning in return for quarters, fuel, food, medical care, land for a garden, and monthly wages. Actual pay per month ranged from $2.00 to $15.00 with $2.00 to $5.00 most common. Some planters added a rest period at noon or Wednesday afternoon off and prizes to attract and keep black laborers. One established a school for freedmen and their children. Many black laborers refused to sign new contracts with their employers in late 1865 because some landowners had paid off their white creditors first and failed to fulfill their labor agreements that year. Negroes in large numbers sought planters who would agree to share-cropping contracts which allowed the cropper greater supervision of his own time and the right to live away from the landowner. Such arrangements widened a bit further the differences between slavery and freedom. Contracts varied from one-tenth to one-third of the crop for the cropper, with one-fourth the usual division. Planters generally provided food, clothing, and medicine.

Landowners complained of broken contracts, theft, "insolence," poor care of animals, and less work than under slavery. In many cases, however, both parties broke contracts and theft became a means of recovering unpaid wages. Various acts of defiance or refusal to obey orders represented assertions of freedom which carried great psychological value to the ex-slaves. Some planters enticed Negroes to break contracts and change jobs. Other landowners blamed the Freedmen's Bureau for letting black people move about and assert their freedom which, in the eyes of whites accustomed to complete control over Negroes, became racial hostility. Planters also disliked the bureau because it provided relief to freedmen hit by natural disaster and because it enforced labor contracts, since both might give black workers some greater opportunity to choose employers and to demand higher wages.

Opposition to Gregory caused President Johnson to replace him with General J. B. Kiddoo in April, 1866. The new bureau chief issued orders for fines against planters and laborers who broke contracts and sent out his agents to require that black laborers make new contracts. Since the thirty-five agents in 1866 included ten planters and one former Confederate colonel, planters generally found their actions more acceptable. In the summer Kiddoo did announce that unpaid wages would be considered liens against crops.

When the state legislature met in the fall of 1866 it enacted a Black Code which included several labor laws. They placed a lien on one-half of a planter's crop to cover wages, allowed contracts to be broken because of harsh treatment, and required the recording of advances to laborers if they were to be liens on wages. But most provisions of the act clearly favored employers. Contracts bound entire families, and youths fourteen to twenty-one years old could be apprenticed if the parents agreed or if they could not support the child. Broken contracts resulted in loss of pay; wages could be reduced by the employer for sickness, failure to labor to his satisfaction, or damage to equipment. Employees could be fined for refusing to obey orders, impudence, swearing, quarrelling, or fighting. They could not leave the plantation or have visitors during working hours without permission. Anyone without a job or means of support could be arrested and fined or forced to labor on public projects at $1.00 a day until the fine was paid. Though based in part on labor, vagrancy, and apprenticeship laws used also in the North, the codes left employers so much discretion and control that conditions under them in some ways would approximate slavery. Kiddoo continued to require elaborate labor contracts with copies filed at bureau offices, but he nullified the more unfair aspects of the code in early 1867. General Charles Griffin, who replaced Kiddoo in 1867, initially allowed the apprenticeship and vagrancy laws to be enforced, but later decided they were being arbitrarily used against freedmen and halted their use.

Some planters tried to organize on the county level to control wages. To develop unity among Negro laborers, Jeremiah J. Hamilton, a black leader who later served in the legislature, called a meeting at Bastrop in December, 1866. Apparently neither effort met much success. A number of planters and state officials sought white southern and immigrant labor to replace Negro workers. Many southern and foreign laborers came to Texas in the late 1860's and early 1870's, but most wanted land of their own and only a minority accepted positions as farm workers or tenants. Matt Gaines, the Negro state senator, favored the promotion of immigration, but urged that agents be sent also to Africa. He received little backing for his views. Other landowners opposed the use of white labor as harder to control. Still others tried to replace black workers with labor saving machines and diversified crops. The Klan used violence and fear to force Negro labor at low wages in a number of East Texas counties. A few planters sent agents to bring more freedmen from other southern states. Despite all efforts to replace or control them as laborers and the different types of contracts offered in the late 1860's, the vast majority of ex-slaves settled down to become sharecroppers or tenant farmers by 1870 and a few had saved enough to buy their own farms.

Most black Texans remained in some type of farming after emancipation, but some became cowboys on Texas ranches and with trail drives which originated in the state. They acted as ropers, cooks, bronc riders, and horse wranglers. Probably Negroes formed one-fourth or one-fifth of the cowboys on drives to Kansas railheads. They shared both the responsibilities and the foibles of their occupation. Ex-slave Ike Word became the best roper on the Charles Word ranch near Goliad. Bose Ikard herded cattle, fought Indians, and guarded money for Charles Goodnight in West Texas. A black cook got drunk when his drive reached Abilene and shot up the town. He became the first occupant of a new town jail and its first escapee when the cowboys from his herd broke him out. Felix Haywood and his father rounded up unbranded cattle along the San Antonio River for a white rancher who payed them in land and a share of the herd. Punching cattle had its attractions for freedmen since they faced less prejudice in such a predominantly male, highly mobile society. A few developed herds of their own, especially by rounding up unbranded cattle in South Texas. Not many, however, could hope to acquire land or even become foremen. For easy identification whites often added the term "Nigger" to the names of black cowboys, such as "Nigger Frank" and "Nigger Add."

An increasing number of black people moved to towns to find non-agricultural positions. In addition to politicians, policemen, and soldiers, Negroes worked as coachmen, butchers, railroad workers, and laundry employees. A few operated small stores and organized musical bands. Many women worked as domestic servants, though some husbands who could support their families wanted their wives to remain at home with their children as a mark of emancipation. In San Antonio during 1870, 63 per cent of the black males worked as unskilled laborers, porters, and servants. Ten per cent served in semi-skilled positions such as teamsters, hack drivers, cart drivers, and hostlers. Twenty-three per cent obtained their livelihood as skilled artisans—carpenters, wheelwrights, stone masons, barbers, blacksmiths, painters, plasterers, and cooks. Only 4 per cent found employment in professions such as policemen, ministers, and teachers. Unskilled, semi-skilled, and skilled laborers formed 90 per cent of Mexican-American males, 68 per cent among European immigrants, and 56 per cent among native whites. Only 14 per cent of the black males in San Antonio owned property, which averaged $288 per person, compared to figures of $3,000 to $1,686 for native whites, immigrants, and Mexican-Americans. Negroes thus fell at the bottom of the socio-economic ladder, somewhat below Mexican-Americans and well behind native whites and immigrants. While figures are unavailable for other Texas towns, these statistics suggest the general condition of urban freedmen.

Black laborers faced opposition from white artisans in some trades who feared that black competition might cost them jobs or reduce wages. Most white union members agreed with the laborer who told a Galveston meeting of the International Workingmen's Association in 1872, if "the colored man is to be taken into full fellowship in this society, socially and politically, I must decline to become a member." The Screwmen's Benevolent Association of Galveston considered but rejected

Negro membership on more than one occasion after its creation in 1866. In response black longshoremen organized their own benevolent association in 1870. Texas freedmen sent delegates to the National Labor Convention of Colored Men at Washington in December, 1869. The Laborers Union Association of the State of Texas invited white and black workers to its meeting at Houston in June, 1871. That same year the National Labor Union (Colored) established a branch in Houston. Yet only a few integrated or black unions could be counted among the limited number of weak unions which existed in Texas during Reconstruction.

In the open frontier society of Texas some freedmen joined their white counterparts in activities beyond the bounds of law. Black prostitutes existed in most of the larger towns. A few Negroes became professional outlaws such as Merrick Trammel who operated in Limestone County until killed in 1875.

In the late 1860's and early 1870's a small minority of Texas freedmen found possibilities to save money and to acquire farms or small businesses. But the vast majority of black Texans could not overcome the variety of racial restrictions, either by law or custom, which kept them rural or urban laborers with limited skills and opportunities for advancement.

Education

Freedmen's Bureau officials made the first efforts toward organized education for black people after emancipation. Gregory appointed Lieutenant E. M. Wheelock, a Unitarian minister from New England, as superintendent of bureau schools. He established the first school at Galveston in September, 1865. Houston had a Negro school in an African Methodist church by

October. By January, 1866, the bureau had created in Texas ten day and six night schools with twenty teachers and 1,041 pupils including many adults. The program continued to expand that spring and reached an early peak in May and June of 100 schools, including Sunday schools, taught by sixty-five instructors and attended by 4,769 students. Almost all existed in towns where they had military protection. Negroes had exhibited a strong desire for education by seeking out or helping to establish bureau schools which they supported with $.25 to $.50 tuitions at different times despite the limitations on their movement and economic conditions.

A cholera epidemic in South Texas during the summer caused a decline to 1,679 pupils in day and night schools by September. The 1866 Texas constitution allowed separate black schools. But it authorized for their maintenance only the taxes paid by Negroes who with little property and low salaries could support only a few institutions in urban areas. The legislature which met the same year did little to promote the idea, though the Texas Teachers' Convention urged white southern aid to educate the black man so he would "understand his duties and his privileges as a freedman." Clearly they had in mind an education which would adapt Negroes to continued white control. Most white Texans because of their racial views assumed black people could acquire only a limited "industrial education" and feared any broader instruction especially if taught by persons with different racial attitudes. To enforce their views most white Texans refused to teach in Freedmen's Bureau schools and would not rent rooms to or associate with northern teachers or other bureau officers. Many also refused to sell or rent land or buildings for the schools. Some opponents burned a few bureau schools, and insulted, tarred and feathered, beat, and even killed some teachers.

Yet in 1867 bureau schools revived through continued black support and an agreement with the Congregationalist American Missionary Society to provide more teachers and aid in establishing more schools. The bureau also sought black teachers from the North, from a Negro regiment stationed at Brownsville, and from within the state. From eight to forty-eight black instructors served the bureau schools in Texas at different times. Kiddoo increased attendance 400 per cent in Galveston and Houston by abolishing the tuition. The number of Texas day schools grew to fifty-five with fifty-three teachers and 2,975 students in July, with another 2,182 pupils in Sunday schools. Then malaria struck killing dozens of children and three teachers during the summer. General J. J. Reynolds, military commander of Texas in the fall of 1867, hurt the school system further by ending bureau payment of teachers' salaries which forced an increase in tuition to $1.00 for the first pupil in each family, $.75 each for two, and $.67 each for three. By January, 1868, bureau day schools reached a low of thirty-four with thirty-two teachers and 1,133 students, though 909 pupils attended twelve Sunday schools.

Freedmen's Bureau schools began their third expansion in 1868 under the direction of Joseph Welch, who replaced Wheelock. Despite continued problems of health and harassment the bureau reached new peaks with ninety-five day and night schools and 4,188 students in the summer of 1869. Planters even provided land for schools in four instances. After a winter decline the bureau conducted sixty-six schools with 3,248 pupils in July, 1870, before orders came to phase out or transfer the schools to state control. Bureau schools generally existed in rough frame buildings with log desks and benches. Some even had tent ceilings. Black churches housed some classes and by 1870 a few brick buildings had been constructed or purchased. The curriculum consisted of reading, writing, arithmetic, geography, and needlework with Bible stories used frequently to teach grammar. Teachers conducted examinations' at the end of each term which were open to parents and public.

Wheelock resigned from the bureau in 1867 to become state superintendent of public instruction when offered the position by Provisional Governor E. M. Pease. Wheelock took as his major task the presentation to the constitutional convention in 1868 of a plan for a free public school system. He proposed a state board of education and a state superintendent of schools to conduct a system of common schools divided into districts by the legislature and open at least four months a year. It would be available to all children, five to eighteen, regardless of race with compulsory attendance unless they enrolled in a private school. The convention accepted the basic plan and provided for its support the use of funds from the sale of public land, up to one-fourth of state tax revenues, a $1.00 poll tax, and local taxes. The Republican majority in the Twelfth Legislature created the system and taxes authorized for its maintenance in the constitution. These laws allowed local boards to decide whether schools would separate black and white children. Segregation became the uniform practice despite some Negro opposition.

Separation failed to silence white Democratic critics of the new public school system. They attacked control by the state board and superintendent over school construction, teacher selection, and the courses of study. Many believed it to be too costly and some refused to pay taxes for its support. Others disliked the northern teachers and the state superintendent Jacob C. DeGress, a German immigrant and former sub-assistant commissioner of the Freedmen's Bureau. Still others opposed compulsory attendance as undemocratic and a threat to private schools. Perhaps as pervasive as any criticism, however, remained the fear of black education because it might make Negroes harder to control and because the federal government might require integrated schools. Yet despite strong opposition Texas public schools taught 129,542 pupils—56 per cent of all school age children in the state—during the 1872-1873 school year. Black students formed about one-fourth to one-third of that number. When Democrats gained control of the legislature in 1873 and decentralized the system, attendance fell to 102,688 pupils, or 38 per cent of all possible students, in 1873-1874.

In 1872 the African Methodist Episcopal Church in Austin founded Paul Quinn College, which began as an elementary and secondary school and later moved to Waco. The black Texas Conference of the Methodist Episcopal Church established in Marshall during 1873 Wiley, the first college level institution for Negroes west of the Mississippi.

Illiteracy among freedmen over ten years of age in Texas fell from over 95 per cent in 1865 to 89 per cent in 1870 and to 75 per cent in 1880, primarily as a result of Freedmen's Bureau schools of the late 1860's and the public school system instituted by the Republicans in the early 1870's. Yet Allen Manning, who was fifteen in 1865, spoke for many other black people when he recalled that in his section of the state, "We don't git no schools for a long time, and I never see the inside of a school," during Reconstruction.

Social Life

In rural areas black social life simply expanded upon patterns that existed before emancipation. Men hunted and fished at night and on weekends. Freedmen held dances and church services on weekends, except in cases of revivals which lasted at times for up to two weeks. Separate Negro towns or villages developed in some rural areas, especially where land became available for several black families. Kendleton in Fort Bend County and Board House in Blanco County had been established by 1870. Black people created at least thirty-nine separate communities in fifteen Texas counties at different times to allow themselves greater control of local political, economic, and social life away from constant white domination.

A more diverse social life developed in Texas towns where Negroes celebrated holidays such as Juneteenth—Texas emancipation day in June—with parades, dances, barbecues, and political speeches. Urban black people organized social, fraternal, and debating clubs, bands, and baseball teams. Freedmen's fire and militia companies also served social as well as civic purposes.

The number of black urban dwellers increased sharply between 1860 and 1870. The percentage of Negro population in Galveston grew from 16 to 22 percent, in San Antonio from 7 to 16 per cent, and in Houston from 22 to 39 per cent. Complete residential segregation did not exist immediately in 1870. Wards in San Antonio ranged from 12 to 19 per cent black, in Galveston from 9 to 29 per cent, and in Houston from 24 to 51 per cent. Yet those figures suggest trends toward segregation in some parts of Galveston and Houston. They also obscure the development of all-black sections which overlapped ward boundaries. Others existed just outside the city limits. Freedomtown, an area of poor Negro shacks, grew up on the outer edge of the Fourth Ward in Houston. Pleasant Hill east of Waller Creek in Austin consisted of both houses and tents. Governor E. M. Pease gave land to his ex-slaves who formed the Clarksville black enclave in West Austin. In such areas health problems with cholera and smallpox remained a constant threat because of poor housing, food, and sanitation.

Religion took on new dimensions among black people after emancipation. Ex-slave members of predominantly white churches generally left to form separate congregations with Negro or northern white ministers. At least one group in Austin continued to hold services in the basement of the white church they had attended as slaves, however, until they received payment for the labor they had contributed to its construction. These actions stemmed from a desire by freedmen for greater control over their own religious life and from increased white hostility toward integrated services with black people they no longer controlled. The Klan in some areas threatened both white ministers and freedmen who tried to continue the old pattern.

In rural areas several Negro denominations used the same building on alternate Sundays, despite their sometimes heated doctrinal differences. Black churches became focal points for social, educational, and political activities. They also provided an opportunity for the development of Negro civic and political leaders even before voting rights had been granted to freedmen. From such a background came men like Meshack Roberts, an ex-slave blacksmith and Methodist lay leader who represented Harrison County for three terms in the state legislature during the 1870's. A greater freedom of expression and participation existed in black churches, whose services generally resembled a revival atmosphere.

Black Baptists and Methodists formed an overwhelming majority among Texas Negroes because the familiar evangelical style of those denominations appealed most strongly to freedmen. The Methodist Episcopal Church—the northern branch of Methodism after the church divided in 1845—organized in December, 1865, the Mississippi Mission Conference which included all black Methodist Episcopal churches in Mississippi, Louisiana, and Texas. At Trinity Methodist Church in Houston during 1867 all Negro Methodist Episcopal congregations in the state met to organize the Texas Conference which grew to 7,934 members with fifty ministers by 1871. Black ministers of the African Methodist Episcopal Church began to establish congregations in Texas during 1866 and claimed 3,000 members within two years. Two white ministers organized the Colorado Colored Conference of the Methodist Protestant Church in 1868. The Methodist Episcopal Church, South, found that it had only 3,269 black members by 1866. When the number continued to decline, the white southern Methodists helped organize the Colored Methodist Episcopal Church in 1870 to create a black

Methodist denomination which was not controlled by northern Methodists.

Black Baptists grew even more rapidly in numbers because of the autonomy granted each local congregation, which matched Negro desires to avoid white dominance. I. S. Campbell, a black minister from the Midwest, organized the first Negro Baptist church in Texas at Galveston in 1865. White Baptists continued to open their services to freedmen in some areas and many opposed separate churches fearing a lack of qualified black ministers. As Negro members steadily left white congregations to hold their own meetings, white Baptist associations began to accept separate churches, "since they never have been, and, we presume, never will be, permitted to exercise equal rights, immunities and privileges with the white members of the church." Some white ministers preached to separate black and white congregations through 1867. Associations of Negro Baptist churches organized in 1868. By 1869 the vast majority of black Baptists attended separate congregations.

The Episcopal Church in Texas lost most of its ex-slave members, though Sunday schools for freedmen existed through the late 1860's at Independence, San Antonio, and Jefferson. Two Negro evangelists held a Church of Christ meeting at Circleville in 1867 and a congregation developed in Waco by 1872. Presbyterian churches ordained a few black ministers in the early 1870's and retained the attendance of a few Negroes including G. T. Ruby. Yet most religious freedmen clearly became Methodists or Baptists.

In response to white hostility and control, during and after slavery, black Texans developed their own social and religious groups and institutions during Reconstruction as did freedmen throughout the North before the Civil War and the South after emancipation.

Some white Texans suggested that Reconstruction had heightened racial tensions because of Republican attempts to guarantee freedmen basic economic, political, and educational opportunities and rights. Verbal and violent expressions of racial hostility did increase because Negroes felt more freedom to protest past and present wrongs, which stimulated most whites to stronger efforts to maintain and defend white control over freedmen. Only black acceptance of continued subordination could have produced less tension. Yet whites who looked with horror on any hint of "Negro domination" could not, because of their assumptions of racial superiority, understand black opposition to "white supremacy."

Though actual Reconstruction in Texas lasted only eight years, it provided freedmen with voting rights and some experience in officeholding. They also acquired the greater autonomy of sharecropping which included some hope of savings for the purchase of land. More black workers found urban jobs; yet they remained generally unskilled and in many cases faced discrimination. Public education through the Freedmen's Bureau and the state began to reduce Negro illiteracy. Freedmen created their own social and religious organizations which allowed them real freedom of expression and an opportunity to develop leaders.

Despite white violence and discrimination Texas freedmen found some hope and at least limited advances during Reconstruction. The future seemed clouded as this time of promise and progress slipped away.

4

Voters
and
Laborers

Politics, Violence, and Legal Status

The end of Reconstruction did not halt black political participation in Texas, though it resulted in a lessening of Negro involvement and influence. Legal segregation began to revive during the late nineteenth century, preceded or accompanied frequently by discrimination through custom. Sporadic violence against Negroes continued with black subordination as its goal.

White Democrats called a new constitutional convention in 1875 to write a new document which reflected their views better than the Republican constitution of 1869. The five Negroes who served in the convention fought for strong school provisions including the creation of a black land grant college. They helped defeat the requirement of a poll tax for voting with the aid of white Republicans and Grangers who feared it would hurt poor whites too and might result in a loss of seats in Congress under the Fourteenth Amendment. But they could not turn back white demands for required school segregation. Gerrymanders of predominantly black counties reduced but did not eliminate the chances of Negro or Republican legislators and judges. Black Texans, who preferred the 1869 constitution, voted overwhelmingly against the new document to no avail. Yet most historians and political scientists of the twentieth century judge the 1869 constitution superior to its 1875 successor, which severely restricted the governor and legislature and forced numerous amendments in the years to come.

Negro Republicans faced perplexing decisions in the late nineteenth century. Because they formed only 25 per cent of the population by 1880, the chances of victory over the white Democratic majority remained dim. For black politicians three choices existed. They could seek greater control over policy and patronage within the Republican party; they could join or attempt "fusion" with dissident Democratic factions or third parties; or they could, by the 1890's, support the Democratic party in an effort to influence its policies. Negro leaders tried each approach at different times with varying degrees of success.

In the late 1870's the primarily white "conservative" faction of the Republican party controlled federal patronage through better ties to the Hayes administration. In a key move the "conservatives" ousted N. W. Cuney from his position in the Galveston customshouse. Yet the larger and predominantly black "radical" wing continued to support E. J. Davis who won election as national committeeman in 1876.

The Greenback party began to organize in Texas during 1877 as a national depression drove farm prices down and the federal government prepared to resume full payments for greenbacks which would hurt debtors. Black delegates appeared in the earliest third party meetings and represented seventy Greenback clubs for Negroes at the state convention in 1878. In addition to their economic program, Greenbackers appealed for black votes by calling for a better public school system. Davis threw his support behind the third party and successfully urged the Republican convention to forego nominations for state office and back the Greenback candidates in 1878. The "conservative" faction refused to accept that decision and nominated candidates including for lieutenant governor Richard Allen, the Negro customs inspector for the port of Houston. Democrats compared the Greenback clubs to the Loyal League. Greenback candidates, who ran second in the state races, divided the Negro votes rather evenly with the dissident Republican nominees, who ran third. But Democratic candidates swept to victory by a two to one margin. Greenback and Republican votes did send nine black representatives to the legislature where they helped defeat a poll tax measure when the Democratic majority divided on the issue.

In an effort to promote harmony in the Republican party and to gain control of federal patronage the Davis faction agreed to a separate

Republican ticket, instead of fusion, in 1880. With Davis as their gubernatorial candidate, the Republicans recaptured most black votes and moved ahead of the Greenbackers, though the Democrats again won all state contests. Davis, with national Republican support, led a second fusion effort with Greenbackers in 1882 behind an Independent gubernatorial candidate who ran well but failed to break Democratic control of state offices. Black legislators declined to five by 1881 and to two by 1883. Democrats used white fears of black domination against all Negro or Negro-supported candidates, though economic, social, and personal issues also weighed in the minds of the white majority who voted against both Greenbackers and Independents.

After the death of E. J. Davis in 1883 black politicians expanded their influence and power in the Republican party to more clearly reflect the fact that Negroes formed 90 per cent of its membership. Cuney and Allen became two of the four delegates-at-large to the national convention in 1884, where Cuney led a majority of the Texas delegates in support of presidential nominee James G. Blaine. When the state convention under Cuney's leadership again voted to back Independent candidates on the state level, the "conservative" faction once more broke ranks to put forward its own nominees who ran a weak third. The dissident effort stemmed from a desire to control federal patronage and opposition to black leadership. At the state convention in 1886 Cuney won election as national committeeman for Texas, which clearly established him as the most powerful black or Republican politician in the state. He did temporarily reunite the party, which again became the major opposition for Democrats as third party sentiments faded in 1886. Republican nominees lost, as they usually did, by a three to one margin.

Unity collapsed in 1888 when Cuney led the majority in support of non-partisan-prohibition candidates, while some white Republicans voted the Democratic ticket which easily prevailed. When Benjamin Harrison won the presidency, Cuney, despite stiff white Republican opposition, became customs inspector at Galveston with control over other customs appointments. But white Republicans controlled justice department appointments in North Texas and shared justice and internal revenue departments appointments in other parts of the state. White Republican clubs organized in North Texas and in all urban areas, although an early effort in Houston failed to develop a separate "lily white" branch of the party.

Racial divisions among Texas Republicans caused them to advise Harrison both for and against the Lodge bill which would allow federal supervision to guarantee fair federal elections. White Republican clubs opposed the Lodge bill and contested, unsuccessfully in most cases, for the seats of several mixed delegations at the 1890 state convention. With Cuney clearly in control of the state organization, "lily whites" held a separate meeting to make "war against negro domination," but could not find a candidate for governor. In the hope of attracting more white southern support to the Republican party, "lily whites" chose separate nominees for state offices in 1892 and sought, without success, seats at the national convention. Cuney continued as national committeeman and agreed to throw Republican support to conservative Democrat George Clark in a race against progressive Democrat James Hogg and a Populist nominee. The black Republican leader hoped to divide the dominant Democrats and increase his personal and party influence in state politics.

Hogg won about half the black votes in his successful bid for reelection because of his concern, however paternalistic, over issues such as education and lynching. Yet some of his white backers rallied traditional Democratic support with cries against "Clark, Cuney, and the Coons." Clark probably won 30 per cent of the Negro votes and the Populists 20 per cent. The "lily whites" polled only 1,300 votes, or less than 1 per cent of those cast.

Efforts to reconcile Republican factions failed in 1894 when "lily whites" demanded control of the party despite their minute electoral base. Populists won over an increasing number of black voters through the capable work at the state and local levels by eloquent Negro organizers such as J. B. Rayner and promises of better education, equal political and legal rights, and economic improvement in the midst of a depression. Yet third party leaders did not advocate social equality and received strong support from some West Texas counties which opposed black settlers. Populists attracted about 35 per cent of the Negro voters in 1894, while the regular Republican nominee with Cuney's support carried 50 per cent. Despite their decline from first to third in black votes Democrats again won the state races. "Lily whites" increased their vote to 5,300, about 1 per cent of the total, but still trailed all major candidates.

A three way struggle developed in the Republican state convention of 1896 between those who supported William McKinley for president, Cuney who favored William B. Allison, and William M. "Gooseneck Bill" McDonald, a black teacher and fraternal leader, who led the backers of Thomas B. Reed. The meeting selected a combination of Reed-Allison delegates to the national convention. But the McKinley men, who had, unlike their counterparts in most southern states. failed to win control of the state party, bolted and sent their own delegation which won seats in the national convention and replaced Cuney with a white national committeeman. When the Republican state executive committee decided on fusion with the Populists that fall, McDonald refused and campaigned for the Democrats. Black voters divided about equally between the Populists and the victorious Democrats.

After Cuney died in 1897, McDonald and Henry Ferguson, a prominent black Republican from Fort Bend County, struggled for Cuney's dual position as party leader and Negro spokesman. Divisions between black leaders and white control of federal patronage opened the way to increasing white dominance of the Republican party as "lily whites" returned to the fold. McDonald led a brief bolt in 1900, but he failed to win seats for his supporters at the national convention. Compromise prevailed in 1902. McDonald accused white leaders of creating a "Lily White machine" in 1904, however, and a largely Negro delegation again sought without success to win seats at the national convention.

Throughout the late 1890's and early 1900's, after the decline of the Populists, Republicans offered little threat to Democratic control of state offices. By 1906 a sense of rejection within the party of Lincoln and defeat in state politics helped reduce support for the predominantly black wing of the Republican party to a mere 5,400 votes. The candidate of the primarily white faction polled 23,700.

White efforts to disfranchise Negroes also stimulated the decline in the number of black voters by 1906. The white majorities in most counties showed no fear of black suffrage except when splits among the Anglo voters allowed blacks to hold the balance of power. Negroes formed majorities in fourteen counties along the coast, in the Brazos River valley, and in Northeast Texas. They constituted 40 to 50 per cent of the population in thirteen other East Texas counties. Black majorities on the local level often elected Negroes to positions such as alderman, county commissioner, justice of the peace, county treasurer, tax assessor, and constable. Whites responded by refusing financial support for high bond requirements and by making often unfounded charges of corruption and inefficiency. Some whites refused to serve with Negroes. The legislature at different times in the late nineteenth century denied seats to three black candidates in contested elections. In at least one case the grounds for denial appeared to be highly questionable. But disfranchisement called for stronger measures.

A white men's party organized in Panola County during 1874 to use economic intimidation and social ostracism against all Republicans. In Harrison County a similar group organized in 1876 but lost the two following elections. After the second defeat in 1878 the members challenged the vote on a technicality, seized the courthouse, and declared themselves elected. Democratic state officials refused to intervene. Harrison County whites thereafter manipulated the vote for their purposes in state and local elections, though the loss of a suit in federal court during 1880 ended such practices in national campaigns. Whites drove ten black leaders from the county and had others arrested when they asked that ballots be counted in public. A new election law of 1879 to reduce fraud actually increased the possibility of confusing illiterate voters because it required only white ballots without any party symbols.

In the late 1870's white men's parties or intimidation of Negro voters developed in the town of Navasota and in Leon, Montgomery, Colorado, Dewitt, and Washington counties. Similar events occurred in Waller, Harris, Washington, Matagorda, and Wharton counties in the 1880's.

White Democrats in Fort Bend County organized in 1888 a club known as the Jaybirds. White and black county officers created a counter group called the Woodpeckers. Whippings, assaults, and killings followed. Jaybirds ordered seven Negro leaders to leave the county, but allowed black tax assessor Henry Ferguson to remain if he supported them in the next election. Yet the Woodpeckers still won. When Jaybirds surrounded them at the courthouse in August, 1889, three men died in the gun battle while Texas Rangers watched. The Democratic governor again left local white Democrats in control, though two of the evicted black leaders sued in federal court and received some compensation.

White men's associations organized in Colorado, Matagorda, Brazoria, Grimes, Milam, and Marion counties to assure "that white supremacy must obtain." In Robertson County Democrats stopped black Populists from voting with rifles, pistols, and baseball bats. The Democratic county judge killed one Negro leader and shot a black attorney in court for an "insolent" remark. By such means the last black legislators found their support cut away and met defeat in the 1890's.

From these organizations and activities also developed local use of the white primary, which spread rapidly across East Texas in the late 1890's and early 1900's. When the legislature adopted a new election law in 1903, it allowed each party to add specific limitations on its membership. The state Democratic executive committee in 1904 suggested white primaries to all county committees which generally accepted the idea.

White Democrats proposed payment of a poll tax as a suffrage requirement sporadically during the late nineteenth century. The leading advocate, A. W. Terrell, held strong racial views and intended the poll tax as a means of eliminating black voters. Yet he and other proponents failed because many Democrats feared it would fall too heavily on poor whites as well as on Negroes. Republicans, Greenbackers, and Populists generally opposed the poll tax as a blow at the bases of their support.

Finally, after several unsuccessful attempts, the legislature in 1902 passed a constitutional amendment allowing a poll tax for voting. Populists, Mexican-Americans, labor unions, and some Anglo papers opposed it. The white primary and loss of power within the Republican party reduced the level of black involvement in this crucial suffrage test and other state elections. The amendment passed by a two to one margin with the support of most whites—especially the native Anglos who strongly favored prohibition and looked upon the poll tax as a means of eliminating election fraud and wet voters. The poll tax did reduce the number of voters in Texas elections, but it fell on the innocent as well as those guilty of selling votes, and had no effect on potential vote purchasers, for some local politicians bought poll taxes for their constituents. Houston adopted a city poll tax for local elections which produced similar results.

White men's associations and poll tax supporters generally used accusations of fraud as an excuse for their actions. Yet the associations resorted to violence rather than to the courts to end supposed "frauds." Many areas favored white primaries and a poll tax without any local cases of corruption. Most whites wanted to eliminate black voters simply because they assumed them to be inferior people who should not have any voice in government.

Negroes consistently fought disfranchisement in Texas through the Republican and third parties and by appeals for federal action in Congress or the courts. Yet they could not stem the tide against black suffrage which ran so strongly through the South at the turn of the century. Because of its smaller percentage of black population, Texas did not follow many other southern states in the adoption of literacy tests and grandfather clauses. But the decline in Negro voter participation from about 100,000 in the 1890's to approximately 5,000 in 1906 suggests the effectiveness of the white primary, the poll tax, and the "lily white" thrust in the Republican party.

While the political participation and power of black Texans slowly dwindled during the late nineteenth century, whites also chipped away at black legal status. Few Negroes had become judges, even as justices of the peace, during Reconstruction. Even fewer continued, only in predominantly black counties, after the Democrats regained power in 1874. In 1876 the legislature adopted a law that allowed county judges to appoint jury commissions which selected jurors from the literate citizens of the county. Seldom did Negroes who could read and write find themselves acceptable to jury commissions. A few Populist sheriffs called black jurors for service in return for their political support. State and federal courts reversed an occasional decision when exclusion of black jurors could be proven. No new attempt developed to exclude black testimony against whites, but white juries clearly accepted the word of most whites over that of most Negroes.

The Texas Court of Appeals in 1877 upheld the national Civil Rights Act of 1875, despite opposition from the Democratic press. Yet black people, concentrated at the bottom of the economic ladder, could not often afford the luxury of restaurants, hotels, theaters, and bars. Some urban Negroes tested their rights to attend or use public facilities and usually met resistance. The legislature repealed all license laws to eliminate ties with the state government and thus make prosecution of the civil rights act against privately owned facilities more difficult. A few businesses closed to avoid integration. A judge threw out a suit in Galveston because the theater owner could not afford the $500 fine. Another theater owner refunded black ticket holders' money to avoid admitting them. In 1883 the Supreme Court declared the Civil Rights Act of 1875 unconstitutional. A state convention of black leaders held in Austin that year accepted the concept of separate accommodations, but only if they were truly equal. Segregation of public accommodations had achieved such wide acceptance by 1885 that when two Negro women protested their removal from a Waco theater, the manager had them arrested for creating a disturbance.

No law on segregation of transportation existed at the end of Reconstruction. In 1877 a federal judge upheld the access of Negroes to first class as well as smoking cars, while accepting the concept of separate but equal facilities. Yet a black minister received only the refund of his fare after a refusal of equal accommodations in 1882. The Democratic governor and attorney general urged separate but equal railroad cars in the early 1880's, but only the Texas Central immediately adopted the practice. Several towns began to require separate waiting rooms during the same decade. The legislature in 1889 passed an act allowing railroads to require separate coaches and made segregation on railways mandatory in 1891, despite the individual and collective protests of several black leaders. Because the lines made only limited efforts to provide equal facilities, a black Methodist bishop won $100 in damages when refused a Pullman car ticket. Few Negroes could afford such accommodations and the law continued to govern other facilities. In 1903 several Texas cities joined a southern trend by adopting ordinances that required separate seating on streetcars. Black leaders protested first before organizing boycotts which lasted several months in Houston and San Antonio. Though the streetcar companies lost money, city councils refused to rescind the laws and the legislature required streetcar segregation on a statewide basis in 1907. This act, which brought transportation segregation to the local level where it affected large numbers of Negroes, marked a crucial stage in the development of segregation in Texas.

White Texans had extended legal segregation to include a ban on interracial marriage in 1858, but only a few cases came to trial before the courts declared the law invalid in 1877. The legislature adopted a new act in 1882 which forbade all interracial sexual relations. The State Convention of Colored Men in 1883 protested, however, that the authorities generally enforced it only with regard to marriage. Thus the caste system continued to wink at white men who visited Negro prostitutes or kept black mistresses.

White Texans, as a part of their assumptions of black racial inferiority, believed Negroes to be criminally prone. Black economic and social status, the inability of Negroes to secure legal counsel, and bias by white juries and judges, however, provide better explanations for the 50 per cent black ratio among Texas penitentiary inmates. Some whites unsuccessfully sought to continue distinctions from the slave period by whipping Negroes for minor offences. Frequent charges against black people included abusive language which often meant simply talking back to whites. Local white officials revived vagrancy and apprenticeship laws which they applied primarily to Negroes. Black people regularly received longer sentences and higher fines. A Negro boy went to prison for stealing a $.20 can of sardines. Many blacks who could not post bond awaited trial for weeks or months in jail on minor charges. Others served for months or years to pay off small fines. Some white law officers tricked Negroes into gambling on pay day so the lawmen could assess fines which they shared.

Crimes by Negroes against other black people generally resulted in much lighter punishment because white lawmen, judges, and juries assumed Negroes to be naturally inclined toward violence and let them channel it against each other. For that reason black violence, actually based on the frustrations of their social and economic status, fell primarily on other Negroes.

Texas jails and prisons offered little comfort and limited facilities for all prisoners, while black inmates also faced the possibility of racial hostility from jailers or guards who were almost without exception white. One Negro died for lack of medical care before his case came to court. Some counties hired out prisoners or worked them on roads. State prisons leased convicts to planters, railroads, and quarries to save money. After being auctioned off under conditions reminiscent of slavery, convicts faced whippings, crowded quarters, and poor food. The death rate among leased prisoners ranged from 5 to 50 per cent in different years, with tuberculosis, typhoid, malaria, and pneumonia the major causes. Guards killed several convicts who tried to escape such conditions, though authorities seldom explored the circumstances behind such cases. Similar events happened in several Texas towns. At El Paso, for example, a policeman killed a Negro businessman who supposedly had threatened the policeman with a pistol while drunk. The officer faced no charges although the Negro had been shot from behind.

Black people at times faced extralegal treatment in criminal matters. Between three hundred and five hundred Negroes met death by lynching in the late nineteenth century in Texas. Most had been accused of murder or rape of white persons, though charges of assault, theft, and slander at times brought violent reactions. White lynchers excused their actions as necessary to stop such crimes or to protect raped women from the humiliation of public testimony. Evidence later proved some victims of lynch mobs innocent.

Some whites and most Negroes opposed lynching, though many white leaders and newspapers condoned such acts. Governor Hogg called unsuccessfully for an anti-lynching law after a mob mutilated and burned alive accused rapist Henry Smith at Paris in 1892 before thousands of people. Five years later a similar event in Tyler stimulated an anti-lynching act which required the prosecution of lynchers and the dismissal of law officers who permitted lynchings. Eight members of lynch mobs received prison sentences in 1899 and a widow won damages from another lyncher. The rate of lynchings declined from eighteen per year in the 1890's to ten per year from 1899 to 1903.

Whites used custom as well as law in attempts to maintain psychological control over black people. According to folklore one store owner required Negroes to ask for "Mistuh Prince Albert Tobaccuh," since the prince had been a white man. Such practices ultimately produced negative self images among some black people. Another Negro folktale of the period suggested that a black person truly converted to Christianity could dream of a white man; those who were not saved could dream only of black men.

The Democratic party solidified its control of the state administration in the mid-1870's by eliminating the integrated State Police and militia. Confident of their power Democrats then organized new white militia companies for emergency use and allowed a few black companies to be raised primarily as social groups. The new full-time Texas Rangers remained all white from their inception. Between 1875 and 1881 Negroes created nine militia companies which the adjutant general organized in 1880 into a regiment under the command of Colonel A. M. Gregory. When Gregory recruited some unauthorized companies in East Texas during 1882, white fears and protests led to the dismissal of both the colonel and the new units. Inspectors' reports resulted in the disbanding of five black and several white companies in 1885. For the next two decades a Colored Infantry Battalion of four or five companies served primarily ceremonial and social functions such as attendance at the Afro-American Fair in Houston during August, 1896. The battalion did hold summer training encampments beginning in 1890, but only one company ever received a call to preserve order. Ironically that company prevented the lynching of a Mexican-American in 1889. Though the use of black militia might have heightened tensions in cases where lynch mobs sought Negroes, some men may have died needlessly because of white reluctance to call black companies. Despite favorable reports by inspectors as late as 1904, the state adjutant general disbanded the battalion in 1906 at the peak of white pressure for more uniform segregation and discrimination.

Although black military power dwindled on the state level after Reconstruction, Negro federal troops remained active along the frontier. The black 9th and 10th United States Cavalry regiments destroyed several camps and forced hundreds of Indians back to their reservations during the Red River War on the high plains in 1874. The 9th Cavalry stopped the Salt War at El Paso between groups of Mexican-American and Anglo settlers in 1877 and served along the Texas-New Mexico border against Apache raiders in 1878. The 10th Cavalry continued to garrison forts on the Texas frontier until transferred to

Arizona in 1885. The black 24th and 25th Infantry, as well as Negro cavalry, captured horse and cattle thieves, chased bandits, built roads, and strung telegraph lines along the Rio Grande. The black soldiers pursued Indians into Mexico to destroy their villages in 1876 and 1877. One small command that lost its way on the unmapped plains suffered four deaths during an eighty-six hour march without water. Negro cavalry and infantry guarded water holes and mountain passes along the Rio Grande south and west of Fort Davis in 1880 and drove back every attempt by Victorio to lead the return of his Apaches into the United States.

In spite of their services the "buffalo soldiers" faced continued racial problems with Texas Rangers, buffalo hunters, and other civilians at frontier posts such as Fort Concho. One ranger captain left the service rather than discipline his men who roughed up off duty soldiers. The cavalrymen later shot up a saloon in retaliation. When Negro troopers fought with buffalo hunters who tried to intimidate them, rangers arrested the soldiers. One received a death sentence but won release on appeal. Black cavalrymen shot up San Angelo again when they thought a white man who had killed an unarmed soldier had been freed. He later won acquittal before a white civilian jury.

Prejudice existed within the army too. Black regiments could expect only infrequent relief from assignments to posts in harsh climates and little recognition of their services. Henry Flipper, the first Negro to graduate from West Point and the only black officer in the army, served capably for four years on the Texas frontier. But a court martial at Fort Davis in 1882 dismissed him from the army for conduct unbecoming an officer, although it found him innocent of embezzlement charges. Flipper claimed, with some support, that the post commander, Colonel William R. Shafter, acted out of prejudice toward him, though Shafter had a reputation for harsh treatment of all subordinates. Despite these problems the black troops in Texas maintained a rate of desertion and alcoholism sharply lower than white regiments. White citizens of Brownsville, unhappy about the stationing of the 25th Infantry at Fort Brown, charged that Negroes raided the town and killed one man on an August night in 1906 to retaliate for local discriminatory practices. Because none of the troops admitted participation or implicated others, President Theodore Roosevelt dismissed the three companies stationed at Fort Brown and white Texas newspapers urged an end to all Negro units and enlistments. But Senator Joseph B. Foraker of Ohio forced an investigation which showed no reliable evidence existed against the black troops. Instead it seemed local smugglers or saloon keepers might have framed the soldiers to force their removal. A few of the troops finally received an opportunity to reenlist.

The Brownsville incident provided further evidence of the deteriorating political and legal status of Negroes in Texas and the nation. Whites in the same year eliminated black militia, extended segregation to streetcars, reduced Negroes to a minority within the Republican party, and held the second all white Democratic primary.

Labor and Economic Status

The majority of employed black Texans–63 per cent–continued to labor at various forms of agriculture in 1900. By the turn of the century landowners formed 31 per cent of the Negro farmers, with 69 per cent sharecroppers and tenants—compared to 50 per cent among white farmers. Cash tenants who paid $3 to $7 an acre and maintained fences were more numerous than sharecroppers. Some rented land at a rate of one bale of cotton for every four to seven acres. Others worked for the landowner part of each week on his crop and spent the rest raising their own crop. Some tenants cleared land in return for a rent free first crop.

Negro tenant farmers often produced little or no profits because they farmed extremely small plots — 59 per cent worked fifty acres of less, 83 per cent worked 100 acres or less. Black farm owners averaged fifty-eight acres valued at $858, while white farm owners averaged 425 acres worth over $3,000. Landowners and storekeepers offered supplies and cash in advance at interest rates such as 25 per cent or 1 per cent each month. Rent on animals and equipment at times reached exorbitant heights. Many uneducated black croppers found themselves unable to check a landowner's figures at the end of a year if he told them their expenses for supplies equaled their share of the crop. A Convention of Colored Men at Houston in 1879 and a Colored Land and Labor Strike at Bastrop protested the level of shares and rents. At least one white newspaper showed some sympathy, noting that the average tenant made only $34 annual profit on cotton and $75 on corn.

Agricultural problems did not wholly separate black farmers from whites. Yet a higher percentage of tenants and the smaller size of farms clearly relegated Negro agriculturists to a lower economic position. Falling farm prices, deflation of currency, and high interest rates for supplies on credit hurt all farmers, black or white, while the reluctance of many whites to sell land or extend credit to

Negroes further retarded black agricultural profits and land acquisition.

Negro farm workers averaged $10 to $20 a month in the late nineteenth century. Cotton pickers could expect $.35 to $1.00 per 100 pounds. Cotton chopping brought $.50 to $1.00 a day. In areas where a high percentage of black population created strong competition for farm jobs, some planters still could employ whip wielding overseers. Other landowners, however, found they could get better results with kinder treatment and incentives. The few strikes for higher wages generally failed.

Black as well as white farmers sought to unite for more effective action on agricultural problems. In the 1870's a Colored Farmers' Association organized on the model of the Grange. A Colored State Grange developed in 1880. These groups provided social gatherings and some unity of resources for the sale of crops or the purchase of land. R. M. Humphreys, a white Baptist minister, established the Colored Farmers' Alliance in Houston County during 1886. Membership spread to twelve states with J. J. Shuffer, a black Texan, as president. The Colored Alliance created an exchange in Houston to provide a collective buying and selling agency for black farmers. For lack of funds and experienced managers the exchange failed in 1891 as did the white Southern Farmers' Alliance exchange. R. L. Smith, who would be one of the last Negro legislators in the 1890's, founded the Farmers' Improvement Society of Texas in Colorado County during 1889 to promote the purchase of farms, better farming methods, and cooperative purchases and sales. Smith drew together 2,300 members by 1900 and added others in several states in the early twentieth century.

Such groups made only limited gains in the face of long term economic and racial problems aggravated in the 1890's by a national depression.

Black men continued to form about 20 to 25 per cent of the cowboys, bronc riders, wranglers, and cooks in the cattle industry during the late nineteenth century. Some established considerable reputations for their ability. Frank, a roper for Ab Blocker, did not stand night watch because of his specialized skill. James Kelly served as a gunfighter for the Print Olive outfit in the late 1870's. Jim Perry on the huge XIT Ranch and Matthew "Bones" Hooks of the Panhandle gained reputations as excellent bronc busters. Bill Nunn and Bob Lemmons won a degree of fame as mustang hunters. A Negro cowboy won the steer roping contest at Mobeetie in 1884. Bill Pickett of Texas became widely known at the turn of the century for perfecting the technique of bulldogging. Al Jones drove cattle to Kansas thirteen times—once as a herd boss. "80 John" Wallace, an ex-slave from Victoria, went up the trail first at the age of seventeen. He began to buy cattle while still a cowboy, acquired land in Mitchell and Navarro counties in the 1880's, and became an influential rancher. Silas Jackson became a prominent black cattleman near Goliad. Although generally better treated than Negroes in more heavily settled areas, black cowboys faced difficulties similar to those of tenant farmers in purchasing land. As the frontier passed the demand for their services declined, forcing them into other occupations. Hooks, for example, became a pullman porter. Negro cowboys faded from memory too as twentieth century white fiction writers omitted them through ignorance or choice from most novels about the West.

Non-agricultural labor involved a growing number of black people, though Texas had a lower percentage than any other state because of its limited urbanization and industrialization. Unskilled and semi-skilled jobs increased while agricultural and domestic workers declined. Personal and domestic services such as servants, laundresses, nurses and mid-wives, restaurant and saloon keepers, hair dressers, and barbers did compose 28 per cent of all employed Negroes in 1900. Younger domestic servants, born after slavery, showed greater independence in seeking better jobs or wages. When they could not improve their situation some worked more slowly or engaged in minor theft to compensate for long hours and low wages. Despite a continued demand for Negro servants, such actions stimulated white grumbling about impudence, laziness, and dishonesty.

In East Texas black lumber workers formed 42 per cent of the 6,350 men employed by that industry in 1890. They averaged 220 to 260 days work a year at $.80 to $1.25 a day, but some received company script redeemable only at a company store. A few Negroes became sawyers at $4.50 to $6.00 a day, though white laborers received most skilled positions. At Harrisburg in 1886 black workers conducted a brief and unsuccessful strike. The Knights of Labor received complaints about working conditions in the timber region which some compared to "chattel slavery."

Railroad construction brought several thousand Negroes to Texas in the 1870's from sections of the South harder hit by economic depression. The lines also employed some black men as porters and in maintenance jobs. Yet white and convict laborers replaced many Negroes especially on construction crews for wages of $1.00 to $1.25 a day in the 1870's and 1880's. Some railroad unions accepted black members, but most refused. Railroads on occasion used non-union Negro workers as scabs to help break strikes.

When white longshoremen excluded Negroes from their union, the black Longshoreman's Benevolent Association organized at Galveston in 1870. Two more Negro dockworkers' locals developed during the 1870's in the island city with members whose wages averaged $500 a year. Wharf and shipping companies with the help of N. W. Cuney used black strikebreakers in 1883 and 1885 in Galveston. The Colored Labor Protective Union thereafter controlled labor on the Mallory wharf. When the union affiliated with the American Federation of Labor and struck for higher wages in 1898, the company brought in Negro scabs protected by state militia after some violence. The first International Longshoremen's Association local west of the Mississippi developed among black dockhands at Sabine Pass in 1898. The union struck for higher wages and won a compromise increase to $.35 an hour, but soon collapsed.

Knights of Labor locals in several cities accepted black members and David Black served on the state executive board in the 1880's. As the Knights faded from prominence as the major national union, T. D. McLeroy, a Negro, acted as vice-president of the 1889 convention which organized the State Federation of Labor. The A. F. of L. as it admitted Texas locals in the 1890's accepted only a limited number of Negro longshoremen's and lumber workers' unions. A coal company imported Negroes from Indiana to break a strike at its mine near Thurber. Few black men found acceptance into apprenticeship programs in skilled trades. Yet most urban areas in 1890 contained at least some black carpenters, blacksmiths, painters, printers, masons, engravers, plasterers, roofers, shoemakers, tailors, furniture makers, machinists, butchers, brickmakers, dressmakers, and cotton or textile mill workers. Some light-skinned mulattoes passed as white to get skilled jobs.

Though more black laborers worked as strike-breakers than as union members, few found it possible to retain those jobs because of opposition from most white workers and employers. While figures are not available on other cities, Negro wage earners in San Antonio during 1870—who were 96 per cent manual laborers, 67 per cent unskilled, 11 per cent semi-skilled, and 18 per cent skilled—experienced only 6 per cent upward mobility over the next thirty years in comparison to 11 per cent for Mexican-Americans, 20 per cent for native whites, and 22 per cent for European immigrants. For elderly indigents who could not find normal labor, counties operated self supporting poor farms or houses which offered food and shelter, though they generally proved unhealthy.

Teachers and ministers formed the vast majority of the black professional class in Texas. W. B. Price became the first Negro attorney admitted to the state bar in the late 1870's, as a few white lawyers encouraged black men to study law. Negro doctors opened offices in Texas during the 1880's and organized the Lone Star Medical Association in 1886 when refused membership by the white state association. Benjamin R. Bluitt established himself as the first black surgeon in

Texas in 1888 and later helped organize the first Negro bank in Dallas. In 1894 Marcellus C. Cooper of Dallas became the first black dentist in Texas. Yet by 1900 no major city claimed more than six Negro doctors or four attorneys.

Negro businessmen in Texas numbered no more than 159 by one count in the 1890's, though only Georgia could claim a larger figure. Black businesses included barbershops, saloons, restaurants, grocery stores, boarding houses, blacksmith shops, laundries, wood dealers, boot and shoe shops, caterers, pawn brokers, and dairymen. Average investments ranged from $1,000 to $3,000, though a few real estate dealers and contractors estimated their property at $10,000 to $75,000. Barbershops seemed to be the most stable black business, perhaps because they could in many instances rely on a more affluent white clientele. Most other Negro businesses lacked capital and served only the black community. An exceptional hotel owner who catered to whites had to hire a white manager to meet his guests. Efforts to organize a black owned textile mill failed. To promote black economic enterprises William M. McDonald in 1887, at Fort Worth, organized the Lone Star Fair Association, which later moved to Marshall. A similar Afro-American Fair operated at Houston in 1896.

Twenty-three weekly Negro newspapers existed by 1900, including five of the sixty-six outstanding sheets in the country—the Dallas *Express*, the Wharton *Elevator,* the San Antonio *Advance*, the Oakland *Helping Hand*, and the Galveston *Gazette.* One young black newspaper editor left Texas during the 1890's to become nationally prominent. Emmett J. Scott, the son of a blacksmith, had attended Wiley College and worked for two white journals before he established the *Texas Freeman* in Houston and became secretary to N. W. Cuney. Then in 1897, on a speaking trip to Texas, Booker T. Washington met Scott and made the young man his secretary. Scott assisted in writing *Up From Slavery* and became known as the "brains of the Tuskegee machine." After Washington's death, Scott became the secretary-treasurer of Howard University.

Lack of economic and educational opportunites, especially in Southeast Texas, stimulated an exodus in 1879-1880 to Kansas, where rumor indicated free land could be found. Some Negroes sold farms and left jobs to emigrate because of intimidation and discrimination. Since little free land actually existed, Kansas officials tried to discourage immigration as did most black leaders in Texas. After Richard Allen spoke for the movement at a Nashville convention in 1879, however, delegates from thirty-eight Texas counties met to promote the exodus. Negroes moved in groups of six to 500 at a rate of 1,000 to 1,300 per week for a short time—a total of at least 12,000. Probably 10 per cent began to return disillusioned by December, 1879.

Other movements developed toward a variety of destinations during the late nineteenth century. Some black Texans crossed into Oklahoma when the territory opened for settlement. The American Colonization Society sent twelve black people from Marshall to Liberia in 1879. A society agent toured the state again in 1890. Other Negroes traveled to New York but could not afford passage to Liberia. Interest lingered through the 1880's although a representative from McLennan County returned from Liberia to oppose emigration. A Boston philanthropist in 1880 won the endorsement of a black convention in Dallas for a Negro colony in Northwest Texas, but it failed to materialize. S. A. Hackworth, a white Republican, bought land in Wharton, Fort Bend, and Brazoria counties and resold it to Negroes in the 1870's and 1880's.

Black people in East Texas unsuccessfully appealed for Congressional appropriations to finance emigration to Liberia in the 1880's. In San Antonio 700 Negroes led by the Reverend Daniel E. Johnson tried to organize a steamship company for emigration purposes during 1893, but sold only 112 shares at $10 each during that depression period. Henry Ferguson arranged the settlement of 10,000 Negroes in Mexico during the late 1880's, but the Mexican government cancelled the contract when he did not immediately fulfill it. William H. Ellis, a black businessman, developed a similar plan in the early 1890's with the same results. He later backed the efforts of Bishop Henry Turner, a black Methodist and prominent emigration advocate from Georgia. When the International Migration Society sent 200 emigrants to Liberia from Savannah in 1895, Texas ranked fifth among states contributing black passengers. Rumors of ship departures from Galveston and emigration interest circulated again in 1899.

Some migrants achieved prominence after their departure from Texas. James C. Thomas, a cabin boy on steamers between Galveston and the Northeast, settled during 1881 in New York City. He established himself as an undertaker and real estate man in Harlem, where he earned the title of "the richest man of African descent in New York" by 1907. Scott Joplin, a singer and pianist, left Texarkana in the 1890's to win recognition as the "King of the Ragtime Writers" by 1901.

Emigration movements attracted primarily lower class black people who felt a great sense of despair over their economic condition even more than increasing disfranchisement and discrimination. Though the exodus never included more than a small percentage of black Texans at any time, only the costs of emigration or total despair held back thousands of others. The vast majority of Negroes in Texas found it impossible to overcome a combination of economic and racial problems which kept them at the level of sharecropping and unskilled labor as the twentieth century began.

Education

The doubts of white Texans about black education in the mid-1870's received reinforcement from the still relatively unsophisticated work of several anthropologists and psychologists as the turn of the century approached. Most whites assumed that black people were intellectually inferior and therefore could acquire only rudimentary reading, writing, and mathematical skills. Some Anglos opposed all education for Negroes because it might reduce white control over black people.

Fear of social contact and intermarriage stimulated strong opposition to any possibility of school integration. Democratic Governor Richard Coke threatened to end all public education rather than accept mixed classes if schools were covered by the Civil Rights Bill of 1875. The new state constitution written that year required separate educational facilities and left control wholly in the hands of local school boards. It allowed no local taxes to be levied for schools. The state provided operating expenses but no funds for new buildings or equipment. In 1879 Democratic Governor O. M. Roberts forced a cut back in state appropriations to reduce the state debt with the support of many persons who opposed public education in general and Negro education in particular. Under those conditions attendance and school construction could not keep pace with the growth of the black or white student population.

In 1881 the legislature allowed towns to tax for support of education. Legislators in 1884 created school districts which could levy taxes, appropriated new state education funds, and sought to establish a six-month school term. Yet they exempted from the district concept fifty-three counties with most of the state's black population. Many districts still did not tax, at least in part because of white opposition to local support for black schools. Negro children generally received a smaller percentage per student of state funds than did whites, because of inequitable distribution by local school boards. Texas Democratic congressmen opposed the Blair bill for federal aid to education in the 1880's, although Southern congressmen divided fairly evenly on the unsuccessful proposal. Populist pressure helped produce a few black school trustees on the local level in 1893, but the legislature abolished their positions in 1899.

Two-thirds of all black public schools met in churches, barns, and other rented buildings. Negroes tried to raise money privately for repairs since white school boards were reluctant to build black facilities. In 1889-1890 school boards constructed 233 white schools, but only thirty-seven for Negroes, though white students outnumbered blacks only three to one. Fifteen years later white schools contained 914 libraries with 150,000 volumes, while black schools had only eighty-two libraries with 8,000 books. Aid from the Slater and Peabody funds, established by northern philanthropists, helped improve some urban schools. The first Negro high school existed by 1890 and nineteen had been created by 1900, all in cities.

Most white southern teachers refused to teach in black schools, which opened the way to Negro and northern instructors more sympathetic to the students. In the early years after the Civil War, however, the number of qualified black teachers remained limited. Some school boards continued to reject almost 50 per cent of the Negro applicants even in the 1890's. Teacher institutes began in the 1880's to upgrade both black and white instruction. Salaries varied with the different types of teacher certificates. Since more white teachers held first class certificates their average pay ranged from 5 to 25 per cent above that of Negroes. Yet black teachers actually held a higher percentage of college degrees or diplomas from normal and high schools. Because of low pay many teachers held other jobs or farmed in their spare time. Thirteen black educational and political leaders organized the Colored Teachers' State Association in 1884 to advance the general status of Negro education. L. C. Anderson, principal of Prairie View Agricultural and Mechanical College, served as the first president of the association.

Even sympathetic teachers faced cultural communications problems. According to black folklore one young woman found her class confused over arithmetic. Finally a boy suggested that, instead of asking the class to "Bring down yo' one an' ca'ie yo' two," "Tell 'em to bring down de one an' tote de two." The other students immediately understood the instructions when translated into familiar words. Lack of school funds and child labor during harvest season by black youths in poor farm families caused most Negro children to average far less than six months of school per year. Despite cultural and financial problems black schools reduced Negro illiteracy from 75.4 per cent in 1880 to 38.2 per cent in 1900. At that time Texas ranked fifth among southern states in black enrollment and average daily attendance, third in number of Negro teachers, sixth in industrial education enrollment, and first in number of black public high schools.

The number of black colleges and academies increased steadily during the late nineteenth century, though the student bodies especially in the college level courses remained quite limited. State supported higher education for Negroes began in 1878 with the creation of Prairie View Agricultural and Mechanical College near Hempstead under the control of the Texas A & M board of directors. Though Prairie View began with eight students, two more than Texas A & M in its first year, the state government converted it into a normal school for teachers the next year under Principal E. H. Anderson. The enrollment quickly grew to sixty students, appointed by legislators and directors, who were not required to pay the high $180 tuition. Private loans by white businessmen helped Prairie View survive a dispute between the legislature and the state comptroller over funds in the 1880's.

Under Principal L. C. Anderson, who succeeded his brother in 1885, Prairie View received one-fourth of the federal funds to land grant colleges in Texas and expanded to include agriculture in the Hampton-Tuskegee pattern.

Although he accepted and promoted the style of education whites preferred for black people, Republican Anderson in 1895 lost his position to black Democrat E. L. Blackshear, who proved to be even less outspoken in defense of Negro rights. Republican and Populist criticism in the 1890's did stimulate the construction of some new buildings and pay raises for the staff. In 1899 Prairie View added an industrial and mechanical department.

Texas voters authorized a state Negro university at Austin in 1882, but the legislature never established one. The Colored Teachers' State Association led a petition drive in 1896 which produced a second act for a separate university. The state supreme court declared it unconstitutional, however, because no public land remained to be used for its support. The legislature then authorized classical and scientific studies at Prairie View in 1901.

Private colleges for black students also expanded, both in size and in number, during the late nineteenth century. Wiley College, which opened during Reconstruction at Marshall, emphasized teacher training as well as high school preparation for its college courses. The first Negro president and a shift to black faculty came in the late 1890's. Negro Baptists built a school at Marshall in 1877. At Denison during 1880 the African Methodist Episcopal Church established a normal school.

The year 1881 proved an especially active one in the field of black higher education. Nathan Bishop of New York left funds which the Baptist Home Mission Society supplemented to establish and operate Bishop College at Marshall in 1881. David Abner, Jr., son of a black legislator and a graduate of Bishop College, became its first Negro professor and later served as president of Guadalupe and Conroe colleges and the National Baptist Convention Theological Seminary at Nashville. The Colored Methodist Episcopal denomination founded a college at Longview in 1881. That same year the Baptist State Convention created Hearne Academy. The African Methodist Episcopal Church, under the guidance of Richard Harvey Cain, a former black congressman from South Carolina and bishop of the Louisiana and Texas district, moved Paul Quinn College in 1881 to Waco where it attracted 150 to 200 students a year. The American Missionary Association of the Congregational Church opened Tillotson Collegiate and Normal Institute in Austin during 1881.

Further expansion followed in the next two decades. In 1884 the Catholic Church sold to the black Guadalupe Baptist Association Guadalupe College at Seguin which increased its enrollment to 300 by the turn of the century. The Baptist Missionary and Education Association of Texas in 1885 founded Houston College with 100 students. In 1886 the Freedmen's Board of the Presbyterian Church created Mary Allen Seminary for girls at Crockett on land given by local citizens and by James Snyder of Illinois. Negro Masons established a college in Dallas during 1887 on land provided by white religious leaders of that city. At Tyler in 1894 the Colored Methodist Church founded Phillips University, though it operated almost exclusively as an elementary and secondary school in its early years. The Freedmen's Aid Society of the Methodist Episcopal Church with local Negro support bought land for a college in Austin during 1883. Construction began in the 1890's and Samuel Huston College opened with eight-three students in 1900. Catholic Bishop James S.

Johnson converted a San Antonio parochial school into St. Phillips Junior College and Vocational Institute in 1902.

Though some black colleges in Texas did not last, they increased in number from two to at least eleven in the three decades from 1875 to 1905. The state ranked near the top in total Negro college students and sixth in black college graduates. Yet the total number of students and graduates represented only a tiny portion of Texas Negroes. And most faculties continued to be predominantly white in the 1890's, a source of growing friction.

Social Life

The social life of black people in isolated rural areas changed little in the nineteenth century. The folklore of the time suggested, "All dey knowed was haa'd work, mean obuhseers, chu'ch onset a-mont', big dinnuha on a Sunday, Saddy night chu'ch suppuhs, an' string ban' flang-dangs."

Housing for most Negroes consisted of one or two rooms with a shed for a kitchen and completely separate sanitation facilities, which were typical conditions for the families of most small farmers. Major floods and storms struck on several occasions in the predominantly black river valleys and coastal counties, leaving hundreds or even thousands homeless, cropless, and even starving. The black population in urban wards during 1890 ranged from 9 to 47 per cent in Galveston, from 4 to 20 per cent in San Antonio, and from 33 to 42 per cent in Houston. Thus the variation in the percentage of Negro population in different wards had grown since 1870 from 20 to 38 per cent in Galveston and from 7 to 16 per cent in San Antonio. In Houston the range apparently had narrowed from 27 to 9 per cent, but black sections actually existed across ward lines or in a portion of a ward. Residential segregation had advanced a pace.

Few black doctors practiced in Texas, and many black people relied on druggists' advice or home remedies because medical services proved costly. Persons who claimed to be government agents cheated some black people by offering them fake immunizations. Negroes suffered and died from smallpox, tuberculosis, pneumonia, diarrhea, nervous disorders, heart disease, malaria, typhoid, and measles. Negro families might place their mentally ill relatives in state asylums, though some met refusal and local authorities locked others in jail where they received no treatment. The state provided no black orphans home to match the one for white children built in 1887. But it did create that same year a Deaf, Dumb, and Blind Institute for Colored Youths at Austin which taught trades to 100 students by 1900.

In comparison to conditions under slavery, family life after the Civil War included stronger marriage ties especially for the small middle class which developed. Figures for 1890 and 1900 indicate a black divorce rate about twice that of the overall population, yet divorcees included only 0.9 per cent of Negro men and 1.8 per cent of Negro women. Some members of the large lower class, however, found formal marriage and divorce a financial burden, which led to common law arrangements and a higher than average rate of illegitimacy. The slave heritage of limited responsibilities and economic restrictions which kept men from adequately supporting their families led to informal separations, and to many mother dominated families.

Juneteenth and other holiday celebrations attracted crowds of up to 5,000 in large towns for speeches, Negro band concerts and parades, picnics, baseball, horse racing, gambling, and dancing. Railroad excursions occasionally brought as many as 1,000 persons to cities or fairs, though they declined after 1890. Several of the larger towns fielded Negro baseball teams on a sporadic basis. Entertainment in urban areas often developed around saloons and red light districts where fights also erupted. Minstrel shows by Negro groups attracted black and white audiences. The black middle class in some towns organized literary, dramatic, and debating societies.

Sutton Griggs, the only important black novelist born in Texas during the late nineteenth century, wrote five novels which established him as more prolific but somewhat less artistic than his Negro contemporaries, Paul Lawrence Dunbar and Charles Chesnutt. Though a Baptist minister, Griggs' in his early novels won a reputation as a black nationalist who in *Imperium in Imperio* (1899) seemed to advocate a separate Negro nation in Texas. Yet the trend of his thoughts reflected the declining status of black people in Texas and the nation. He continued to protest against white racism in three novels from 1901 to 1905, but in *Pointing the Way* (1908) he appeared to favor upper class white protection for Negroes against lower class whites.

Social segregation stimulated the growth of separate social and fraternal groups in the black community. Fraternal organizations also provided limited insurance benefits to their members. The first Negro Masonic lodge developed in Galveston, with six in the state by 1875. Annual conventions of the state Grand Lodge in various cities attracted hundreds of delegates who usually paraded at some time during their meetings. The Grand United Order of Odd Fellows in Canada and Britain created Negro chapters in Texas during the late 1870's, which held parties, picnics, and balls. In 1885 the Grand Lodge of the Knights of Pythias organized in Texas as a primarily social order, though it claimed over a million dollars of insurance in the state. Several local societies and marriage unions developed to bring couples together. Negro fire fighting and militia companies also served as social groups in the towns where they existed.

Separate black religious denominations, especially the Baptists and the Methodists, continued to grow during the late nineteenth century. Negro Baptists organized a state convention in 1874, which counted twenty-three associations with about 50,000 members by 1880 and grew to 111,138 in 1890 because of its participatory style and the autonomy of congregations. Sunday schools, a journal, and annual meetings of up to 2,000 persons also stimulated their steadily expanding efforts. The partially black Methodist Episcopal Church divided into a Texas and a West Texas Conference in 1874, with 27,453 members by 1890. The African Methodist Episcopal Church, which created a conference in Texas during 1875, numbered 23,392 members in 1890. With 14,895 members that same year the Colored Methodist Episcopal Church ranked third among the Methodist denominations with black congregations. After local supporters developed the first African Methodist Episcopal Zion Church in Grimes County during 1883, the denomination grew to 6,927 by 1890.

Presbyterians undertook a variety of efforts with limited results. The Cumberland Presbyterian Church, Colored, counted thirty congregations with 1,740 members in twelve counties by 1890. Black Presbyterians organized their first congregation of the Presbyterian Church of the United States at Crockett in 1874. Seven churches existed in 1888 when their members organized the Negro Presbytery of Texas. A new congregation at Texarkana founded an industrial school for girls in 1903, but it closed after only eight years for lack of funds. Support for black ministers in Texas from the Presbyterian Church of the United States peaked at about $900 in 1889. Southern Presbyterians created a separate Afro-American Synod for the entire South in 1898. White leaders of Cumberland Presbyterian churches in Texas generally opposed union in 1905 with the U.S.A. Presbyterian Church which favored integration. One white Texas minister argued that "no people ever retained their faith in God and followed his teachings who became amalgamated with an inferior race."

Other denominations involved themselves even less with black people. The Episcopal Church established a mission at Galveston 1884 and ones at Marshall and Tyler during the 1890's. A few evangelists for the Churches of Christ conducted services for Negroes in East Texas and organized a church at Texarkana in 1898. Catholic Bishop Nicholas A. Gallagher and the Dominican Sisters opened a school for Negro children at Galveston in 1886. A church for black Catholics which developed in connection with the school became Holy Rosary Parish. Missionary efforts in Houston began in 1887 and led to the establishment of St. Nicholas Parish in 1896. Gallagher in 1901 invited the Josephite Fathers, an order dedicated to work with Negroes, to assume support of the new church. Margaret Mary Murphy, an Irish immigrant and widow of the mayor of Corpus Christi, established St. Peter Claver church and school for the black people of San Antonio in 1888 and four years later founded the Sisters of the Holy Ghost to conduct instruction in the school.

Black congregations generally remained small with poor buildings and severe financial problems, though some sent limited amounts for missionary work in Africa. Most held fairs and picnics to raise money. A few whites provided land or funds. Others had only criticism for the emotionally involved responsive style of the numerous evangelical congregations. Negro churches often held summer revivals for two to three weeks attended by dozens and at times hundreds of people from all areas within traveling distance. Both revivals and routine church meetings continued to serve as social as well as religious gatherings.

In many ways the Negro churches paralleled their white counterparts, though few could compare with the more affluent urban Anglo congregations. Men held most positions of leadership, but women probably contributed more time to the routine affairs of the black church. As political opportunities declined the black ministry attracted increasing numbers of able leaders. But not all held the same views on religion. While some followed a pious approach, others carried pistols and swore with considerable ability, which could help maintain social status and leadership in a state still emerging from frontier conditions. Many served more than one church and received their pay in food and clothes. Others farmed to supplement their salaries. Many Negro ministers began with little education, though the percentage of illiterate preachers declined with that of black people in general. Some studied with white ministers and a few attended seminaries. White planters opposed revivals or even Sunday night services during cotton picking season. They made some exceptions for preachers who told field hands to "work haa'd an' 'bey yo' boss-man." Yet most Negro ministers walked a fine line between accommodation, to maintain their acceptability with the powerful and affluent white society, and protest, to retain respect and status in their own black community.

Richard Henry Boyd achieved the greatest prominence of any Negro religious leader from Texas. An ex-slave, cowboy, and mill hand, he rose through the Baptist ministry to become secretary of the black Baptist Convention and a successful advocate of religious pamphlets for Sunday schools. In 1897, after he became secretary of the home mission board for the National Baptist Convention, he organized the National Baptist Publishing Board to print for the first time denominational literature for Negroes. This followed his philosophy that black people should control their own religious and educational affairs as much as possible.

Black social life in the late nineteenth century became even more self contained than during Reconstruction, because of continued economic limitations and anti-black violence coupled with growing segregation and discrimination by law and custom. Negro fraternal organizations and churches attained more importance as literacy increased while opportunities for political participation and leadership virtually disappeared. Black people who

had been at least voters and laborers in the post
Reconstruction period found themselves virtual
outsiders in Texas society of the early twentieth
century.

5

Outsiders

Politics, Violence, and Legal Status

Few black Texans participated in state or
national politics by the elections of 1908. Bill
McDonald and M. M. Rodgers, an internal revenue
collector through his friendship with Booker T.
Washington, continued to struggle with little
success against white domination within the
Republican party. A predominantly black group
bolted the state convention that year, but failed to
win recognition at the national convention. Most
Negroes favored Senator Joseph B. Foraker as the

Republican presidential nominee because he had defended the troops accused in the Brownsville riot. But Taft won the nomination with the support of white Republicans in Texas and the South and went on to victory in the fall. Black Texans who voted at all generally remained Republican as the lesser of two evils.

Black political leaders then turned to the rising prohibition movement to regain political power and to discredit the concept of widespread Negro drunkenness. Rodgers became chairman of a state wide black prohibition organization. Texans also led the Anti-Saloon League of Southern Negroes. Yet other blacks opposed prohibition. The Colored Teachers State Association instead urged temperance. The Reverend J. L. "Sin-Killer" Griffin, a prominent black evangelist, and former Populist J. B. Rayner accepted fees from the Texas Brewers Association to speak against prohibition. According to some estimates two-thirds of the 50,000 Negro poll tax holders did not vote in 1911 on the bitterly contested prohibition amendment to the state constitution because of intimidation. The small turnout undercut any immediate hope of reestablishing the significance of black political power.

In 1910 black leaders in search of a political home organized a Negro Democratic League which claimed 600 members within two years. Yet most Democratic leaders feared Negro support and refused to seek black votes. The overwhelmingly Democratic state house of representatives in 1910 passed a resolution which called for modification of the Fourteenth Amendment and repeal of the Fifteenth Amendment. In 1912 the leading candidates for the Democratic gubernatorial nomination agreed no Negroes should vote in the party primary.

Rodgers and McDonald backed Taft for the Republican nomination in 1912 because dominant white party leaders in Texas, who had reduced black influence in the state organization, favored Roosevelt. Taft men gained control of the state party but black influence increased only to a limited extent. Roosevelt's Progressive party showed little interest in black votes. Both Republicans and Progressives ran well behind the Democrats in Texas, while the Democratic national victory eliminated Republican control of federal patronage and further frustrated black political aspirations. In 1914 the Progressive party completely barred Negroes from its organization. But when most Progressives returned to the Republican party in 1916, black and white "regular" Republicans beat off their effort to totally exclude Negroes.

When World War I began, black Texans generally supported the war effort through food conservation programs, Red Cross drives, purchase of Liberty Bonds, and patriotic meetings in Austin and Dallas. W. L. Davis, a Houston fraternal leader, became secretary of the Negro Division in the Federal Food Administration. McDonald and others traveled about the state to make pro-war speeches. Privately some Negro leaders in Texas expressed resentment that black men faced conscription when their rights were being ignored at home. Some white leaders and papers opposed black military service because they feared any armed Negroes. Yet Negroes provided about 25 per cent—31,000 men—of the troops called up from Texas, though they formed only 16 per cent of the state's population. For some the army provided better clothes, food, housing, and pay than they

114

previously had been able to afford. A few black Texans achieved honor and distinction. Spencer Cornelius Dickerson of Austin served as a doctor with the army in 1918 and later rose to brigadier general. Hugh McElroy of Houston, who had served in the Spanish-American War and on the Mexican border with Pershing, won the Croix de Guerre for gallantry in action while temporarily attached to the French army. For others, however, the war brought death and discrimination.

A white mob lynched a black man near Huntsville because he refused to serve and later killed his family when they resisted removal from their home. Another Negro faced arrest for publicly hoping the Germans would win since black people already lived in slavery. At Camp Bowie Negro troops received separate quarters surrounded by a high barbed wire fence. In France black troops met fair treatment from most Frenchmen. But the army assigned them white officers and relegated many to labor battalions in sea ports. It often restricted them to small areas in towns and allowed military police to treat them more harshly. Negroes received no Red Cross services in many areas. Whites opposed the presence of black troops in Texas, which resulted in clashes at Del Rio, San Antonio, and Waco. Negroes of the 24th Infantry met discrimination and segregation in Houston for several days. When police roughed up a black soldier and woman and arrested a Negro military policeman on August 23, 1917, the incident stimulated a retaliatory raid by about 150 troops in which seventeen persons—police, soldiers, and civilians—were killed and sixteen wounded. Thirteen of the soldiers involved received the death penalty and forty-one life imprisonment.

In 1919 Negroes organized an Equal Rights Association to promote democratic government and equal justice. But breakthroughs of black participation tended to be the result of close Democratic primaries, such as the Pat Neff-Joe Bailey runoff for the gubernatorial nomination in 1920. In some East Texas counties Neff or Bailey supporters sought to increase their vote by opening the ballot to Negroes. Some blacks in their thirties voted for the first time.

Whites continued to dominate the state Republican party, but could not avoid a split in 1920 when several contesting black delegations failed to win seats. The white wing polled 90,000 votes, while the "black and tan" ticket received 26,000 votes in the gubernatorial race that fall. Thus the return of Republicans to national office, which strengthened white Republicans in the South through federal patronage, produced a mixed reaction among Texas Negroes. A sense of powerlessness continued to rankle black Republicans, though the party took a stand against the Ku Klux Klan in 1922. The new Klan, which claimed over 100,000 members in the state, proved powerful enough, however, to help elect Earle B. Mayfield, a Klansman, to the United States Senate from Texas. Some black people voted for the Progressive candidate, Robert LaFollette, or the Democrat, John W. Davis, in 1924, as a protest against the "lily-white" attitudes of state Republican party leaders. In the gubernatorial election that year the remnant of Negro voters favored Miriam Ferguson, who opposed the Klan, over her Republican opponent.

In 1928 Negro Republicans supported the attempt by Congressman Harry Wurzbach to wrest control of the party from the established leaders.

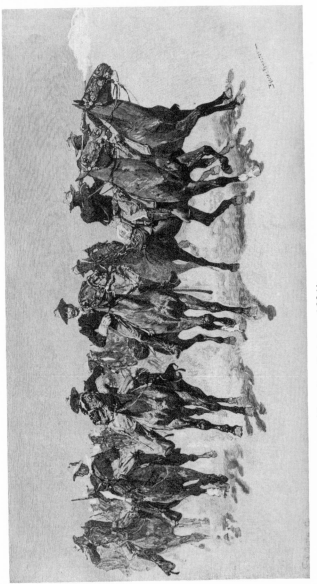

Ninth Cavalry (From *Century Magazine*, October, 1891)

Henry O. Flipper (From Texas Memorial Museum, Austin)

Norris Wright Cuney (From M. C. Hare, *Norris Wright Cuney,* courtesy of The University of Texas, Institute of Texan Cultures, San Antonio)

Robert L. Smith (From J. M. Brewer, *Negro Legislators of Texas*)

Bill Pickett (From Southwest Collection, Texas Tech University)

Lynching of Jesse Washington (From Library of Congress)

Lawrence A. Nixon (From Mrs. Lawrence A. Nixon, El Paso)

Charles Bellinger (From A. W. Jackson, *A Sure Foundation*)

Etta Moten (From The University of Texas, Institute of Texan Cultures, San Antonio)

Mary Branch (From The University of Texas, Institute of Texan Cultures, San Antonio)

A. Maceo Smith (From The University of Texas, Institute of Texan Cultures, San Antonio)

Heman M. Sweatt (From Houston *Post*)

Mrs. Charles White (From The University of Texas, Institute of Texan Cultures, San Antonio)

Mack H. Hannah, Jr. (From The University of Texas, Institute of Texan Cultures, San Antonio)

Barbara Jordan (From The University of Texas, Institute of Texan Cultures, San Antonio)

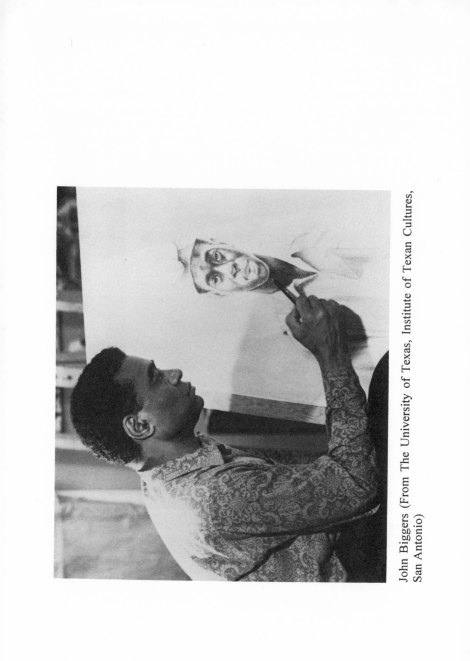

John Biggers (From The University of Texas, Institute of Texan Cultures, San Antonio)

When that effort failed, McDonald and others threw their support to Democrat Al Smith, although he had been nominated for president at Houston in a convention which segregated spectators. Black support probably hurt Smith among the white Protestant majority in Texas, as did his anti-prohibition views and Catholic religion. Soon after the election of Herbert Hoover, however, the overwhelmingly Democratic Texas legislature condemned his wife for entertaining Negro Congressman Oscar DePriest. But the acceptance by Hoover of continued white Republican dominance in the Texas party combined with the depression to thrust the limited number of voting Negroes into the Democratic party by 1932, four years before a national majority of black voters made that transition. Participation in New Deal programs kept most black voters in Texas in their new political home during the 1930's.

White Texans had reduced black involvement in state politics and parties to an ineffectual level during the first four decades of the twentieth century. Yet Negroes continued to be active in some cities such as Dallas, Galveston, Fort Worth, and San Antonio. Local politicians generally conducted campaigns on a nonpartisan basis with appeals by all candidates for the black vote. Galveston Democrats faced a local challenge from a "People's Party" which sent both groups in search of Negro support. Black people in Fort Worth backed a reform ticket, which instituted a city-manager form of government, in hopes of removing the red-light district from the black section of town. W. L. Davis ran unsuccessfully for the state senate from Houston in 1920, while three Negroes also failed to win Harris County offices.

133

Dallas Negroes organized an Independent Voters League in the 1920's to work for street lights, better schools, and other local issues. Similar groups formed in other communities and established a state league in November, 1927, with R. D. Evans, a Waco attorney, as president, and Clifford Richardson, editor of the Houston *Informer*, as secretary. The state organization served as a clearing house for ideas and efforts to promote greater black participation in both Texas and local politics.

Charles Bellinger, a real estate man who also provided loans for other Negroes in San Antonio, organized the black vote through Negro ministers and the purchase of poll taxes for voters. In return for the black vote he usually could deliver, white politicians provided street paving, sewers, better schools and parks, fire houses, a library, and a public auditorium for the black section. Dallas Negroes achieved similar concessions by providing the margin of victory in a close city election during 1937. Bellinger also won tacit acceptance from political allies in city offices for his control of local bootlegging and gambling.

A legal case against a non-partisan white primary in Waco during 1918 brought from the district court a favorable decision which opened the local primary to black voters. Yet Houston Negro leaders failed to win an injunction from the Supreme Court in 1921 against the white primary in Houston because the election had passed before the case could be heard. When the loser in a San Antonio political race complained publicly about the black bloc vote, it further stimulated the building white demands which caused the legislature in 1923 to adopt a law against Negro participation in party primaries. The winner of the

San Antonio election then pushed through a revision of the city charter to allow a non-partisan primary which would include black voters.

H. C. Chandler of San Antonio immediately tested the new state law in a federal district court, which ruled that the primary was not a state election and thus was not protected by the Fourteenth and Fifteenth amendments. After being refused the right to participate in the 1924 primary, Lawrence A. Nixon, a Wiley College graduate and physician in El Paso, challenged the law in court with NAACP financial and legal aid. In 1927 he won a Supreme Court judgment against the act as a violation of the Fourteenth Amendment. The legislature then adopted a new law allowing rather than requiring parties to hold segregated primaries. Suits in state and federal courts failed to stop the white primaries in Houston, San Antonio, and Waco during 1928 and 1930. Despite an appeal from Negro leaders, the Democratic state executive committee voted by a narrow fourteen to thirteen margin in 1930 to continue segregated primaries. Nixon also returned to court in 1929 after again being refused the right to a primary vote. When his case reached the Supreme Court in 1932, the justices threw out the second state law because it made political parties into state agencies by authorizing them to discriminate on the basis of race.

The Democratic party then resumed its pre-1923 practice of allowing white primaries in all counties under local party rules without any support from state law. Major newspapers divided on the issue and Democrats in San Antonio, Corpus Christi, and Waco accepted some Negro voters. But party leaders in Beaumont, Dallas, Fort Worth, and Houston turned away potential black participants. Julius White, chairman of the Harris County Negro Democratic Club, lost a suit in local court to stop the segregated primary. To develop greater support for further court tests Antonio Maceo Smith and the Reverend Maynard H. Jackson of Dallas cooperated with Clifford Richardson and Richard R. Grovey of Houston in 1936 to reorganize the Independent Voters League as the Progressive Voters League. Grovey, a Tillotson College graduate and barber shop owner, again took a case to federal court, but the Supreme Court rejected his plea on the grounds that the Democratic party was a voluntary association. Thus the poll tax, the Democratic white primary, and white Republican leaders combined to keep most black Texans outside the political arena and to allow little voice to those who entered it from 1904 to 1944.

White racial views on social, economic, and political issues stimulated some white individuals or groups to violent acts and allowed others to condone them as another means of maintaining white control and restricting black status. One unsuccessful lyncher excused his actions with the comment: "No one should try to stop a nigger from being mobbed that had killed a white man, because mobbing Negro[e]s put fear in Negro[e]s that keeps them in their places. A nigger isn't a citerzen [sic] any way." Texas ranked third in the nation in lynchings with over a hundred between 1900 and 1910. Lynch mobs took twenty-four lives in the peak year, 1908. Seventy-three counties. primarily in East Texas, had lynchings. Harrison County led with fifteen over a period of about thirty-five years. Black victims of lynch mobs faced accusations ranging from rape and murder to assault, theft. quarrels with whites, and being related to a criminal. Evidence suggested that several were clearly or probably innocent. Crowds of up to 10,000 persons gathered in a holiday atmosphere to watch some lynchings. Most mobs hanged their victims, though others resorted to beating, shooting, and burning. A Waco mob in 1916 beat, stabbed, mutilated, hanged, and finally burned Jesse Washington. At Sherman in 1930 a mob burned down part of the black section and the county courthouse where a Negro was being held for trial, despite the presence of the sheriff, police, rangers, and national guardsmen.

Fears of black retaliation, much exaggerated like fears of slave revolts, arose frequently. Such false rumors circulated at Silsbee in 1904, at Waco in 1905, at Colmesneil in 1906, and at Haskell in 1908. When black passengers on an excursion train entered the white section seeking seats, fighting erupted near Beaumont in 1902. One Negro died and others received wounds along with three whites. Militia stopped a violent confrontation at Wragleys Mills in 1904 after a Negro wounded a white man by mistake. At Beaumont in 1908 whites burned two black amusement parks and police arrested unemployed Negroes following a rape charge against a black man. Fears of labor competition in San Angelo during 1909 caused whites to beat a black janitor and drive other Negroes from the town. A year later in Anderson County white fears developed because of rumors about a white man in debt to a Negro, whites working under a black overseer, and black meetings to organize attacks on whites. White mobs killed eighteen Negroes in the series of raids that followed. Fearful of black riots, the legislature in 1910 barred films of the boxing match in which Jack Johnson, a black Texan, defeated Jim Jeffries.

"Whitecapping," a term generally applied to violent intimidation short of death, occurred in many areas of East Texas. Whites employed whippings, warning shots, threats, and destruction of property to hold down Negro wages and economic competition, to enforce black social subservience, and to stimulate conformity to middle class social behavior.

White newspapers and politicians frequently approved or at least condoned lynching, mob violence, and whitecapping. White newspapers also offered a one-sided view of the black community by concentrating on Negro crime or humorous events which furthered white stereotypes of black ignorance or childishness. In the second decade of the twentieth century, however, the Dallas *News* and the San Antonio *Express* editorialized against mob violence. The state government also exhibited some concern over such events, which declined in number for a time.

In 1919 two race riots occurred in Texas during a period of similar clashes across the nation, stimulated by white fears of black migration to cities, labor competition, and demands for greater equality by returning Negro soldiers. At Port Arthur in July twenty whites and fourteen Negroes clashed with several persons injured, including two blacks who required hospital treatment. In Longview white concern developed over the efforts of black farmers to raise cotton prices and the appeals of the Chicago *Defender*—a Negro paper—for black migration to the North. A July 2 article in the *Defender* suggested that the lynching of a Negro for rape near Longview actually resulted from his love affair with a white woman. A group of whites badly beat Samuel Jones, a black teacher suspected of authoring the story. When the mob later entered the Negro section of town to attack Jones again, black defenders wounded four of the whites. They retreated but returned to burn the teacher's home and several other houses and shops. Local police arrested only Negroes, but other white leaders called in the militia and Texas Rangers who restored order with a curfew, collection of firearms, and arrests of both blacks and whites. Most later gained release, but Jones and some other Negroes could not return to Longview.

Texas Democrats in Congress opposed a federal anti-lynching bill in 1921, though the lone Republican congressman from San Antonio supported its passage. Mob violence increased in the early 1920's with the rise of a new Ku Klux Klan. Klan members attacked Catholics, Jews, immigrants, and supposedly immoral white Protestants, but dealt most harshly with Negroes. Klansmen branded a black bellhop in Dallas with acid and castrated a light-skinned Negro accused of relations with white women. They raided the office of the Houston *Informer* and threatened the Dallas *Express*, both black papers. Hooded groups beat a black youth in Texarkana, removed two Negroes from the Denton jail to flog them, and forced black cotton pickers near Corsicana to end their strike for higher wages.

White Texans did not agree uniformly with mob violence. The governor sent a representative to the Interracial Congress which met at Texarkana in 1920. The following year business and professional men organized the Texas Committee on Interracial Cooperation, to oppose violence and to seek better housing, jobs, transportation, and education for black Texans. State militia and local leaders broke up some potential lynch mobs. The last Texas lynching occurred in 1935 at a time when Congressman Maury Maverick of San Antonio broke Texas Democratic ranks to support federal anti-lynching legislation.

Such efforts against violence included no attack on the caste system or its supporting Jim Crow laws. The legislature added a law in 1909 which required separate waiting rooms in railroad stations and another in 1911 for separate employee compartments. A Negro in Dallas who refused to sit in a segregated section of a streetcar was shot. When black soldiers violated such laws in San Antonio, President Taft considered removing them from the city. Yet the facilities remained far from equal. Some trains included no "colored" car, diners and Pullman cars remained closed to Negroes, and separate black cars and waiting rooms seldom received equal care. White taxi drivers generally refused to carry Negro passengers. Streetcars and buses, however, introduced movable signs which allowed some flexibility in the separation of black and white customers according to their numbers on a specific vehicle.

Residential segregation developed as a result of custom in Texas cities until Dallas passed a law in 1916 after a petition from the white Deere Park Improvement League. Negro leaders and the Dallas *News* opposed its adoption and 3,000 whites voted against the new act to no avail. White real estate men challenged the law because it limited profits on land sales. The Texas Court of Civil Appeals agreed and invalidated the act in 1926. But Dallas legislators in 1927 led a successful fight for a state law which allowed segregation by city control over the issuance of building permits. River Oaks Corporation restricted the area it developed in Houston to whites only. Despite the higher cost of comparable houses in segregated sections, most

Negroes did not challenge such restrictions because blacks in integrated areas faced the threat of fire bombs and other forms of harassment. The Dallas Negro Chamber of Commerce initially accepted segregation, but protested the police decision to control vice by allowing prostitution and gambling only in the black section. Between 1915 and 1924 several cities also passed acts against any form of interracial sex, though state law already forbade intermarriage.

State facilities — such as insane asylums, juvenile rehabilitation schools, and deaf, dumb, and blind schools—remained segregated through the early decades of the twentieth century. Six private orphanages for Negroes existed, but the state maintained no home for black orphans until it was given a former private institution at Gilmer in 1929. The legislature in 1909 required racial separation in state prisons. Whipping continued as a means of discipline for black prisoners after it had been dropped for whites. Negro girls went to the black women's prison, although the Colored Women's Clubs gave the state land at Crockett in 1923. The legislature failed to appropriate funds for the operation of a rehabilitation school on the site until 1945. The state provided no funds for the treatment of black epileptics and tuberculars until 1935.

Most city and county facilities excluded or discriminated against Negroes. Galveston created the first black branch library in the South during 1904, followed by Houston in 1909. The legislature authorized separate county libraries for Negroes in 1919. Such segregated facilities represented an improvement, but some black leaders pointed out their inferior quality in comparison to white libraries. Not until 1927 did all of the larger Texas cities have Negro nurses on their staffs. Houston used the donation of an oil man to construct the first public hospital for Negroes in the South during 1926. By 1931 black hospitals existed in six Texas towns. Other urban areas offered only separate sections of public or private hospitals—generally inferior in facilities and services. Houston in 1916 became one of the first Texas cities to provide any funds for separate parks in its black section and to allow Negro children to visit the city zoo on special days. Custom and local laws segregated recreational facilities including swimming pools and rest rooms. The legislature in 1907 allowed theaters and private amusement parks to segregate Negroes or refuse them admittance. Houston and other towns segregated all facilities in their city halls, from separate public drinking fountains to floors in the jail. The Houston city auditorium could be rented by blacks for segregated programs. Segregation in hotels and restaurants remained a matter of custom, though most chose to discriminate. A few accepted an occasional well dressed Negro.

Texas courts generally did not call Negroes for jury duty or sent them home to avoid their participation. Two whites threw Professor G. F. Porter of Wiley College out of the waiting room of a Dallas court when he refused to leave after being dismissed as a juror. Decisions reflected jury composition. White or black assaults on Negroes resulted in short jail sentences. Black assaults on whites produced lengthy prison terms.

When Maury Maverick wrote in 1937: "I do not hate colored people; neither do I claim greater knowledge of them than Yankees," it represented the more advanced Southern racial sentiments possible in a world where scientists had begun to doubt the validity of innate racial differences and Nazi treatment of Jews cast shadows on all racial discrimination. Maverick spoke out in favor of equal protection of the law, economic opportunity, health care, and education, and against the poll tax, though he did not support social equality. His stand won him enough recognition in a black poll during 1940 to be one of five whites in the nation cited for their contributions to race relations. Yet Maverick hardly spoke for a majority of white Texans.

In response to disfranchisement, segregation, and violence, most black Texans chose accommodation and self-help within the caste system as the safest methods of advancement in the early twentieth century. The prominence of Booker T. Washington and the development of partially self-sustaining black ghettoes in Texas urban areas strengthened that philosophy. Middle class Negroes organized local law and order leagues and a Negro Protection Congress of Texas in 1906 to fight crime among the black lower class and to set themselves apart from the Negro masses in the hope of better treatment from whites. A few black vigilante organizations including a Colored Clan in San Antonio, arose briefly to threaten or punish "trouble makers" in Negro society for similar reasons.

Yet even many outwardly accommodationist Negroes responded at times with subtle rejoinders to white assumptions of superiority. When a white worker thanked his fellow employee, a black boy, for assistance with the comment, "Two heads are better than one, even if one is a goat's head," the youth quickly replied, "Yassuh, and one a little nigguh's."

In the second decade of the twentieth century

black Texans turned to more positive and outspoken responses to their problems. In 1912 Houston Negroes formed the first Texas chapter of the new National Association for the Advancement of Colored People. By 1919 thirty-one chapters existed with 7,000 members—over 1,000 in both Dallas and San Antonio. Whites reacted against the organization because it openly protested segregation and violence and functioned on an integrated basis at the national level. The state government harrassed the NAACP by requesting records of local branches, which might be used to pressure individuals. When its white executive secretary, John R. Shillady, appeared at Austin in 1919 to defend the association, local officials including a county judge and constable beat him into unconsciousness and permanently injured his health. Yet the offenders faced no arrest or even reprimand; Governor W. P. Hobby publicly condoned the attack. Nevertheless the NAACP remained active in Texas and achieved at least some success in support of the white primary challenge by L. A. Nixon.

Other sources of protest also developed. A few black attorneys, such as J. Vance Lewis of Houston, provided more than a perfunctory defense of Negro clients despite occasional threats of mob violence. During the World War I crusade to "make the world safe for democracy," editor W. E. King of the Dallas *Express*, President L. L. Campbell of the Baptist State Convention, and other Negro leaders revived open criticism of injustice. In the months immediately after the war Waco minister A. A. Lucas publicly demanded that whites give up their paradoxical stereotype of all black people as "no good" or "sassy." Negro Methodists. Masons, and additional Baptist leaders including N. P. Pullum of Houston, A. S. Jackson of Dallas, and A. M. Moore of Marshall added their voices to the protests. In the 1920's black businessmen, like Charles R. Graggs of Dallas, spoke out despite threats of arrest or violence. Houston editors C. N. Love of the *Texas Freeman*, W. L. Davis of the *Western Star*, and Clifford Richardson of the new Houston *Informer* joined the attack on segregation, discrimination, disfranchisement, and violence. The *Informer* described as lies the idea that white southerners were Negroes' "best friends" and the concept of "separate but equal."

Protests produced greater self-respect, but the limited results caused some Negroes to consider other alternatives. Many flocked to cities in Texas while others left the state. Ned Eastman Barnes moved from rural Montgomery County to Houston to concentrate on his numerous inventions to improve railroad tracks, engines, and station facilities. A Negro from Gonzales explained that he and several friends "would like to better our conditions by coming North." From Houston a black freight handler wrote that he "would like Chicago or Philadelphia But I don't Care where so long as I Go where a man is a man." Newspapers such as the Chicago *Defender* kept many Texas Negroes informed about conditions and possibilities in the North. Black migrants to Texas outnumbered emigrants in the late nineteenth century, but the trend reversed after 1900. Considerable numbers moved to the neighboring states of Oklahoma and Louisiana, while 17,000 lived in the North by 1920. Some Negroes supported unsuccessful proposals to make Texas or an area along the Texas-Mexico border into a black republic or colony. A number of black Texans

145

journeyed to Galveston in 1914 with the hope of sailing to Africa under the leadership of Chief Alfred C. Sam, an African who developed the movement primarily in Oklahoma. Few if any could find space on the small ship Sam provided for the voyage. Texas Negroes held mixed views about Marcus Garvey, who advocated black pride and organization as well as emigration to Africa when he spoke at Dallas in 1922 to found a local chapter of his Universal Negro Improvement Association.

Support for emigration ideas came generally from members of the large black lower class who faced greater problems with fewer alternatives than the much smaller middle class in Texas society. Migration north involved a more varied group as the Dallas *Express* explained. "This exodus is not by any means confined to the worthless or the ignorant negro. A large per cent of the young negroes in this exodus are rather intelligent. Many of the business houses in Houston, Dallas and Galveston, where the exodus is greatest in Texas, have lost some of their best help." Some of those who left rose to considerable prominence elsewhere. Maud Cuney Hare, daughter of N. W. Cuney, moved to Boston where she became a pianist, playwright, lecturer, and author. Chester Franklin of Denison edited the Kansas City *Call* in Missouri from 1919 to 1950. William J. Nickerson, founder of the Houston *Observer* during World War I, later became a major insurance executive in Los Angeles, California. Jesse Mitchell graduated from Prairie View before he went to Washington where he became a real estate man and in 1934 founded what was for a time the largest black bank in the nation.

A new burst of organizational and protest

activity by black Texans developed in the 1930's. The key figure in those efforts, Antonio Maceo Smith, has been described as "the organizing genius of the movement for equality and first class citizenship among Texas Negroes." A native of Texarkana with degrees from Fisk and New York universities, Smith helped reorganize the Dallas Negro Chamber of Commerce in 1932 and became its first executive secretary. In 1936 he led in the creation of a Texas Negro Chamber of Commerce with twelve chapters. With Smith as state secretary, these civic groups expressed broad interests in business, employment, education, housing, and neighborhood development. Smith personally became racial relations officer of the Federal Housing Administration in Dallas during 1936. He also helped establish the Progressive Voters League and the Texas State Conference of Branches of the NAACP, which he served as secretary. The Reverend Ernest C. Estell guided the development of the Inter-denominational Ministers Alliance in several Texas cities to further black unity and support for the state wide Negro organizations. Though black Texans remained largely outside the political and legal systems of the state through the first few decades of the twentieth century, the Negro middle class became increasingly active in protesting and seeking means to overcome their exclusion.

Economics

About half of the black workers in Texas during the early twentieth century continued to labor in agricultural pursuits. In 1900, 35,000 Negroes worked as farm laborers, 45,000 farmed as tenants, and 20,000 owned the land they tilled. The percentage of black landowners fell well below that of whites, as did the size of their farms. Wages for black farm workers averaged $.50 to $.75 a day, or $12 to $15 a month, at the turn of the century. Cotton continued as the major crop for 86 per cent of these black agriculturalists, who sold it for $25 to $40 a bale in 1900.

By 1910 the number of Negro farm laborers had increased to 75,000. In the next decade that figure declined while the number of farmers increased. The number of blacks engaged in agriculture remained at 48 per cent of the total Negro work force. By 1930 the number of black farm workers had fallen to 41,000, while Negro tenants had increased to 65,000, and black farm owners remained about 20,000 in number. Wages ranged from $5 a day to $40 a month during World War I, and the value of a cotton bale increased to $129 by 1929, though inflation diminished the purchasing power of both figures. Ku Klux Klan activity in the 1920's reduced efforts to improve wages in some counties. Local lawmen in other areas forced Negroes to pick cotton or face vagrancy charges. Mechanization and the attractions of industry and cities also helped reduce the percentage of all Negro wage earners engaged in agriculture to 36 per cent by 1930. Up to two-thirds of the black farm laborers in some counties actually lived in or near towns where they sought jobs during the agricultural off seasons. Thus they remained in a type of limbo between the rural and urban economies. Others supplemented their scant income by operating illegal stills during the prohibition period.

The Farmers' Improvement Society, founded by R. L. Smith in the 1890's, had grown to 2,300 members by 1900. It counted over 9,000 members in 1907, and expanded to include 21,000 persons in several states by 1909. Under Smith's guidance the organization urged its members to avoid credit buying, to purchase land and homes, and to reduce costs and increase profits through cooperative buying and selling. The society associated itself with Booker T. Washington and his Negro Farmers' Congress, and sponsored an agricultural college, a bank, a women's auxiliary, fairs, and a truck growers' union. Leaders who organized the Colored Farmers' Educational and Cooperative Union at Dallas in 1905 emphasized joint purchasing and sales efforts. Negroes created county farmers' institutes and cooperative associations at different times, though they generally died out after relatively brief periods. Such organizations helped sustain black farmers through a variety of problems, but they could not markedly change the general agricultural situation which remained largely static.

Most black cowboys turned to other occupations when cattle drives ceased and the demand for their services declined. Those who had acquired land, however, lasted well into the twentieth century. D. W. "80 John" Wallace moved about between Texas, Oklahoma, and New Mexico, but died in Texas on his 10,000 acre ranch in Mitchell County.

Black Texans in urban areas during the early twentieth century found themselves limited primarily to unskilled jobs. As craft unions developed they generally closed their membership to Negroes, which caused a decline in the number of black masons, printers, and miners. Tremendous urban demands for carpenters caused the number of black carpenters to double from 1900 to 1930, but combined with union exclusion to produce their decrease from 35 to 5 per cent of all carpenters in the state. Technological change reduced the demand for Negro and white blacksmiths.

Negro males engaged in non-agricultural labor numbered 57,000 in 1900—38,000 of them personal and domestic servants and unskilled laborers. Blacks provided 4,300 railroad employees, 3,200 workers for trucking and delivery lines, and 2,500 sawmill operatives. By 1910 Negro mill hands had doubled in number, though they still labored for $.75 to $1.00 a day under conditions some compared to slavery. Black porters and construction workers on railroads increased to 8,300 by 1924. Urbanization raised the number of non-agricultural Negro laborers to 98,000 by 1920, with the major increase in the building trades, iron and steel industries, and oil refineries. Over 2,000 black longshoremen worked for $.30 an hour in 1915. Other Negroes labored in coal and lumber goods, glass and stone factories, and as mechanics. Wages jumped 20 to 25 per cent during 1918 as employers sought to slow the flow of black migrants who left the state to seek jobs in northern war industries. Yet only a limited number of public positions remained available to Negroes. Dallas had one black postal employee, one truant officer, three public health nurses, and two school nurses. By 1937, Austin, Beaumont, Galveston, Houston, and San Antonio employed a few Negro policemen, though in some cities they could arrest only other black people.

Many Negro women also entered the job market because income for Negro families remained quite low as a result of the limited employment opportunities for black males. The vast majority of black women labored as domestic and personal servants, seamstresses, and school teachers. Throughout the early twentieth century a higher percentage of Negro women worked than did white women, though female black employees had become a minority of all working women by 1930.

Black laborers remained largely unorganized because of opposition from both business and most white controlled unions. Separate Negro unions existed for hod carriers, cotton jammers, bar porters, and longshoremen in some of the larger cities. But they exercised little influence in the State Federation of Labor. The few black union members sought typical workingmen's goals—recognition of their organizations and better wages and conditions—as well as the race oriented goal of ending job discrimination. Even the relatively strong Negro longshoremen divided dock work equally with their less numerous white counterparts after 1924. The Houston and Texas Central Railroad refused white union demands for the replacement of black switchmen in 1909 to retard the development of labor organization. A Negro strikebreaker died after being stoned during the Southern Pacific Railroad strike of 1922.

Some professions showed substantial growth in the early twentieth century along with the size of the Texas black community which they served, but others remained static. Negro ministers increased in number from 1,150 in 1900 to 2,300 by 1930. Black doctors during the same period advanced from 136 to 205, while dentists experienced a phenomenal growth from 5 to 99. Thus the Lone Star Medical, Dental, and Pharmaceutical Association became the largest Negro medical organization in the nation with over 300 members by 1928. The number of black attorneys actually declined from 28 to 20 during the same three decades, as a result of white opposition, both subtle and violent. Clearly most whites agreed that "Negroes have no part of law operation in the State of Texas."

In the larger urban areas such as Houston, black businessmen saw some opportunities for individual advancement and community development in those services denied to Negroes by segregation. Thus they appealed to black pride by advocating self-sufficiency within the Negro community. From these segregated beginnings developed some of the limited number of wealthy Negroes in Texas, such as Hobart Taylor, Sr., of Houston, who began with an insurance company and later expanded into the taxicab business to become a millionaire by the early 1930's. Yet black businesses remained relatively few in number and limited in size because Negroes lacked the capital or experience to establish or expand entrepreneural operations. With the exception of a few barbers and others providing personal services, most black businessmen also faced a market limited largely to poor Negro consumers and divided in many instances with white competitors. In 1929 Negroes in Texas owned 1,736 retail stores which employed only 3,000 persons. Grocery stores, drug stores, and restaurants formed 53 per cent of those establishments. Some new businesses developed during the early twentieth century, such as funeral homes which grew from one in 1900 to 148 by 1930. A Negro Masonic Lodge organized the New Century Cotton Mills at Dallas in 1901, through the sale of stock primarily to white investors. Sixty workers produced 3,000 yards of yarn daily. A black owned Penny Savings Bank opened in Dallas during 1909, but closed in 1912.

That same year in Fort Worth "Gooseneck Bill" McDonald founded his Fraternal Bank and Trust which continued through the depression. Yet Texas contained only four contemporary black banks in 1928.

Negro businessmen organized local chapters of Booker T. Washington's National Negro Business League in Dallas and Galveston during 1904, and at Fort Worth in 1905. Local leagues and leaders established a state league in 1907, with R. L. Smith, a friend of Washington, as president through its first decade of existence. The black community of Dallas acted as hosts for the Negro National Bankers' Association in 1911. But economic progress remained quite limited, which provoked a split in the Dallas league during 1926. The dissidents then founded a Negro Chamber of Commerce to represent more actively the interest of local black people. Negro chambers of commerce quickly sprang up in several other cities, though the depression greatly retarded their impact.

The Great Depression, which began in 1929 and continued through most of the 1930's, struck hard at black Texans. Negro unemployment increased from 4.8 per cent in 1930 to 8.8 per cent in 1933, while white unemployment only rose from 4.2 per cent to 5.4 per cent in the same period. In agriculture the depression stimulated the use of tractors, the reduction of cotton production, declining farm prices, and reduced credit. These trends forced over 50,000 Negroes off the land and reduced thousands of others from farmers to laborers. The number of black farm owners continued at about 20,000 in 1940; Negro tenants declined in the 1930's from 65,000 to 32,000; black farm laborers increased by 25,000.

Rural economic problems thrust thousands of black people into Texas towns and cities and helped drive almost 20,000 to seek better conditions outside the state during the late 1930's.

In urban areas the depression cut into the wages and family income of Negro workers in addition to increasing unemployment. Average wages for black laborers in Austin fell from $.40 or $.50 an hour in 1928 to $.25 an hour in 1933. Family income declined from an average of $978 for Negroes in 1928 to $874 in 1933. Both figures rose by 1935, to $.40 an hour and $942 a year. Yet at least 60 per cent of all black families still earned less than $1,000 a year by the mid-1930's.

As a result of their greater problems during the depression, Negroes contributed a higher percentage of the unemployed and persons on relief than their population percentage. In Austin, where black people formed 18.5 per cent of the population, they provided 35.6 per cent of the unemployed in 1931-1932 and 33.5 per cent of the relief cases in 1935. Similar ratios existed in other Texas cities. Negroes on relief in 1933 had been manufacturing workers in 16 per cent of the cases while domestic servants contributed 31 per cent, and agriculture provided 42 per cent. Perhaps 90 per cent of all black farm laborers in some areas could not find work in 1935. As late as 1937 Negroes formed 25 per cent of all unemployed persons in the state, though they composed 14 per cent of the population. Racial barriers did fade at least temporarily among black and white unemployed who often slept together in dugouts and shared police harrassment. Only two black banks, the Farmer's Bank and Trust of Fort Worth and the Farmer's Bank of Waco, and two Negro insurance companies. the Excelsior Mutual of

Dallas and the Watchtower Mutual of Houston, had survived the depression by 1937.

New Deal programs and state and private efforts helped relieve the suffering of thousands of persons, black and white, yet even in such agencies discrimination existed. In Walker County only thirteen of the more than 1,300 black farm families received direct relief, while ninety-three others labored on Works Progress Administration projects in 1939. The Farm Security Administration assisted Negro farmers with loans and marketing guidance. The Sabine Farms resettlement project in Harrison and Panola counties involved 120 black families. Some planters allowed their tenants to remain on the land, but forcefully drove away any labor organizers who appeared in their area. Communists faced arrest in Dallas for "agitating" the unemployed and advocating black equality. In Houston the relief benefit per month for Negroes averaged $12.67, compared to $16.86 for whites. At one time Houston officials told blacks not to apply for assistance. Negro work relief families in Austin averaged almost five persons each, but spent only $1.35 to $7.99 a week for food. Even the Civilian Conservation Corps accepted only 300 black youths into its Texas camps by 1935, though 43 per cent of the Negroes between the ages of sixteen and twenty-four drew relief. Black participation in Agricultural Adjustment Agency programs in Texas varied from 5 to 90 per cent in different counties, but averaged 47 per cent for farm owners and 32 per cent for tenants in 1945. Despite some efforts by county extension, A A A, and soil conservation agents, many Negro farmers failed to become involved from lack of time or knowledge of the programs. Federal programs to reduce farm production and increase prices saved many landowning farmers and stimulated the economy. But they forced many tenants and laborers completely out of agriculture as the land they had worked was taken out of production or converted to grazing.

Education

In 1900 black Texans recorded the lowest illiteracy rate in the South, 38 per cent, and led in number of high schools with nineteen. Yet Negro schools in the state continued to suffer from lack of sufficient funds, adequate buildings, and well trained teachers. Black teachers in 1909-1910 averaged $46 per month, compared to $62 for white teachers. Low family incomes forced many black children to leave school at an early age or seasonally to work. Health problems and the cost of textbooks and materials, which often proved ill suited to Negro students, also retarded attendance. Black speech patterns, which differed from formal English, also led to problems for students because teachers viewed them as mispronunciations, although many represented imaginative language creations which allowed more flexible expression. "Ageable," as a description of a person not yet old, or "journeyproud," as a verbal picture of someone excited about a forthcoming trip, suggest some of the possibilities. As pupils fell behind their dislike of school increased as did their drop out rate. Thus the highest attendance rates in the state remained 47 per cent of the potential Negro students in Galveston and 46 per cent of those in San Antonio. The average black school term for Texas in 1909-1910 lasted 135 days, four less than the average white school term in the state, but the longest in the South.

Some white Texans continued to express fears

156

that education would stimulate black opposition to their restricted economic, social, and political status. Other whites, who believed Negro education would advance the interests of the state, successfully urged larger state appropriations to provide improvements. Yet the emphasis remained heavily on industrial, mechanical, and agricultural education, which would raise the level of black skills within the occupational areas already acceptable to whites. White paternalistic concern appeared in several theses on Negro social and health problems written at the University of Texas and Southern Methodist University. A study of black schools by the Texas Education Survey Committee in 1925 stimulated some improvements.

Periodic studies revealed the limitations of black education in Texas. In most areas a time lag existed between the development of white and black facilities. Texas City opened a white school in 1904, but waited until 1915 to offer black education. In 1910 Texas school districts spent an average of over $10 per year on white students compared to $5.74 on Negro pupils. In McLennan County apparently less than half the funds appropriated for Negro education were actually spent on black students. When a district constructed a new building for whites the older one often became a black school. Ironically that shift frequently represented an improvement, since many school districts owned no buildings for the use of Negroes. In 1924, 75 per cent or more of the black schools in Texas had no librarian, industrial rooms, or playground equipment. No textbooks were available for 38 per cent of the schools, while 11 per cent had no toilets. As late as 1929 over two-thirds of the black schools had only one room and one teacher. By 1925 Negro high schools had increased in number to 150, but only thirty-four had received accreditation by 1929 because most did not include a full four year curriculum. Black teachers' salaries by 1928-1929 averaged almost $92 a month, compared to $121 for white teachers, although in San Antonio they received the same pay. Advancement proved difficult for the Negro teacher who could not acquire graduate education in Texas.

Funds to improve black education came from several public and private sources inside and outside the state. Federal aid for vocational training came through the Morrill Act and later the Smith-Hughes Act of 1917, which helped establish four Negro and twenty-eight white high schools. The John F. Slater Fund in the twentieth century also assisted in the creation of county training schools, similar to high schools. In Texas the number grew from one in 1912 to over thirty by 1930. Over three hundred new rural school buildings existed by 1924 as a result of stimulation by the Julius Rosenwald Fund. Texas responded with more matching state funds than any other state. The General Education Board supplemented teachers' salaries primarily through the philanthropic assistance of John D. Rockefeller. Rural home improvement courses developed under the guidance of county supervisors supported by the Anna T. Jeanes Fund established in 1907. The supervisors numbered over twenty by 1930. Baptist academies for black students offered the equivalent of a high school education in six East Texas counties. The Catholic church supported six schools for Negroes at Galveston, San Antonio, and Ames by 1917. Black and white leaders in Walker County drew on local, state, and national sources of private funds to found Sam Houston Industrial Training School in 1903.

The Colored Teachers State Association favored industrial education as a means of attracting white support, though some members expressed doubts about white motives and the long range results of such an emphasis. Administrators dominated the association, which served as a source of status for its officers. Thus it maintained generally conservative positions, though it served as a forum for the discussion of new approaches to black education. After its reorganization in the mid-1920's, the association began to publish the *Texas Standard* as a source of further information for its members. Negro school principals held annual conventions, while parent-teacher associations and mothers' clubs functioned on the local level. To promote athletic and oratorical competition black educators organized the Interscholastic League of Negro Schools in 1920.

Statistics for 1930 revealed some clear advances in black education. Illiteracy had fallen to 13.4 per cent though it varied in counties with black populations of over 1,000 from 25 per cent in Liberty and Rockwall counties to 3 per cent in Potter County. Attendance by Negro children six to fourteen years old had risen to 87 per cent, although black students averaged only 104 days a year, sixth in the South. By 1929-1930 Texas spent almost $40 a year for each black pupil, compared to nearly $47 per white pupil. That figure, the highest in the South, represented an increase from 55 to 85 per cent of the white expenditure level. Yet black schools still lagged behind white schools in several crucial areas. White school property in 1938 stood at three times the value per pupil of Negro school property. A ratio of thirty-nine students per teacher in black schools during 1935-1936 compared to thirty students per teacher in white schools. Negro teachers averaged $581 a year, while white teachers received $950 a year. The depression caused reductions in funds, widened the gap between expenditures on black and white schools, and forced some schools to close temporarily. To help offset such problems the WPA provided funds for basic adult education in English and math.

As the twentieth century began a considerable overlap existed between black high school and college education, since most Negro colleges in Texas offered classes at both levels. Schools which concentrated their efforts almost wholly on non-college courses, included Houston Baptist College, Conroe Normal and Industrial College founded by Baptists in 1903, Christian Theological and Industrial College in Palestine, and Brenham Normal and Industrial College established in 1905. The Farmers' Improvement Society Agricultural College founded at Ladonia in 1906, St. Paul Industrial and Normal College created in Mexia during 1925, Baptist supported Beaumont Normal and Industrial College, Central Texas College, operated by the Baptist Church in Waco from 1901 to 1928, and Fort Worth Industrial and Mechanical College, which closed its doors by 1929, offered a similar type of education. Only a few of the older colleges such as Bishop and Paul Quinn resisted the trend toward industrial training or shifted away from a high school emphasis. Even Wiley College, generally considered the best black institution of higher education in Texas, counted a majority of its students below the tenth grade. In 1914 only 129 students enrolled in college credit courses at all of the Negro colleges in the state, but the number increased to 600 by 1921.

A few new educational institutions and trends appeared in the ranks of Negro colleges during the early twentieth century. In 1905 at Tyler the Baptist Church established Texas Baptist Academy, which became Butler College in 1924. Jarvis Christian College began its efforts at Hawkins in 1912 through support from the Disciples of Christ. Texas College, Jarvis, and Tillotson remained junior colleges through the 1920's, though Tillotson expanded to senior college status in 1930. Guadalupe College, which lost its state recognition earlier, gained accreditation in 1929. That same year Bishop and Samuel Huston dropped their non-college courses.

Public support for the higher education of Negroes remained quite limited. Houston in 1927 established the only public junior college for black students, who provided much of its finances with their fees. Prairie View, the only state supported Negro college, offered courses which ranged from the elementary to the university level to meet the varied backgrounds and interests of its students. Yet the emphasis remained on agricultural, industrial, and teacher education, to fit black people for their "place" in society. E. L. Blackshear, who had guided the early twentieth century development of the school, lost his position because he publicly advocated prohibition. J. G. Osborne in his years as principal upgraded more courses to college level and increased faculty salaries.

W. R. Banks came to Prairie View in the 1920's after building Texas College at Tyler from a struggling school of less than a hundred students to an institution with an enrollment of over 600. Yet he faced doubts or opposition by some faculty, the president of Texas A. & M., and one prominent black editor in Houston. Prairie View achieved accreditation in 1926, established a division of arts and sciences in 1931, and won a class A rating from the Southern Association of Colleges and Secondary Schools in 1934. The depression then caused a 25 per cent budget cut and a reduction of faculty. In the late 1930's, however, Banks received approval to create graduate courses in agriculture and home economics because white politicians had begun to fear court ordered integration in fields where the state offered no courses for Negroes. The General Education Board, a funnel for private philanthropic funds, selected Prairie View as one of five black colleges in the South to receive aid for graduate work. Some black and white liberals feared these limited advances might retard more extensive efforts to improve black education through integration or the creation of a separate liberal arts college for Negroes.

Despite some twentieth century advances, black colleges in Texas during the 1930's continued to face a variety of pressing problems. Among the Negro schools Wiley possessed the largest library with just 14,500 volumes. Only Bishop joined Prairie View with a class A rank, while four others received B ratings. Though Prairie View stood second in the nation behind Howard with an enrollment of 1,500, only 3,000 black college students attended Texas schools.

Despite their limitations these colleges produced many political, business, and educational leaders within the black community in Texas. Occasionally their faculty or graduates rose to national prominence and even challenged the restrictions on the system from which they had come. Wiley president Matthew Dogan showed real courage in allowing his faculty to join the NAACP as early as World War I. Mary E. Branch, the first black female college president in Texas, helped increase the enrollment at Tillotson during the 1930's. James Farmer was born at Marshall, Texas, in 1920, while his father taught at Wiley College. He later received his undergraduate degree there in 1938, before he helped organize the Congress of Racial Equality in 1942. During the 1950's he acted as national program director for the NAACP, became director of CORE in the early 1960's, and served as Assistant Secretary of Health, Education, and Welfare in 1969-1970.

Social Life

Segregation and economic discrimination continued to limit the living conditions and social life of most black people in Texas. Working class Negro families, who formed the vast majority of all black families, generally lived in small, delapidated houses on dirt roads or streets with no plumbing or screens. Frequently more than one family crowded into a dwelling to share the rent. Less than 30 per cent of Texas Negroes owned their own homes in 1910, though the figures ranged from 14 per cent in Dallas to 45 per cent in Denison. Ernie Banks, who later became an all-star baseball player, slept three to a bed as a child in a Dallas house with a wood stove and an outhouse in the 1930's.

Most Texas cities did not follow the Dallas example and pass laws requiring residential segregation, but local white customs and control of most real estate also stimulated the trend toward greater separation, though the degree varied from one urban area to another. Concentration of Negroes in specific sections of Texas towns increased also because of the general trend toward urbanization. Black urban dwellers advanced from 19 per cent of Texas Negroes in 1900 to 39 per cent by 1930. The percentage of black population in urban wards during 1910 ranged from 20 to 38 per cent in Houston, in San Antonio from 2 to 20 per cent, in Dallas from 5 to 37 per cent, and in Fort Worth from 1 to 46 per cent. By 1930 over half of the 22,234 black people in Fort Worth lived in six of its wards. Negro population percentages varied from zero in three wards to 88 per cent in another. In Galveston almost 11,000 of the 15,400 black residents lived in three of the twelve wards in the city by 1940. Three of the ten wards in Waco contained 8,000 of the 11,000 Negro residents at the end of the 1930's.

Although Anglo-Texans subjected black people to poverty and crowded living conditions and shut them off from varied aspects of social and cultural life, most whites failed to recognize these factors as causes when some Negroes did not conform to middle class life styles. The gap between black and total divorce rates actually narrowed from 1900 to 1930. At the turn of the century .4 per cent of all males and .7 per cent of all females were divorced, compared to .9 per cent of Negro men and 1.8 per cent of Negro women. By 1930, 1.4 per cent of all males and 1.9 per cent of all females were divorced, in comparison to 1.9 per cent of black men and 3.2 per cent of black women. Negroes continued to resort to separation more often, as did the poor in most societies, because of the costs of formal divorce. To some extent black family relations foreshadowed mid-twentieth century concepts of incompatibility as a valid cause for divorce, for many separated persons soon settled down with another partner.

Others reunited with their original spouse when economic improvement allowed the husband to be a "good provider" and thus win back the respect of his wife. Such conditions never evolved for some individuals who became part of an itinerant population which floated from town to town in search of employment and companionship or in despair settled into the "red-light" districts and worst slums of Texas cities. Despite white criticism of black morality and fears of miscegination, some wealthy whites in every large Texas city kept mulatto mistresses.

Black folk songs reflected the tensions within Negro society. The verse

A yaller gal sleep in a bed,
A brown skin do de same;
A black gal sleep on de floor,
But she's sleepin jes de same,

suggested both hostility and jealousy toward mulattoes and at the same time pride in blackness. Other songs possibly expressed both a negative self image and resentment at racial discrimination. "God made de nigger, Made him in de night, Made him in a hurry, An' forgot to paint him white."

Churches continued to be the focal points of religious and social life among black people. They supported education and provided forums for discussion, outlets for frustrations, and an organizational structure for the development of Negro leaders. Black church membership in Texas reached 396,157 in 1916, then fell to 351,305 ten years later. Baptists formed a clear majority with 285,000 members in 1916, followed by the three Methodist denominations. By 1936 Negro Baptists numbered 388,044, which established them as the largest single denomination, black or white, in the state. Congregations remained generally poor and fundamentalist with some interest in foreign missions. Their small size also limited the effectiveness of most black congregations. By 1930 Houston counted 160 Negro churches which averaged 390 members and annual expenditures of $2,300. The fifty black churches in rural Fort Bend County averaged seventy-seven members and yearly costs of $400. Each denomination held annual state meetings which usually adopted conservative accommodationist positions, though internal divisions existed over leadership and programs. In 1939 the northern and southern branches of the Methodist Church reunited, but retained two separate black conferences in Texas which participated in a separate Central Jurisdiction for Negroes. Black Catholics, Congregationalists, Episcopalians, Presbyterians, Disciples of Christ, and members of Churches of Christ, all with connections to white denominations, numbered less than 10,000 members each. They generally worshipped in a less evangelical, more middle class style, but also took conservative positions on most social issues.

Urbanization stimulated the rapid growth from 1,500 members in 1906 to 18,000 in 1926 by holiness or spiritualist groups including the Church of the Living God, the Christian Workers for Fellowship, the Pillar and the Ground of Truth, the Apostolic Church, and the General Assembly. In Houston they claimed 31 of 160 congregations by 1930, second only to the Baptists. Some won even ministerial converts from the older denominations. J. Gordon McPherson, the "Black Billy Sunday," and "Sin Killer" Griffin ranked as the leading Negro evangelists who were active in early twentieth century Texas. The Reverend Lacey Kirk Williams, who served churches in Marshall, Dallas, and Fort Worth, became president of the black Baptist Missionary and Education Convention in 1916 and president of the National Baptist Convention in 1922. Despite their continued importance among black people, Negro churches in the early twentieth century had begun to feel the strains of urbanization as membership declined or more splinter groups appeared.

Lodges generally ranked close behind churches as important centers of social and civic affairs as well as sources of burial insurance. The members held weekly or monthly meetings of local chapters and an annual state convention. Lodge halls often doubled as recreation centers, schools, and churches. Several groups became public advocates of improved community health facilities for black people and supporters of other civic projects. While the Masons made an astounding leap from 2,000 members in 1903 to 30,000 in 1921, the Knights of Pythias surpassed them by expanding from 2,500 members to 800 lodges with 35,000 members—the largest number of any state. In 1905 the Texas Federation of Colored Women's Clubs joined the list of sixteen black fraternal and civic groups which already included three women's organizations, the Court of Calanthe, the Household of Ruth, and the Negro Women's Christian Temperance Union. L. H. Lightner of Hearne became an officer of the American Woodmen in 1911 and supreme commander from 1933 to 1950. For the black middle class such orders played an increasingly important role in a society which involved both greater concentrations of people in urban areas and rigid segregation.

Black Texans continued to seek recreation through separate county fairs and observations of national and state holidays as well as Juneteenth with parades, picnics, and speeches. Black people in Houston during 1909 organized De-Ro-Loc, a fall carnival patterned after the white No-Tsu-Oh festival. Dallas Negroes held a special fair in 1901. Almost three decades passed before the National Negro Progressive Society of El Paso organized a similar fair in Fort Worth. Managers of the state fair at Dallas began to set aside a Colored People's Day as a special attraction, with Booker T. Washington as the festival speaker one year. Negroes in some towns and cities developed or persuaded the municipal government to provide parks in black sections. Such facilities generally remained fewer than those for whites in comparison to population percentages. Negro sections of Texas towns also supported separate movie houses, saloons. cafes, bowling alleys, pool halls, dance halls, and soft drink parlors. Black people established YMCAs in Beaumont, Dallas, Fort Worth, and Houston; while Negro YWCAs existed in Beaumont, Dallas Houston, and San Antonio by 1931. Sports ranged from "craps" in red-light districts and slum areas, such as the "Deep Elm" section of Dallas, to organized teams on the sandlot, school, and semi-pro levels.

The two most famous black sports figures from Texas in the early twentieth century achieved their fame only after leaving the state. Andrew "Rube" Foster, the son of a Methodist minister in Calvert, won his nickname by out pitching "Rube" Waddell of the Philadelphia Athletics in an exhibition game during 1902. Because Negroes could not participate in white professional baseball leagues, Foster created and managed the Leland Giants, a black team based in Chicago. In 1920 he then organized the National Negro Baseball League which continued until the white leagues integrated in the 1940's.

Jack Johnson worked as a dock hand in his native Galveston before he became a boxer at the turn of the century. After a two year sturggle to get a championship fight, Johnson knocked out Tommy Burns in Australia during 1908 to become heavyweight champion of the world. He defeated several challengers including middleweight champion Stanley Ketchell in 1909 and former heavyweight champion Jim Jeffries in 1910. Johnson lost his title to Jess Willard in Havana, Cuba, during 1915, but continued to box for several years. Ironically the Texas legislature banned films of his victories over white boxers for fear they would cause Negro riots.

Black cotton pickers in East Texas gathered on large plantations or in small towns on Saturday night to sing and dance after long days in the fields. From the numerous amateur and part-time professional musicians who entertained them came a few of exceptional ability such as "Ragtime Time" Henry Thomas and Blind Lemon Jefferson who eventually recorded for Paramount Records. Jefferson also influenced the vocal and guitar styles of Josh White and Huddie "Leadbelly" Ledbetter. After playing in North Texas before World War I, "Leadbelly" spent several years in Texas and Louisiana prisons before he won national recognition for his renditions of folk and blues songs such as "C. C. Rider," "Jail-House Blues," "Ballad of the Boll Weevil," "Midnight Special," and "Irene." As larger numbers of Negroes moved into Texas cities in the twentieth century, professional black bands developed including outstanding groups led by Alphonso Trent and Troy Floyd. A later generation of black musicians from Texas included Teddy Wilson, Oscar Moore, Henry "Buster" Smith, and Budd Johnson who played with many of the nationally known bands and singers of the 1930's and 1940's. Wilson, with a formal background of study at Tuskegee and Talladega colleges, went on to win several national awards, taught at the Julliard School of Music, and became a staff musician for the Columbia Broadcasting System. Julius Bledsoe, who began his career singing spirituals in a Baptist Church in Waco, won acclaim when he sang "Old Man River" in Ziegfeld's New York production of "Show Boat" during 1928. He later played the lead in "The Emperor Jones" on Broadway and sang in several operas in Europe. Etta Moten, who left Texas early in life, achieved success as a radio and later as a television singer and appeared in movies and on the stage during the 1930's and 1940's.

Few Negroes of the early twentieth century could economically afford to acquire the educational background common to most poets, novelists, actors, and artists. Those who sought to develop their talents frequently faced problems of segregation and discrimination which thwarted their efforts. "Can a colored boy be an artist and make a white man's salary up there," a fifteen year-old cartoonist from Palestine asked the Chicago *Defender*. Most black writing concerned religion, education, or prominent figures within the Negro community from a self-help viewpoint. Negro newspapers ranged from open opposition toward segregation and discrimination by the Galveston *New Idea* to counsels of patience from the Dallas *Express*. Black papers appeared in Amarillo, Austin, Beaumont, Calvert, Dallas, Denison, Fort Worth, Houston, Port Arthur, San Angelo, San Antonio, and Waco by the 1930's. The *Informer* group, based in Houston, traced itself back to the *Texas Freeman* of the 1890's and published editions also in Dallas and San Antonio. Others lasted for only brief periods.

In 1936 John Mason Brewer published *Heralding Dawn: An Anthology of Verse* by Negro poets of early twentieth century Texas. Some selections appeared for the first time, while others had been printed earlier in black newspapers, other anthologies, and national or regional magazines. The contributors generally represented middle-class, college educated backgrounds. Yet their works ranged widely in topics and philosophy. Middle class self-help views appeared in poems such as "The Will to Do," while "On a Birthday" and "My Rainy Day" offered romantic or sentimental themes. "The Encampment Choir" and "Death Scene" reflected a religious note. "Watermelon" and "Deep Ellum and Central Track," about the Dallas red-light district, reflected the influence of the Harlem Renaissance during the 1920's with its increased acceptance of realistic literature about the social life of the black masses. Poems about hypocritical "Church Folks" and Negro leaders in "Sister Mandy Attends the Business League" explored some of the opportunities for social criticism within the black community. "A Naught's a Naught and a Figger's a Figger, All fer de White Man an' Nuthin' Fer De Nigger" and the "Question to a Mob—Who gave the life of man to you?" suggested an increased willingness by black spokesmen to question white racial attitudes and actions.

The federal government provided $100,000 for the collection, transportation, and housing of Negro exhibits at the Texas Centennial Exposition in 1936, after Texas and Dallas refused funds. Despite segregated facilities and problems with the building contractor, the exhibits and entertainers

171

such as Cab Calloway and Duke Ellington attracted crowds of up to 70,000 Negroes on special days. The exhibits impressed some white observers, though others could not overcome traditional racial assumptions about black people and admit their creativeness.

From the first decade of the twentieth century to World War II black Texans, like most Negroes in the South and the nation, remained outsiders in their relationship to the mainstream of society. Despite a variety of protests and legal efforts they retained little opportunity to participate in or influence politics, except on a limited basis in some urban areas. Black people continued to supply large quantities of unskilled or semiskilled labor for the expanding Texas economy, but only small numbers broke through racial and economic barriers to become landowning farmers, businessmen, practitioners of professions, or skilled craftsmen. Those who did generally found themselves reaping the restricted and ironic benefits of providing segregated services to the separate black community which resulted from discriminatory laws and social practices adopted by the white majority. Segregated schools and churches remained clearly weaker than their white counterparts because they served predominantly poor people who could offer only limited support to their churches and hope for only inequitable public support of education. Yet these institutions remained focal points for black social life and sources of the Negro middle class leaders who continued to channel both anger and hope into protests against the various forms of discrimination faced by all black Texans.

6

People of Anger and Hope

Politics, Violence, and Legal Status

When only 50,000 black voters in Texas participated in the fall presidential election of 1940 and 33,000 in the fall congressional contests of 1942, state politics of the 1940's seemed a continuation of partial disfranchisement and restriction of Negro involvement to unimportant contests. Yet the state NAACP conference of 1940 outlined a ten year program to eliminate the white primary, achieve educational equality, and end segregation by law. A test case during 1940 against the white primary in Houston sought unsuccessfully to establish that county clerks who assisted in primaries were "election officials," that the Democratic primary was the real election in Texas since the Republicans offered only weak opposition in the fall, and that the primary served as part of the official balloting process because it was regulated by the state election laws. Maceo Smith urged several organizations to join the NAACP in support of the primary court test. To formalize that cooperation representatives of nineteen groups met in Dallas on January 10, 1941, and created the Texas Council of Negro Organizations with Smith as chairman.

In 1942 Lonnie Smith, a Negro dentist in Houston, filed suit against the white primary rule of the state Democratic party which eliminated black participation in party decisions. The local chapter and the national office of the NAACP provided attorneys who included W. J. Durham of Sherman, Carter Wesley of Houston, and from the national level William Hastie and Thurgood Marshall, who later became the first black justice on the Supreme Court. In 1944 the Supreme Court reversed lower court decisions, as well as the Supreme Court judgement against R. R. Grovey in 1935, and declared the white primary unconstitutional since it formed an integral part of the election process prescribed by state law.

Immediate Anglo responses to the decision generally took the form of opposition or hope of circumvention. Former governor Dan Moody suggested a return to convention instead of primary nominations. Some legislators considered the repeal of all primary election laws. The chairman of the Democratic executive committee in Dallas County announced he would defy the decision. Harris County Democrats segregated the seating in their convention when some precincts selected black delegates. Congressman Wright Patman vowed that Negroes would vote in his district only "over my dead body." But by 1946 he and other Texas Democrats solicited their support. A poll in 1946 revealed that 44 per cent of white Texans believed Negroes should be allowed to vote in the Democratic primary, while 49 per cent disagreed, with majority opposition in East Texas. When local officials called out the National Guard to halt black voting in the 1946 primary at Marshall, a quick challenge by local black leaders forced its withdrawal. Colorado County officials gave Negroes only state ballots to keep them from participating in local elections. Some cities, however, appointed Negro poll tax deputies for the first time. As a result the 1946 primary attracted 75,000 black people, at least 25,000 more than any recent voter turnout. Yet that figure amounted to only 14 per cent of the potential Negro vote in an election which attracted 33 per cent of the white voters in Texas. In recognition of the increased black influence in Texas politics, white gubernatorial candidates advertised in Negro newspapers and spoke to black organizations. Homer Rainey, the liberal ex-president of the University of Texas, won 85 per cent of the Negro vote but lost the Democratic nomination for governor to Beauford Jester who also sought black support.

Negro voting became more significant in the late 1940's despite some continued opposition. Waxahachie officials in 1947 refused to allow black participation in a city election because they feared a possible Negro majority after heavy registration. Across the state 100,000 black people—18.5 per cent of the potential Negro voters—qualified to vote, which placed Texas fourth in the South behind Oklahoma with 29.6 per cent, Tennessee with 25.8 per cent, and Georgia with 18.8 per cent. In 1948 Negroes in Texas voted overwhelmingly for Harry Truman in the presidential election and supported the more liberal loyal Democrats in party battles on the state level. Yet educational level, forty years of enforced non-participation, registration difficulties, and lack of concern for black problems by white politicians kept a majority of Negroes away from the polls in many elections. In larger cities the existence of two or three separate black ghettoes reduced cooperation among Negro leaders, organizations, and voters. To overcome that problem in Houston black leaders created a local Council of Organizations in 1944. The new group interviewed candidates for office, met with local officials, and organized voter registration drives. The Progressive Voters League and the new Texas Club of Democratic Voters with chapters across the state sought to serve organizational and informational needs of Negro voters.

In 1951 and 1953 federal courts extended their decisions against white primaries to include the local citizens party primaries in Harrison and Fort Bend counties. This left the poll tax as the only remaining legal qualification on voting with racial overtones. A 1948 opinion survey indicated that 56 per cent of white Texans favored the poll tax, while 71 per cent of black Texans opposed it.

Negro Democrats in 1952 opposed the stand of Democratic Governor Allan Shivers, who endorsed the national Republican ticket after the national Democratic party took stands in favor of black civil rights and against return of the tidelands oil fields to state control. Black voters in Houston supported Adlai Stevenson for president by a margin of 20,641 votes to 925. The Democratic primary for governor in 1954 provided the next indication of Negro political views. Black precincts backed liberal Judge Ralph Yarborough by margins of at least eight to one over Governor Shivers, who won renomination for a third term by a smaller percentage than ever before. When the national Democratic party failed to adopt a strong platform on civil rights in 1956, it blurred party differences on the issue. Dwight Eisenhower's personal popularity also helped swing a larger minority of blacks to the Republican candidate. In Houston 11,592 Negroes backed Stevenson, but 6,006 supported Eisenhower in his re-election to the presidency.

By 1958, 226,495 Negroes had registered to vote in Texas—38.8 per cent of the potential black voters in comparison to 49 per cent registration of the possible white voters. Percentages ranged widely from year to year, however, according to county and interest in forthcoming elections. In San Antonio black registration ranged from 11 to 70 per cent during the 1950's. Thirty-six of the forty-four counties with 40 per cent or more Negro registration lay in rural East Texas. While bloc votes for liberal candidates had become common in black urban precincts, white paternalism and the economic power of employers and landowners strongly influenced Negro voters in some rural counties. Both major parties adjusted to black voting in the late 1950's by placing Negroes on their state executive committees—Republican doctor L. G. Pinkston and Democratic attorney W. J. Durham, both of Dallas. Although most black voters had shifted to the Democratic party, the

Republican candidate for governor in 1958 polled 15 to 20 per cent of the votes in Negro precincts.

The Democratic national platform took a strong stand on civil rights in 1960 and John F. Kennedy exhibited a personal interest in the arrest of Martin Luther King Jr. during a protest march in the South. These factors attracted black voters in Texas; 22,156 Negroes in Houston supported Kennedy, while only 3,393 backed Richard Nixon. Texas thus became one of the seven states where black voters provided the margin of victory for Kennedy in closely contested elections. Those seven states in turn swung a majority of electoral votes to Kennedy and made him president.

In the Democratic gubernatorial primary during 1962 the Texas Council of Voters, made up of black leaders from across the state, could not decide whether to endorse Don Yarborough, a liberal attorney from Houston, or Attorney General Will Wilson. Yarborough won his way into a primary with moderate conservative John Connally, former Secretary of the Navy and personal friend of Vice-President Lyndon Johnson. Connally, in his runoff victory, polled 35 per cent of the Negro vote because black business and professional leaders opposed Yarborough's emphasis on economic issues over civil rights and organized the United Political Organization to aid Connally. As governor, Connally maintained some black support by appointing Negroes to several state agencies and boards and by advocating greater expenditures for state educational and health institutions.

In 1964 black voter registration in Texas increased to 375,000—57.7 per cent of the Negro voting age population. Black precincts voted at least 95 per cent to re-elect President Lyndon Johnson and Senator Ralph Yarborough, who had supported the Civil Rights Act of 1964, and against Barry Goldwater and George Bush who opposed the bill.

The Supreme Court in 1966 struck down the poll tax as a requirement for voting. Since the period for payment of poll taxes had ended, the Texas legislature then allowed a free registration period, which expanded the total number of qualified voters in Houston by over 20 per cent. Negroes formed only 11 per cent of the free registrants, however, compared to 15.6 per cent of those who already had purchased poll taxes. Total black registrations in 1966 rose to 400,000 or 61.6 per cent of the potential Negro voters. When the Supreme Court also ordered the redistricting of state legislatures to provide "one man, one vote," the decision opened the way for the election of black legislators from new districts in large urban areas. After two previous defeats Barbara Jordan, a native of Houston with a Boston University law degree, won a contest in Harris County to become the first black state senator since 1881. Curtis M. Graves, a twenty-seven year old graduate of Texas Southern University and Houston public relations man, won one of the house of representatives seats from Harris County. Joseph E. Lockridge, a locally little known Negro attorney from Dallas, also joined the Texas house at the age of thirty-four because he received the endorsement of the integrated but conservative and business-oriented Democratic Committee for Responsible Government. After his death in an airplane crash during May, 1968, Zan Wesley Holmes, Jr., a young Methodist minister and SMU graduate, won a special election to the same seat with similar support. Although black people formed 25 per cent of the Dallas population, Holmes remained their only representative among fifteen local state representatives because they all had to win election in a county-wide multimember district.

Qualified black voters increased in 1968 to 540,000, or 83 per cent of the voting age Negro population. Paul Eggers, the Republican gubernatorial nominee, won 25 to 30 per cent of some black precincts in Dallas, by making a greater effort to gain Negro support than any other modern candidate of his party. The liberal Democratic presidential nominee, Hubert Humphrey, carried Negro precincts by 90 per cent or more, however, as he won the state by a plurality over the moderate Republican, Richard Nixon, and the segregationist American party candidate, George Wallace. In the 1970 Democratic primary for the United States Senate nomination, conservative Lloyd Bentsen defeated incumbent liberal Ralph Yarborough who retained the support of most black voters. Yet Bentsen in the fall election swept the black precincts in Dallas with 27,000 votes to 2,600 for Republican George Bush. Democractic governor Preston Smith ran slightly behind Bentsen's percentage, but also carried all of the Negro precincts by wider margins than in 1968 over Paul Eggers. Since all four candidates ran as moderate conservatives, the overwhelming black support for Democrats stemmed from continued distrust of the modern Republican party and the presence on the ballot in Dallas and a few other areas of Negro Democratic candidates. Voting by Negroes in large numbers reduced the amount of public anti-black comments by most white politicians in Texas. Yet as late as 1969 Congressman O. C. Fisher criticized interracial marriage in his newsletter.

On the local level older styles of manipulative politics continued into the 1960's in small towns and rural counties of East Texas, such as Marion, Upshur, and San Jacinto. Low income, elderly, unskilled, and less educated black people who were more numerous in such areas faced various degrees of economic pressure to accept white views on voting. Credit, loans, jobs, welfare payments, and legal and medical services could be cut off by landowners, storekeepers, lumber companies, doctors, attorneys, and white officials. In hotly contested local elections some Negroes refused to vote to avoid offending either candidate. Whites urged and assisted older blacks to vote absentee. Black leadership in such areas came from the small black middle class, but varied even then in attitude. Negro educators faced yearly contract renewals which kept most of them accommodationist in attitude. Black doctors who attained greater independence advocated registration and voting and led private discussions of desegregation. Whites supported those Negro leaders they considered "safe" to avoid the rise of more militant ones. To defeat some strong black candidates, however, white officials apparently as a last resort manipulated the vote count.

In attempts to retain Negro support, white politicians in small towns and rural areas became increasingly attentive to small individual problems and began to appeal in person for black votes at Negro meetings. White officials also financed barbecues for black voters and promised equal though not desegregated schools and better roads and street lights. The larger Negro vote forced more courteous treatment within a still segregated system and led to the defeat of several officials unsympathetic especially to the economic problems of the great mass of lower class black people in such areas.

Urban machine politics continued in San Antonio into the 1940's as Valmo Bellinger followed his father as political "boss" of the Negro precincts. After an unsuccessful attempt to reach an understanding with liberal Mayor Maury Maverick, Bellinger assisted in his defeat in 1941 and again when Maverick attempted a comeback in 1947. Thus Bellinger apparently assured the continuation for a time of a system in which he organized black votes in return for better public facilities and police treatment in the Negro section, and control of gambling for himself. Yet signs of change appeared when the local chapter of the new Progressive Voters League endorsed Maverick. Somewhat reluctantly Bellinger also backed Rainey for governor in 1946, rather than jeopardize his own position of leadership in the San Antonio black community.

In several of the other larger towns and cities in Texas black leaders began to seek offices themselves or to organize Negro voters behind more sympathetic white candidates. In 1949 the Reverend L. H. Simpson ran unsuccessfully for the Houston city council to reestablish in the minds of both black and white citizens the concept of Negro officeholding on the local level. Apparently because that possibility seemed quite real, Austin in 1951 changed its city council representation from geographical districts to an at-large basis which guaranteed control of all seats by the white majority. In 1952 black voters in Houston helped elect as mayor Roy Hofheinz, who worked quietly for desegregation of public facilities, appointed Negroes to city boards, and paved streets in the black sections. A Negro-Mexican-American coalition, led by returning black migrants and soldiers and by the G. I. Forum and LULAC, elected a Negro minister to the Slaton city commission in 1959 and then defeated an effort to change from a ward to an at-large system. By 1970 Texas counted forty-two black officials on the local level, which placed the state nineteenth in the nation for elected Negro officeholders. Black city councilmen had been elected in Austin, Bryan, Fort Worth, Galveston, Hearne, Houston, Huntsville, Malakoff, Port Arthur, San Antonio, Waco, and Wichita Falls by 1971.

During the late 1950's and early 1960's in Houston, black voters continued to back white moderates and liberals. Negro leaders in the "Bayou City," generally middle class business and professional men, emphasized coalition politics as a means to gain their primary goals of civil rights and desegregation. They employed a variety of groups ranging from the NAACP and the broad Harris County Council of Organizations to church, business, civic, fraternal, and civil rights associations. Yet black leaders and voters often felt a sense of powerlessness within the coalition, because they doubted that Mexican-Americans and Anglo laborers who formed the other large groups within it would back a Negro candidate. That suspicion seemed to be borne out by the race for mayor in 1969. Curtis Graves, the black state representative from Harris County, won 32 per cent of the vote when he unsuccessfully challenged incumbent Mayor Louis Welch. Graves received almost 88 per cent of the Negro vote, but less than 27 per cent of the Mexican-American vote and less than 13 per cent of the white labor vote. Welch, though not reactionary in his views, generally had opposed labor unions and had done little for Mexican-Americans. Though race never publicly became an issue in the campaign, it clearly influenced many votes.

Negroes in smaller urban areas could not even count on participation in a liberal coalition. Often they faced the continued frustration of white leaders making decisions which affected black people after consultation only with "Uncle Toms" who did not reflect Negro views. Black people thus faced lingering limitations on their political power even after they regained the right to vote and hold political office.

While Negroes sought to reclaim an equal political status in Texas, they also struggled to reestablish their civil rights. Black Texans in 1940 faced not only disfranchisement but also several forms of public segregation required by state or local laws. Most cities separated the races in publicly owned facilities. The legislature in 1950 elaborated on past laws which segregated swimming pools and public rest rooms by banning joint use of facilities in state parks. A poll in 1948 indicated that 66 per cent of white Texans opposed equal rights for Negroes, while 98 per cent of black Texans desired equality. Protests by local black organizations and court cases brought the integration of publicly owned restaurants, golf courses, parks, beaches, and rest rooms in Houston, Dallas, Beaumont, and other Texas cities during the 1950's.

Events in Houston suggest the general course of action and reaction by black and white citizens and leaders in dealing with segregation. In 1948 the leaders of black business, civic, and church groups requested a golf course, since Houston provided such courses for its white citizens. The city council let the case go to the federal courts which ruled in favor of equal facilities in 1951. Houston and most major Texas cities finally integrated their golf courses in 1954 after the Supreme Court decision on school desegregation. After the Supreme Court banned segregation of interstate transportation in 1950, the Houston NAACP chapter protested to both airlines and local officials about plans for separation in the new city airport. Mayor Hofheinz desegregated all air terminal facilities in 1953, except the restaurant. When a federal court ordered desegregation of the restaurant in 1955, white public opinion accepted the decision with little protest because of the criticism Houston received after the ambassador to the United States from India had been refused a meal at the airport.

The Houston branch of the NAACP requested in 1949 that the city and county end separate local library facilities and allow black doctors to use the city-county hospital. Hofheinz agreed to library desegregation in 1954. Medical associations or hospitals in Bexar, Dallas, Harris, and Travis counties desegregated in 1955, though no Negro physicians held full staff membership at the city-county hospital in Houston as late as 1963. When a federal court ordered Harris county to open its courthouse cafeteria to all citizens, the county instead closed the facility to all persons except employees and their guests. A suit by the Harris County Council of Organizations finally brought reopening of the cafeteria on a desegregated basis in 1962. Negroes also sued in 1960 to open the Harris County recreation area at Sylvan Beach. A federal court ordered desegregation of the park in 1962, after an appeal to the county commissioners failed. A request in 1961 from several black organizations for an end to separation in all city facilities brought official agreement in 1962. The desegregation of public buildings and parks followed a similar course in the other major cities of Texas, though San Antonio moved more rapidly without forcing its black citizens into the courts for favorable results. Yet questions lingered in some cases such as the Lubbock city cemetery which apparently segregated graves until 1969.

A Negro doctor in Wichita Falls won $500 damages from a policeman who assaulted him in an attempt to enforce separation in a waiting room, after the Supreme Court had ruled against segregation of interstate transportation in the late 1940's and early 1950's. Yet the Houston railway station remained segregated even after sit-in demonstrations in 1961 by freedom riders and students from Rice and Texas Southern universities. Five protestors received $500 fines for unlawful assembly. Others who received $1,000 fines won reversals on appeal to the Texas Court of Criminal Appeals. In Dallas during 1954 a black woman won $1,500 damages for her arrest when she left a city bus after refusing to sit in the rear. Between 1954 and 1956 all of the major cities in Texas ended separation on buses as a result of new rulings by the Interstate Commerce Commission and the Supreme Court.

In the early 1950's the subtleties of segregation and discrimination still included refusals by many stores to allow Negroes to try on clothes and the use of "girl" and "boy" by whites addressing black adults. As early as 1952 Carter Wesley, editor of the Houston *Informer,* protested hotel segregation in Texas. In the early 1960's black and white students from Texas Southern University in Houston, the University of Texas in

Austin, and other colleges across the state began to protest restaurant and theater segregation. Bishop and Wiley college students in Marshall undertook one of the first series of nonviolent demonstrations in Texas during the spring of 1960. Prairie View students with limited white support boycotted Hempstead merchants in the fall of 1963. Local chapters of the NAACP and the Congress of Racial Equality also picketed, petitioned, and boycotted against segregation in Austin, Houston, and San Antonio. The Harris County Council of Organizations raised $10,000 to pay the fines assessed students for picketing in Houston. In El Paso, where Negroes formed only 2 per cent of the population, the city council desegregated public accommodations by ordinance in 1962. Fears of negative publicity and economic losses began to produce voluntary desegregation by hotels, restaurants, and theaters in Texas as in other parts of the South during 1963.

Most Anglo-Texans opposed a federal civil rights bill which would ban separation or exclusion in such businesses, but President Lyndon Johnson supported the bill and Senator Ralph Yarborough voted for it in 1964 as a step toward equal opportunity and treatment for all citizens. A majority of white Texans accepted the legislation, though most felt integration was coming too quickly. After passage of the bill 54 per cent of black Texans believed the speed of integration to be satisfactory, while a considerable minority still considered it too slow. In some smaller East Texas towns, such as Huntsville and San Augustine, sit-ins and protests remained necessary even in 1965 to bring integration of public accommodations.

Violence and law enforcement continued to be major areas of tension and conflict for black people after 1940. Thousands of Texas Negroes served in the armed forces during World War II, the Korean War, and the Vietnam War. Doris Miller, who became a high school football star and boxer after his birth on a farm near Waco, left his segregated messman's duties on a battleship to win the Navy Cross by shooting down four Japanese planes and assisting the wounded at Pearl Harbor. Yet he died in action in December, 1943, still a messman. White politicians and newspapers in Texas opposed the stationing there of black troops from the North. Though part of the Negro 2nd Cavalry trained at Fort Clark, such views caused another segment of the unit to be diverted elsewhere. Local white protests brought the removal of the black 54th Coast Artillery from Camp Wallace near Galveston despite objections from Negro citizens. Black troops at Fort Bliss outside El Paso retaliated against white troops who beat Negro soldiers in June, 1943. To reduce local tension based on similar harassment of black servicemen, civilian and military officials in Houston organized an interracial citizens committee. Negro airmen stationed at Pampa Army Air Field met less hostility, but found few recreation facilities or local black citizens to help them break the monotony of their day-to-day routine. Negro cadet navigators trained at Hondo Field in 1944 with integrated mess and recreation halls, but separate barracks and classrooms. Prairie View claimed one of the few Reserve Officer Training Corps units at black colleges in the United States. Yet it only prepared Negro cadets for the limited number of positions available in the segregated armed services. A poet captured the ultimate irony of military segregation when he wrote:

On a train in Texas German prisoners eat
With white American soldiers, seat by seat,
While black American soldiers sit apart,
The white men eating meat, the black men heart.

With integration of the armed forces during the 1950's, more Negroes joined the military services because they offered greater social equality and economic security than some could expect in civilian life. Yet the Korean and Vietnam wars produced some unrest over the draft because the number of black draft board members for the entire state as late as 1968 totaled only twenty-six. The Texas National Guard contained a mere 177 Negroes out of 17,713 members in 1965.

On June 16, 1943, the rumor that a Negro assaulted a white woman set off a riot at Beaumont by whites who burned and wrecked property and beat people in the black section. Local police, national guardsmen, and rangers finally restored order after twenty hours and over sixty injuries. Though white riots and lynchings of Negroes became less common, incidents still occurred such as the whipping in Houston during 1960 of Felton Turner by four whites who cut KKK in his chest and stomach. The Houston Ku Klux Klan as late as 1971 published a *Rat Sheet* which listed various individuals it disliked including some designated as "niggerlover."

Strained relations between black people and white police continued in many Texas communities. C. C. White knew that some members of his congregation received beatings in the Jacksonville city jail during the 1950's and 1960's, but he tried to cooperate with the local police in the hope that he might influence their treatment of Negroes. An East Texas jury in 1958

189

acquitted a police chief of murder because he claimed the black man he killed had a knife, though other officers testified the man held no weapon and had raised his hands. When a Houston policeman killed a Negro accused of stealing a loaf of bread in February, 1966, only rain cooled the frustration and bitterness of the large crowd which gathered. Two white policemen in Fort Worth faced a civil damage suit in 1970 on charges of rough treatment against two black women and a boy. In May, 1971, two highway patrolmen claimed self defense when they killed or wounded three members of a black family near Shiner, though the Negroes claimed they resisted only rough treatment and fired no shots at the officers.

Efforts by the Harris County Council of Organizations and similar local black groups began to stimulate the hiring of black policemen in the late 1940's. By 1966 forty Negroes served on the Houston police force, fifteen in Dallas, seven in Fort Worth, and a scattering of others in Jacksonville, Lubbock, Midland, Paris, and other Texas cities. Of fourteen major cities in the United States surveyed in 1971, Dallas ranked last in ratio of black police, 2 per cent, to black population, 25 per cent. Because Negroes formed less than 4 per cent of the Houston police, the mayor began a special recruiting program in 1971. Few Negro policemen attained administrative positions where they could influence law enforcement policies and introduce some broader understanding of the black community and its problems to entire police departments. Instead black patrolmen often felt they had to prove themselves to white superiors by being "tough" on black suspected offenders. The Department of Public Safety and the Texas Rangers remained completely white as late as

190

1966, although the state attorney general added two Negro lawyers to his staff. Appeals for police review boards from the Houston NAACP and other local groups generally met with hostility from police departments and many white citizens and apathy on the part of mayors and other elected officials sensitive to a possible white backlash. In 1966, 46 per cent of the Negroes in Houston held a favorable image of the police while 31 per cent held an unfavorable image. But the unfavorable percentage rose sharply after police shot up student dormitories in the Texas Southern University "riot" of 1967.

Negative images of law enforcement among black people extended beyond the police to include also the courts, where there were few Negro judges and most prosecutors made a consistent effort to eliminate black jurors from all cases which involved a Negro defendant. In cases of murder and rape, which blacks committed almost exclusively against other Negroes, blacks averaged shorter sentences than white offenders. Yet the limited instances of black violence against whites probably accounted for the fact that 231 of the 361 men executed by the state since 1924 were Negroes. In cases of robbery, more often an interracial crime because of the economic structure, Negroes received longer sentences than Anglos. Those statistics indicated a lingering double standard of justice which black people had long perceived.

Protests and demonstrations against segregation and discrimination led to confrontations and a variety of charges or actions against black activists which many Negroes saw as new forms of police harassment. Lee Otis Johnson, who led anti-war protests at Texas Southern

University and publicly criticized the mayor and police of Houston at a Martin Luther King memorial rally, received a thirty-year sentence for giving a police undercover agent a marijuana cigarette. Black people questioned not only the length of the sentence but also the fact that the police waited six weeks to indict Johnson while the jury deliberated only thirty minutes. In Dallas, Student Nonviolent Coordinating Committee leaders Ernie McMillan and Matthew Johnson, who had organized boycotts against ghetto grocery stores, received ten year sentences for actions which resulted in $211 in damages at one store. Nacogdoches police arrested Mickey McGuire, a field organizer of the National Association of Black Students, for leading a protest march in May, 1970, and held him under $105,000 bond. McGuire in turn filed charges against the police for harassment which violated his civil rights.

Tension spilled over into violence on at least two occasions, once in 1967 and again in 1970, in Houston. Black protests over a drowning in a garbage dump and inequitable public school discipline as well as false rumors that a Negro had been shot stimulated debates and a gathering of students on the Texas Southern University campus during May 16, 1967. Police, who had been sent to head off action by the students, became a focal point of frustrations in the form of a rock and bottle barrage. About 10:40 p.m. a shot was fired. Police then fired on the dorms from which they believed the shot had come. Between 11:00 p.m. and 2:00 a.m. black community leaders tried three times to negotiate a truce, but apparently no organization or leadership existed among the students in the dorms. During the three hours students fired forty to sixty shots and police responded with about 2,000 rounds. The only person who received more than a flesh wound, Policeman Louis Kuba, died out of the main line of fire from what may have been a recochet by a police bullet. At 2:00 p.m. the police rushed the dorms, conducted a hurried and at times destructive search of the rooms, and arrested 488 occupants, though few weapons could be found. Many students who had taken no part in the exchange of shots felt they were roughed up unnecessarily and estimates of damage to the dorms ranged from $10,000 to $30,000. Yet a Houston grand jury exonerated the police of physical violence or property damage and indicted five activist students for murder on the assumption that they incited a riot which led to the policeman's death. Eventually charges against all five were dropped in 1970 for lack of evidence.

White newspapers emphasized the policeman's death, blamed school administrators or "agitators," and failed to present black views or explain the social and economic problems which had provided the setting and background for resentment and frustration by Negro students. With only that restricted view of events three-fourths of white Houstonians told pollsters they preferred forceful responses such as "shoot the rioters" or "call in the army." The Houston police, underpaid, understaffed, and without a course on race relations until 1968, thus felt little pressure to review their policies and practices. In 1969 and 1970 policemen claimed self defence in the shootings of three black youths suspected of crimes, although two were shot in the back. Police who conducted a mass search for a robbery suspect in the Negro Sunnyside section during the summer of 1969, entered several homes without warrants and became irate when some residents objected. When two Houston police apparently beat to death one black man and hospitalized another after their arrest, the police were suspended from the force but acquitted of murder despite eyewitness testimony from other police officers for the prosecution. Those who testified, however, felt themselves ostricized and resigned from the force.

In response to those events and continued economic and social problems a group of young blacks in the summer of 1970 formed Peoples Party II—patterned on the Black Panthers—to protest police action, to collect clothing and other second hand goods for poor people, and to set up a free breakfast program and health clinic for poor children. They also armed themselves and talked of watching police in the black section to stop unnecessary treatment. When a Negro former social worker, not directly connected with the group, told the city council that police must not enter the area around the party offices, the mayor and the police judged Peoples Party II a revolutionary organization. On July 26, after two members of the group were arrested in a confrontation with a policeman, other members stopped traffic near their headquarters to ask for donations. Some openly carried rifles or shotguns, a legal act in the state of Texas. Police arrived and some plainclothesmen climbed to the roof of a nearby church where they believed they were fired upon from the street below. Some black people unrelated to Peoples Party II, however, later testified the police fired first. In the brief exchange of shots which followed, the police suffered no casualties but killed Carl Hampton, chairman of Peoples Party II, and wounded three other Negroes and a white supporter of the black group.

White Houstonians and Texans generally accepted the police version of the event and agreed with the mayor of Houston who continued to describe Peoples Party II as "revolutionary." Few white newspapers or public officials tried to explain that the black community in Houston and across the state viewed the incident as another in a long history of harassment and overreaction by police. While Houston suffered the two major moments of violence, Negroes in many Texas cities continued to complain that police stopped and searched them without reason, used dogs to move non-violent persons or groups, and still used "nigger" and other profane terms in addressing black people.

Social and economic discrimination combined with rising expectations to produce deep frustrations which errupted in a series of riots against symbols of white authority and property by Negroes in the black sections primarily of northern urban areas during the 1960's and 1970's. Because of some civil rights progress and lower expectation and unemployment levels in Texas and the South, such reactions developed less frequently in those areas during the mid-1960's. But Midland became the site of one disorder in July, 1968. Local problems and frustrations in Lubbock, which stimulated the creation of a city grievance committee during the summer of 1971, burst forth during September in two nights of sporadic rock throwing and the wounding of a policeman after a white youth shot and killed a black fellow student following a fight at their high school.

In the period from 1940 to 1970 black Texans, with the support of the federal government and a minority of white Texans, almost completely eliminated political disfranchisement and the legal segregation practices which had circumscribed their status in the state. Yet discrimination lingered in some aspects of law enforcement to produce tension and conflict, especially when combined with continued economic problems.

Labor and Economic Status

Between 1940 and 1970 black rural population in Texas declined steadily as Negroes moved to urban areas both inside and outside the state. Trends toward mechanization, diversification, larger farms, and more livestock speeded those shifts. Poor educational backgrounds and lack of capital or sources of sufficient credit made it more difficult for Negro farmers to participate in such changes. Even in the 1960's black farmers found federal aid more difficult to acquire. In Marion County Negro farmers constituted 46 per cent of all agriculturalists, but received support for only 15 per cent of the government aided conservation plans. The rural black population of 504,281 in 1940 fell to 256,750 by 1960, while the number of Negro farmers was reduced from 52,751 in 1940 to 15,041 by 1960. White rural population and the number of white farmers also declined, but at a slower pace. The average size of black farms increased during the same period from fifty-seven to seventy-six acres, but the average size of white farms almost doubled over the same years. White farmers collectively owned slightly more acres in 1960 than they had twenty years before, while Negro farmers held only about one-third their total acres in 1940. Black tenants and sharecroppers conducted the greatest exodus from agriculture, for their numbers declined from 32,610 in 1940 to

3,138 by 1960. Farm income improved during the forties and fifties, but 42 per cent of the black rural population still lived on less than $1,000 a year as late as 1960. To supplement low incomes a majority of Negro farmers by 1954 also sought part-time jobs of other types. By 1960 only 8 per cent of all black workers in Texas remained in rural areas—a sharp decline from the 32 per cent of two decades before.

Urban black population in Texas grew from 420,110 in 1940 to 905,089 in 1960, stimulated by farming trends and industrialization speeded by World War II. In 1940, 35 percent of all Negro workers held service jobs, 10 per cent were in trades, 7 per cent in manufacturing, 5 per cent labored for public utilities, and 4 per cent held professional positions—percentages consistently below the white level except in the poorly paid service jobs. Among black industrial laborers 67 per cent occupied unskilled positions. Negro unemployment hovered near 11 per cent, almost 4 per cent above the white level.

World War II almost doubled the number of black industrial workers, from 150,000 to a peak of 295,000 in 1943, and increased their percentage of the state's industrial work force from 7 to 10 per cent. Most entered the shipbuilding, food and tobacco processing, metal products, aircraft, chemical, petroleum, and apparel industries. Yet wartime placement came overwhelmingly in unskilled positions, which meant that Negroes were hardest hit by postwar reductions. Some plants, such as Vultee Aviation, segregated their assembly lines. Others, including Baytown oil refineries paid higher wages to whites than to blacks who did the same types of work. By 1951 a study of 989 Texas manufacturers indicated that 75 per cent employed

Negroes, though only 8 per cent used them in clerical, professional, or managerial positions.

In the period from 1940 to 1960 several Negro occupational trends appeared. The percentage of black domestic servants declined from 29 to 21 per cent of all black laborers. This group in turn included most of the Negro women who worked—29 per cent in 1940 compared to 15 per cent of all white women. Black people sought other types of labor because of low domestic wages, which averaged $6.20 a week in 1941, and more openings in industry. Increases occurred in the percentage of construction, manufacturing, trucking, utilities, wholesaling, restaurant, retail sales, educational services, and welfare and hospital employees. Collectively those industries doubled the percentage of their Negro workers. A small new industry, menhaden fishing, developed at Sabine in the 1950's with all-black boat crews. Yet most of the new positions still fell in the unskilled or semiskilled labor categories.

In 1940 Texas counted 1 Negro designer, 2 architects, 4 veterinarians, 6 chemists, 6 engineers, 21 authors and editors, 23 lawyers, 31 pharmacists, 46 social workers, 85 dentists, and 164 doctors, compared to hundreds or thousands of whites in each category. By 1960 the number of black professional and technical positions, excluding clergy and teachers, had grown to about 3,700—though the percentage still fell far below that for whites.

Public employment also involved discrimination. In every city the percentage of Negro municipal employees fell below the black population percentage in 1940. A majority of those employed ranked low on the economic scale in positions such as unskilled street maintenance and garbage men. By 1960 in some cities, such as Houston, Negroes held a percentage of jobs similar to their population percentage, but still ranked low on any scale of skills and pay. Until the 1960's the state highway and education departments offered black people only menial jobs. Ironically the Texas Employment Commission, though it served many Negroes, hired few until the 1960's, and cut off unemployment assistance to black people who sought normally segregated positions which were unlikely to be opened to them. The State Board of Control, however, employed Negroes in 25 percent of its positions by 1966. Federal offices generally had better records of employing blacks but often did not promote them. A white protest developed briefly over the advancement of three Negroes to supervisory positions in the Dallas post office during the early 1960's. In building the Manned Spacecraft Center near Houston the federal government accepted the employment of segregated construction trades unions because no others were available.

Between 1940 and 1960 the median income for black Texans—higher than in ten other southern states—increased from 37 to about 50 per cent of the median income for white Texans. Yet during the early 1960's, 50 to 60 per cent of the Negroes in Houston earned less than $4,000—25 per cent earned less than $2,000. In the period from 1967 to 1970 the black unemployment rate in the state ranged from 5.7 to 7.6 per cent, compared to a white range of 2.7 to 4 per cent. C. C. White expressed the feeling of many lower class Negroes when he admitted that in 1960 "nobody in Jacksonville paid much attention to" the Civil Rights Movement. "We was more concerned here with helping people find work, and seeing that they didn't go hungry." A majority of black people in Houston ranked jobs their main problem, far ahead of education, housing, or legal and civil rights in 1966.

A survey of the opinions of white college students—presumably among the best educated and more broadminded members of their race—in the early 1940's indicated the extent of Negro economic problems based on racial views. Half of the students favored job segregation; 45 per cent agreed with unequal pay scales, and almost 60 per cent preferred segregated unions.

To overcome such opposition the state conference of NAACP chapters and the Texas Negro Chamber of Commerce, with forty-one local chapters, joined other black groups in the Texas Council of Negro Organizations during 1941 to press for equal job training and employment. They supported defense programs, vocational training in public schools, black participation on city planning boards, and job information for returning soldiers. Though unsuccessful, they also fought for a permanent federal Fair Employment Practices Commission to check for discrimination in industries with federal contracts. In the 1950's Negro chambers of commerce negotiated with their white counterparts to open up jobs for all qualified applicants regardless of race.

Black union members joined the struggle as Negro longshoremen and oil field workers charged discrimination in promotion lists during the 1950's. Construction unions and a number of other labor organizations in the skilled trades remained segregated even in 1970, despite public statements and efforts in favor of integration by both national and state AFL-CIO leaders throughout the 1960's.

Several approaches to black economic

problems developed in the 1960's. The federal government funded locally run community action agencies to locate and attack poverty in several Texas cities. Programs included emergency food and medical supplies, job information, child day care centers for working mothers, and legal aid to the poor. Two job corps training centers in San Marcos and McKinney, to teach specific skills, also developed out of the federal "war on poverty." VISTA workers—Volunteers In Service to America—worked in some Texas counties to assist with community organization and self help for the poor. But local white officials in Harrison and Panola counties forced the removal of VISTA workers because they provided some assistance for a black boycott of a store in Marshall and for a newsheet critical of race relations in the area. The United States Equal Employment Opportunity Commission, after hearings in Houston during June, 1970, reported that several companies had made commendable efforts to hire minority workers. But it also criticized the fact that the vast majority of minority employees remained in blue collar positions and that other companies and several unions had made little effort to recruit members of minorities.

Private groups also sought to grapple with black economic problems in a variety of ways. SNCC organized a boycott of white owned supermarkets in Dallas, which had been accused of offering poor merchandise and service at high prices in black sections while discriminating in employment. SNCC hoped to buy out the chain of stores, which in turn brought charges of customer intimidation against pickets. In Houston the Reverend Earl E. Allen, a Methodist minister and former community action agency worker, organized HOPE Development, Inc., with support from local churches and individuals, black and white. The organization provided job training courses, a youth work and culture program, and advice to Negroes about consumer, welfare, and legal problems. Some city officials accused Allen of being a "militant" and a "racist," but his white supporters and most Negroes saw him as a man of pride who stood up for the interests of poor blacks. An international program for vocational training, founded in Philadelphia by a black minister, the Reverend Leon Sullivan, established its first Opportunities Industrialization Center in Texas at Dallas during the late 1960's and expanded to Houston and Lubbock in the early 1970's.

Because Negroes continued to have difficulty acquiring capital, credit, and business training or experience, black businesses in Texas remained quite limited in number through the 1960's. Bankers were unwilling to risk loans on businesses in ghetto areas where buildings were older and the crime rate higher. Black consumers had less to spend because of their poverty. Although Negroes formed 20 to 25 per cent of the population in Dallas and Houston, they owned only about 3 per cent of the businesses in each city. Whites owned a majority of the businesses in the black community, which became a source of friction at times. Black businesses were almost unknown in towns of less than 50,000 total population. The existing Negro businesses fell heavily in the grocery, restaurant, tavern, and barber and beauty shop categories, with some small retail shops, gasoline stations, and funeral homes. Individuals owned most black businesses and, because of their financial problems, a majority lasted less than ten years. Most had one or no employees, while virtually none had as many as ten workers.

Major black businesses in 1947 included nine insurance companies with headquarters in Houston, Dallas, Austin, Galveston, Marshall, and Waco. The Fraternal Bank and Trust of Fort Worth existed into the 1950's when credit unions began to develop in some of the larger cities. In the 1960's Negroes with some white support founded the Riverside National Bank and the Standard Savings and Loan Association in Houston. The wealthiest black businessman in Texas during the 1960's, Mack Hannah, Jr., of Houston, operated a rubber plant in Beaumont during World War II. With the profits he then went into the insurance and building and loan businesses.

To aid in the development of black businesses the Small Business Administration began in the 1960's with local bank participation to make high risk loans in ghetto areas. The largest government loan to a minority firm in 1970 went to a Dallas company operated by three Negroes, to expand production and supply the Defense Department with $5,000,000 in canned hams. Both the Urban League in Dallas and the Negro chambers of commerce cooperated with government agencies to stimulate black business and with local colleges to promote business education.

Despite the success in business of a few Negroes, generally with unusual white financial connections or government aid, black people who wished to enter the business world still faced major problems. Basically the trend was toward large manufacturing and retail corporations with several plants or stores across a city or even the country. Few small businessmen could successfully meet such competition.

Education

In 1940 black educational opportunities in Texas remained clearly unequal. But a more responsive federal administration, World War II against German racism, and better organization on the local level made it possible for Negro leaders to pursue equality in the 1940's with greater hopes of real success.

At its meeting in November, 1941, the Colored Teachers State Association established the Texas Commission on Democracy in Education, with President Joseph J. Rhoads of Bishop College as chairman, to promote equality in teachers' salaries, school terms, funds, quality and breadth of courses, administrative positions, and accreditation. The commission in March, 1942, published *Democracy's Debt of Honor,* which outlined the inequities in Texas education and the resulting economic problems. In July, as a result of meetings with the presidents of the University of Texas and Texas A&M, a conference of seventy-five black and white civic and educational leaders met in Austin to work for equal education. This new Commission for the Improvement of Educational Opportunities for Negroes in Texas took up some of the goals of the Colored Teachers State Association and also sought to place two Negroes on the staff of the state department of education. That same year the state board of education dropped its separate standards of accreditation.

Because voluntary change seemed slow and uncertain, however, the Texas Commission on Democracy in Education and the Texas Council of Negro Organizations in November, 1942, threw their support behind equalization of teachers salaries in a case which had been before the Dallas school board since May, 1941. When the board refused to act, the Negro Teachers Alliance of Dallas brought suit to require equal pay. The board agreed in February, 1943, to a plan which would take three and a half years for completion. The Houston school board reached a similar agreement in April and a number of other major cities and towns had conformed by the 1944-1945 school year. Yet twenty school boards continued to resist equalization as late as 1947. The state attorney general ruled illegal the attempt by Texarkana to drop all black schools from the accredited list to avoid equalization. Some superintendents fired better trained Negro teachers to escape higher salaries. Other superintendents refused to renew the contracts of teachers who joined the NAACP, voted in the Democratic primary, studied outside the South, or showed any sign of discontent. A successful attempt to expand black influence came in San Antonio where in 1948 Negroes and Mexican-Americans combined to elect G. J. Sutton, a black businessman, as a trustee of the city's junior college system.

Despite progress toward equalization of teachers salaries, a variety of other problems plagued black public schools in the 1940's and early 1950's. In 1944-1945, 81 per cent of the Negro schools still had only one or two teachers, compared to 68 per cent among white schools; only 32 per cent of the black high schools met all standards, compared to 68 per cent of the white high schools; and Negro schools averaged 147 day terms, compared to 172 days for white schools. Negro schools generally had less funds for counsellors, vocational and science classrooms, health facilities, libraries, cafeterias, gyms, stadiums, and in rural areas buses. Even though the number of library books per black pupil doubled between 1940 and 1950, Negro students still had available to them less than half the average number of volumes available to white pupils. Black schools generally cost less for original construction and deteriorated more rapidly as a result of inferior materials. Negro students could expect a much more limited range of courses, both academic and vocational. Thus conditions in Texas as in other southern states bore out the Supreme Court decisions during 1954 and 1955 in the Brown case that segregated schools were unequal and therefore unconstitutional.

A poll of public opinion in Texas after the Brown decision showed whites four to one opposed and blacks two to one in favor of school integration. Succeeding polls in the late 1950's indicated a slowly but steadily increasing minority of whites who favored gradual integration. Yet Allan Shivers won reelection as governor in 1954 on a platform of opposition to desegregation by all legal means.

Friona in Northwest Texas integrated its three black students in 1953-1954, primarily for financial reasons. Sixty-six school districts including Austin, San Antonio, San Angelo, El Paso, and Corpus Christi, began at least token integration of a few students as early as 1955-1956. When segregationists in Big Spring challenged school integration they lost before the state supreme court which declared state school segregation laws unconstitutional. Yet integration remained limited because some districts allowed white students to transfer out of integrated schools and others fired Negro teachers after integration. The white Texas State Teachers Association initially refused to accept black members after the court decision.

Forceful opposition to school integration developed at Mansfield near Fort Worth in the fall of 1956 when over 250 whites stopped the entry of black pupils into formerly white schools. Governor Shivers used Texas Rangers, not to disperse the mob, but to remove the students. Mansfield schools remained segregated for at least two more years.

White Citizens Councils formed in several East Texas cities and towns and claimed a membership of 20,000, though only 250 delegates attended their convention in 1955. The councils supported three referendums on the 1956 election ballot—one against compulsory attendance at integrated schools, a second against intermarriage, and a third in favor of interposition by the state government against federal laws and their enforcement. All passed by margins of four to one. At least one local official of the NAACP met enough harassment from individual whites and local law officers to move his family out of the state. The state government tried to limit NAACP action on legal technicalities and to gain access to its membership lists, but only succeeded in solidifying Negro support for the organization. Over opposition from some white church groups, the Young Democrats, and Mexican-American legislators from South Texas, the legislature considered several new segregation bills. It finally adopted only two. One forbade school integration unless local voters approved, and withdrew state funds if a district integrated without such approval. A second bill allowed local officials to continue segregation under a variety of other pretexts—space, transportation, ability, psychological effect, sex, and morality. After the Little Rock crisis the Texas legislature voted to close schools if military force was used to integrate them and released children from compulsory attendance if the parents objected to desegregation.

By 1957-1958 over 120 school districts had made some effort to integrate. But among the districts which refused to act were most of those in East Texas, including both Dallas and Houston, the largest segregated school system in the nation. Negro parents filed suits in each city and won court orders for integration in 1957. Despite the election to the Houston school board in 1958 of Mrs. Charles E. White, an articulate Negro PTA member and former teacher who polled a large vote from white moderates, and appeals from ministers in Houston and Dallas, the majorities on both boards continued to delay action. Finally federal judges in 1960 and 1961 issued court orders to integrate one grade a year in both cities because the boards could not agree on integration plans. Yet the Houston school board interpreted its order so severely that even then only eleven black students could enter former white schools. In 1962 the federal judge threw out the board restrictions in order to speed the integration process.

By 1961, of the 722 biracial districts in Texas, 128, which contained about 10 per cent of the state's black pupils and 30 per cent of its white pupils, had been integrated to some extent. But careful zoning to match residential segregation, easy transfer plans which more affluent whites could use, and lack of transportation for poorer black students kept the overwhelming majority of Negroes in all-black schools. Fears of social and educational problems with hostile white parents, students, and teachers also retarded integration efforts by some Negro pupils and parents. Some supposedly integrated schools actually segregated students by classroom. Other schools cancelled all social activities or made them optional after school where they often remained exclusively white. The dismissal of well qualified black teachers and administrators and the closing of even some relatively new black schools also stimulated Negro criticism that they bore the burden of desegregation.

In 1962 the national government warned fifty-three districts which included federal installations that they might lose their "impacted area" funds if they did not integrate. By 1964, ten years after the Supreme Court decision, only 373 districts had desegregated, with the result that only 18,000 of 325,000 black students—about 5 per cent—attended integrated facilities. Yet those statistics placed Texas first in integration among the eleven ex-Confederate states.

After passage of the 1964 Civil Rights Act, which allowed the federal government to withdraw its financial support from any segregated school district, progress in integration spurted ahead. By 1965 all but sixty-six districts had undertaken some form of desegregation or filed plans to do so with the Department of Health, Education, and Welfare. That same year the Future Farmers of America and the Future Homemakers of America finally merged with their black counterparts, the New Farmers of America and the New Homemakers of America. The Colored Teachers State Association also combined that year with the Texas State Teachers Association. By 1966 twenty-six of the thirty-eight federal "head start" programs to provide pre-school preparation for poor children in Texas were integrated, the highest percentage in the South. The school year 1966-1967 saw 160,000 Negro pupils, about 47 per cent, attending integrated schools. About one-third of that number, however, were in schools with over 80 per cent black students. That same year predominantly Negro high schools began to participate in Texas Interscholastic League sports competition. By 1968 black members had served on the school boards in Houston, Dallas, Austin, Beaumont, Port Arthur, and several smaller communities. Yet Negro parents and the Justice Department found it necessary in 1967 to challenge Houston school board plans to construct new schools in a pattern which would increase segregation.

In 1969, fifteen years after the original desegregation decision, the Supreme Court ruled that schools districts could no longer delay integration nor could they avoid real compliance through freedom-of-choice plans and clever zoning lines. The Department of Health, Education, and Welfare then challenged the desegregation plans of twenty-six school districts in Texas, including most major cities in the state, because they maintained racially identifiable schools which were "visible vestiges of the dual school structure." The Texas Education Agency in the spring of 1970 reported that over 75 per cent of the black pupils in Texas went to desegregated schools. But HEW estimated that only 35 per cent of the Negro students in Texas attended predominantly white schools, compared to 38 per cent for the entire South. In San Antonio 87 per cent of the black students still attended predominantly Negro schools. In Houston and Dallas the percentages were 92 and 97 per cent. The NAACP and local parents joined in court tests of existing school plans in Houston, Dallas, and other cities. A major issue in several cases hinged on whether Mexican-American students should be considered a separate minority group or part of the Anglo majority for integration purposes. Federal district judges differed on that issue, but they increased school integration by redrawing school zone boundaries, pairing formerly black and white schools to place half the grades in one school and half in the other, closing some schools to produce consolidation of students in one building, and limited busing.

Opposition to the new court orders took several forms. Some white parents moved or rented apartments to give addresses outside integrated areas. Such actions caused the scrapping of one court ordered desegregation plan in Austin. A small group of Anglos bombed school buses in Longview to avoid their use for integration purposes. In Tyler three Negroes were convicted of conspiracy to bomb the school administration building. Fires destroyed buildings in two communities. Scuffles and protests by black or white pupils developed briefly in some schools over personal differences, lost football games, uneven representation among cheerleaders, teacher transfers, dress codes, and school names—such as Robert E. Lee—which offended black students. Mexican-Americans boycotted Houston schools for three weeks because the court order there did not recognize them as a separate minority to be integrated into the overall system.

In the fall of 1970 and the spring 1971 a federal judge in Texas eliminated the last nine all-black school districts in East Texas by combining them with adjoining biracial or white districts. He also ordered the Texas Education Agency to review districts with over 66 per cent minority enrollments or more than 90 per cent Anglo students and to enforce non-discrimination by withholding accreditation or funds. That ruling rendered more difficult the continuation of segregation in gerrymandered or suburban school districts.

In the summer of 1971, after the Supreme Court approved of busing as a means to increase school integration, HEW, the NAACP, and local Negro and Mexican-American citizens filed new suits in Dallas, Fort Worth, Austin, Corpus Christi, Amarillo, Odessa, and Midland. Republican Senator John Tower, no doubt concerned about the effect of federal action on the political future of his party in Texas, joined President Nixon in a condemnation of busing, despite the fact that almost 40 per cent of the pupils in the United States already were bused to school for other reasons. Local white citizens groups expressed opposition to busing on grounds ranging from cost to somewhat exaggerated fears of physical harm, a decline in morality, or an increase in drug use. Opponents talked of residential moves, boycotts, and creation of private schools such as already existed on a limited scale in other southern states. Black parents also protested especially the school board plans in Austin and Dallas because their children would bear the major burden of busing and school closing. Federal judges varied in their reactions to plans presented by HEW, local school boards, and the Texas Education Desegregation Technical Assistance Center at the University of Texas. In most cases judges sought to limit busing as much as possible, though all employed it to some extent. In Dallas and Austin judges accepted controversial plans for television or field trip contact between Anglo and minority students instead of actual school integration, though the Dallas television plan called for greater expenditures than busing. Cluster concepts which involved five or six elementary schools with limited busing also were accepted in other plans, such as the one in Fort Worth.

Catholic private schools in Texas led the way toward integration under the direction of Archbishop Robert E. Lucey. In the 1940's he began to educate Catholic parents on the issue and to promote integrated contests and other meetings between black and white Catholic schools. By 1954 at least 100 Negroes attended formerly white Catholic schools in San Antonio, although over 600 others continued in all black schools. By 1956-1957 the number of Negroes exceeded 1,100 in twenty-four integrated Catholic schools. In 1970 and 1971 Catholic schools at times limited their enrollments to avoid becoming havens for white students fleeing integrated public schools.

In 1943 the Texas Council of Negro Organizations despaired of ever pressing the state into a grant of equal higher education for black people and began to consider an attack on segregation of public colleges. The legislature officially constituted Prairie View a university in 1945 to avoid integration of the University of Texas or the creation of a Negro university. Black people felt insulted by that action, since it included little increase in funds. In June the TCNO and the state NAACP chapters agreed to a court test of segregation at the University of Texas.

In February, 1946, Heman M. Sweatt, a graduate of Wiley College and a World War II veteran who worked for the Houston post office, unsuccessfully attempted to register in the law school at the University of Texas. Sweatt filed suit in Texas district court during May, to desegregate the state institution. In June the judge ruled that equal facilities must be provided within six months or Sweatt could attend the University of Texas. All candidates for governor in 1946 promised continued segregation while the state created a law school by hiring two Negro attorneys in Houston to teach courses in a building next to their offices. Many white professors and students at the University of Texas sympathized with Sweatt and contributed funds for his case.

The legislature in the spring of 1947 authorized $3.2 million to build and operate a Negro university in Houston as recommended by Governor Beauford Jester and his advisors. In the interim the state moved its temporary black law school to Austin where classes would be taught by University of Texas law professors in a basement near the state capitol, with access to both state and university libraries. The Houston *Informer* expressed an inclination to accept the new provisions as a step forward, but did not oppose the decision of Sweatt, his attorneys, and the NAACP to pursue the case. When they lost in district court during May they appealed to the state supreme court, which rejected the appeal in October, 1948.

By the fall of 1947 the state had taken over Houston College for Negroes and expanded it into Texas State University for Negroes, a name later changed to Texas Southern University. That institution opened with 2,000 students, but critics accused the state of stereotyping Negroes because 42 per cent of the courses were vocational.

In 1947 and 1948 the state NAACP voted to continue its efforts to test segregation and discrimination through the courts. Forty-two black students who applied for admission to the graduate, medical, and dental schools of the University of Texas in April, 1949, peacefully demonstrated on behalf of their cause at the Austin campus and at the state capitol. In August the medical school accepted Herman A. Barnett to sit in regular classes, though a facade of separation remained because Texas State University for Negroes would issue his degree. The legislature hurriedly appropriated $185,000 to add a black medical school in Houston. In Austin the University of Texas graduate school accepted W. Astor Kirk, a Negro government instructor at Tillotson College, during February, 1950. He later withdrew upon learning he would be taught in separate classes, but returned to achieve a Ph.D. in the 1960's. Polls indicated that 76 per cent of all Texans opposed college integration in 1950, but 74 per cent of Negroes favored integrated higher education and 56 per cent of University of Texas students would accept desegregation of graduate courses.

In June, 1950, the Supreme Court, which had been considering the Sweatt case for almost a year, rendered a decision in his behalf because the new law school in Houston could not compare to the older one at Austin in faculty, library holdings, general facilities, or reputation. That summer three Negroes entered graduate and professional schools at the University of Texas, followed in the fall by Sweatt and fourteen others. The University of Texas medical school also accepted black students in 1950 as did the dental school in 1951.

Integration of undergraduate college education began in 1952 at Del Mar Junior College in Corpus Christi and about the same time at Amarillo College, at Wayland Baptist College in

Plainview, and at Southwest Baptist Theological Seminary in Fort Worth. The University of Texas and Southern Methodist University accepted black undergraduates in 1955. Other public and private colleges followed with only limited protest or violence. A white crowd prevented Negroes from enrolling at Texarkana Junior College in 1955, but white pickets failed to accomplish a similar goal at Lamar State College in Beaumont during 1956. Thirty-eight of the fifty-seven formerly white colleges in Texas had been integrated by 1958. But Texas Tech, Baylor, Texas Christian, and Rice universities did not desegregate until the early 1960's—Rice only after breaking the will of its founder, William Marsh Rice, in court. Five state colleges and four junior colleges remained segregated as late as 1964. Black professors joined the faculties of the University of Texas and Rice University for the first time in 1964 and 1965. The University of Texas did not integrate its dorms until 1965, the year the Southwest Conference also integrated its athletic competition. Ironically, by tightening entrance requirements and forbidding admission of minority students under a special Council of Legal Educational Opportunity program which had operated in 1968 and 1969, the University of Texas regents made its entering law class "lily white" again in 1971.

While Negroes remained excluded from white colleges in Texas during the 1940's, the thirteen black colleges—more than in any other state—grew steadily. When integration offered the Negro student a wider educational selection, however, most black schools leveled off in enrollment or suffered mild declines, except for the state supported former Negro colleges with lower tuitions. Samuel Huston and Tillotson

216

colleges merged as Huston-Tillotson College in 1952 to strengthen its faculty, student body, and financial status. Among the private colleges only Bishop, after its transfer to Dallas in 1961, attracted more than a thousand students. Some black colleges, such as Butler, Paul Quinn, and Mary Allen, could not gain accreditation because of weak faculties and libraries. Bishop and Jarvis faced probation for similar reasons. Prairie View had the largest budget in 1959, at $2 million; Texas Southern the best library, with 79,000 volumes; and Huston-Tillotson and Bishop the highest percentage of Ph.D.'s on their faculties, with 33 per cent. The United Negro College Fund and the Ford Foundation provided financial assistance to several of the predominantly Negro schools. By 1968 Prairie View received over $7 million in state and federal funds. Yet its student body, though one-fourth the size of its related land grant school, Texas A & M, received only one-sixth as much in federal funds and only one-ninth as much from the state budget.

Participation of students from black colleges in civil rights activities, tensions between campus groups, or campus protests against highly restrictive and outdated rules and regulations for students resulted in the expulsion or suspension of students at Prairie View in 1968 and 1971, and at Texas Southern and Paul Quinn in 1970. The American Association of University Professors and the Southern Association of Colleges and Secondary Schools conducted investigations of possible arbitrary administrative action in some cases. Yet in spite of their numerous problems black colleges continued in the 1950's and 1960's to serve the needs of many Negro students who came from weak public school backgrounds. As

217

late as 1961, a majority of the freshmen at Texas Southern took remedial math or English. Texas Southern students also could attend the University of Wisconsin for a year through an exchange program.

Black students at predominantly white schools also made their presence felt in the late 1960's with protests against various forms of discrimination and demands for black studies courses and programs to improve race relations and enhance their sense of cultural pride and identity. Afro-Americans for Black Liberation at the University of Houston became the most active and controversial group because of its off-campus programs to aid the ghetto and charges of violence on campus. While Texas A & M initially rejected such requests, most larger universities, including the University of Texas at both Austin and El Paso, the University of Houston, Southern Methodist, and Texas Tech, moved to implement black or ethnic studies programs. Negro legislators and professors also applied pressure on the Texas Education Agency to revise the public school curricula and include more and better balanced treatment of minorities in history and social studies courses. Thus they passed well beyond the long established stage of celebrating "Negro History Week" in all-black schools and at times throughout the Negro community.

Despite major advances after 1940, the evidence of lingering educational and economic discrimination appeared in the 1970 figures for high school and college graduates in Houston. Of the white population in the city above the age of twenty-five, 59 per cent had completed four years of high school and 13 per cent had finished four years of college. Only 40 per cent of the black people in Houston had completed four years of high school and only 7 per cent had finished four years of college.

Social Life

By 1960 three-fourths of the black people in Texas lived in urban areas. The Negro percentage of the total population in Houston increased from 21 per cent in 1950 to 26 per cent in 1970, while in Dallas it grew from 13 per cent to 25 per cent. Beaumont led both of the larger cities with 30 per cent. Total figures on the increase in black urban dwellers proved far more impressive—in Dallas from 58,000 to 210,000, and in Houston from 125,000 to 317,000 over the same twenty-year period. Of the new arrivals in any major city, half to two-thirds came from rural areas in Texas, while the remainder moved from some other urban area in the state. Most of the Negro city dwellers fell between the ages of twenty-five and thirty-four with men outnumbering women. Migrants generally fell into two categories—persons with no more than four years of education or persons with at least a full high school education. Such movements also stimulated marriage, divorce, and birth rates. Yet the black birth rate in Houston during 1941 was fifty-three per 1,000 women between the ages of fifteen and forty-four, compared to sixty-six white births per 1,000, primarily because more Negro women worked. Migration out of the state continued to attract many bright young Negroes such as Percy Sutton, who moved to New York city during World War II and in the 1960's became a state legislator and president of the borough of Manhattan. The largest single group of migrants from Texas, however,

219

moved west, primarily to California, in the 1940's and 1950's.

Black migrants to Texas urban areas swelled the size of the existing ghettoes. By 1960 one of the twenty-four census tracts in Austin contained 13,260 of the 24,413 Negro residents of the city. Two other tracts held 5,000 more black people, while eleven tracts each included less than 100. Dallas had no Negroes in thirty-six of its over 200 census tracts, while black people formed over 90 per cent of the residents in at least six others. In Fort Worth fifty-three of the eighty census tracts recorded less than 100 Negroes each while black majorities lived in eleven others. Houston showed slightly greater dispersal of its Negro population with less than 100 black people in only fifty-nine of its 164 census tracts. But one of its suburbs, Pasadena, numbered only twenty-nine Negroes in its entire population of 58,737. Yet Pasadena represented only an extreme example of the statewide trend, for whites in the metropolitan suburbs of Texas during the 1960's increased 45 per cent compared to a black increase of only 16 per cent. Between 1940 and 1960 Texas cities averaged almost an 11 per cent increase in residential segregation, which left the seventeen largest urban areas in the state with a range of segregation from a low of 80 per cent in El Paso to a high of 98 per cent in Odessa. Twelve of the seventeen cities were over 90 per cent segregated. By 1970 Texas counted three of the twenty most segregated major cities in the nation—Dallas ranked fourth, Houston ninth, and San Antonio fifteenth. The state segregation level declined 2.8 per cent in the 1960's, however, because of increased house construction and new laws against residential discrimination.

The housing available in such ghettoes ranged widely, but 63 per cent in the black section of San Antonio ranked as delapidated or lacked a bath, toilet, or· running water as late as 1950. Housing units also increased at only half the rate of population growth for Negroes in San Antonio during the 1940's, because contractors assumed all blacks to be poor and none wanted "to become known as a 'nigger' builder." In 1952 out-of-town competition built and easily sold 200 new homes in the Negro section which stimulated local construction of houses to some extent. In Houston 52 per cent of the black housing was substandard in 1950, but city contractors showed more interest in providing new houses and Negroes bought into white areas west and south of the central ghetto. White home owners tried to organize against black buyers and newly purchased Negro homes were bombed in Dallas and Houston in the 1940's and 1950's. Such efforts failed and the white exodus which followed, rather than Negro entry into residential areas, caused some decline in property values. Yet as late as 1966 the black Settegast area of northeast Houston still suffered from open sewers, unpaved streets, a lack of city water, and rats. Because 25 per cent of the homes had no inside toilets, seepage from outside facilities polluted water wells in the vicinity. Similar conditions existed in sections of the other major Texas cities.

By 1970 black people formed almost 13 per cent of the Texas population. They held only 10 per cent of the owner occupied homes in the state, but rented 15 per cent of those leased in some manner. Negroes occupied 19 per cent of the dwellings with more than one person per room and 25 per cent of those without complete plumbing facilities. The results of economic discrimination and residential segregation thus appeared quite clearly in such statistical studies.

Public housing and urban renewal projects proved a mixed blessing to Texas Negroes. In Dallas and Fort Worth black people occupied about half of the public housing in 1959, though it remained segregated by custom and location. As a result of the Kealing urban renewal project in Austin during the 1960's the area had more paved streets, lights, and parks. Yet one-third of the families in the "renewed" area did not get decent homes, 70 per cent paid more rent or higher house payments afterward, and 19 per cent of the pre-project home owners had become renters. Highway construction in Austin went far toward eliminating the small black enclave called Clarksville on the overwhelmingly white west side of the city. Urban renewal in Lubbock caused dozens of poor Negro families who could not afford new public housing to move into a largely shack section outside the city limits where some raised gardens and animals which provided it with the nickname "Pig City." Preston Smith, the governor of Texas and a Lubbock resident, showed little understanding of the situation when he used it as an example of his view that "Some people like to live in slums."

Because such social conditions, coupled with low income, continued to prevail through the 1960's, black people approached their situation with varied attitudes. Some saw no hope and escaped into alcoholism and into drug addiction. Others became stoics who accepted conditions as they were and made the most of them. J. D. Sonny Wells, the son of an alcoholic and a prostitute, remembered "the flashy clothes of the gamblers

and pimps and the sharp automobiles. I recall that
I had been very anxious to grow up so that I could
be one of them." Some, such as one Houston
businessman and church deacon, exploited other
Negroes as a tenement owner, "loan shark,"
numbers operator, and purveyor of prostitutes.
Some released their frustrations through violence,
almost entirely against other black people. Negroes
formed 67 per cent of the murderers and murder
victims in Houston during the mid-1950's. A
survey of 327 murder charges against black people
revealed that 321 of the victims also were Negroes.
The chances of robbery or rape ranged from 350 to
400 per cent higher in the black section than in
other parts of Houston in the 1960's. Such
conditions also disrupted family life to the extent
that 24 per cent of black families in Texas by 1970
had female rather than male heads. Bobby Seale
grew up in Dallas, Port Arthur, and San Antonio
during World War II as the son of a carpenter who
was forced by economic and social conditions to
raise his own three children and a nephew in
houses shared with other families. The Seales later
moved to California where they faced similar
problems and Bobby became chairman of the
Black Panther Party in 1966.

Black urban folklore of the 1960's provided
some insight into the quite different culture of
Negroes with limited and often unstable incomes,
who still faced discrimination in a number of
forms. Clearly resentment of white power and
exploitation of black people existed as a major
element in ghetto folklore. Older folk tales
suggested accommodation or subtle rejoinders as
the proper response, but newer ones reflected
greater pride and desire to fight back. Negro urban
folklore showed no sense of attachment to place, a

product of both minority status and migration. Both powerlessness and lack of roots produced certain logical consequences. Black people who could not attain or retain status in middle class ways sought recognition through verbal contests, such as "playing the dozens," and other activities including sex which displayed their virility. That emphasis in turn placed greater strain on male-female relationships and caused suspicions of hypocrisy and self interest toward middle class Negroes who professed different standards or seemed to lack race consciousness.

Yet out of the turmoil and differences within the black community new leaders emerged to attack Negro social problems. In Dallas Albert Lipscomb organized black homeowners to fight for just compensation when the city chose to expand Fair Park and offered Negroes seventy-five cents a square foot while some whites were reported to have received $4.50 to $20 per square foot. Ruth Jefferson of Dallas organized a sit-in at the state welfare department when it reduced from $135 to $123 a month the payment for her and her five children. While some whites complained, the black community elected her a community organizer in the local poverty program.

Frequently business, professional, and political figures began to replace black ministers as community leaders, especially in larger urban areas, although some ministers participated in the NAACP or local civil rights organizations. Some white ministers and church organizations actively supported integration efforts in Texas during the 1950's and 1960's. The United Methodist Church in the late 1960's eliminated its separate black conferences in Texas, though its congregations with a few exceptions remained totally white or black. Black members of the United Methodist Church in Texas had grown in number between 1950 and 1968 only from 36,000 to 38,500. Although membership figures for black denominations are difficult to determine, this rate of increase, which was less than the rate of population growth for the same period, suggests some probable decline of church influence within the black community. Other predominantly white denominations continued to retain a small and relatively stable Negro membership and opened their educational institutions to black students in the 1960's. Negro churches continued to serve social as well as religious functions in the black community and provided some stability amidst population shifts and social change. Yet the trend toward urbanization destroyed many rural churches and did not necessarily replace them with comparable city congregations, even though recent migrants showed more church orientation than other urban dwellers. The Muslims established mosques in Fort Worth, San Antonio, Dallas, and Houston during the 1960's, with related business and social functions, to upgrade the lives of lower class black people.

Leadership in the Negro community also came from its newspaper editors. From the 1940's through the 1960's black people supported papers in Beaumont, Dallas, Forth Worth, Lubbock, San Antonio, Waco, and Marshall because most white edited Texas papers still failed to fully or fairly cover the Negro community. The Beaumont *Enterprise-Journal*, for example, refused to print black wedding pictures until 1968. Houston Negroes by the 1960's could choose from four black weeklies. Fort Worth served as the publishing headquarters for a series of monthly magazines,

225

such as *Sepia*, which achieved national circulations.

Sports provided an increasing number of heroes for black youth in Texas despite the fact that recreational facilities and public school athletics in the state remained segregated until the late 1950's. Dave Hoskins, who later played for Cleveland in the American League, integrated Texas League baseball as a pitcher for Dallas in 1952. I. H. "Sporty" Harvey, a San Antonio boxer, successfully challenged the twenty-year-old state law against integrated boxing and wrestling in 1954.

From the segregated sand lots of Dallas and Beaumont came two stars of major league baseball in the 1950's and 1960's. Ernie Banks, a shortstop-first baseman with the Chicago Cubs, led the National League twice in home runs and runs batted in, was voted its most valuable player in 1958-1959, and won a place in the Texas Sports Hall of Fame in 1970. Frank Robinson, an outfielder-first baseman, won most valuable player in the National League with Cincinnati and in the American League with Baltimore when he led the league in home runs, batting average, and runs batted in during 1966.

Texas also provided the birth place of several outstanding black football players. Abner Haynes starred at North Texas State University on two Missouri Valley Conference championship teams in the late 1950's before he led the professional American Football League in rushing and became its player of the year in 1960. The Beaumont-Port Arthur area alone produced several professional football stars of the late 1960's and early 1970's including Mel Farr, Bubba Smith, and others who played for schools such as UCLA and Michigan State while Southwest Conference coaches continued to claim they could not recruit black players who could pass entrance requirements. Jerry LeVias finally integrated the Southwest Conference and won All-American honors while playing for Southern Methodist University from 1965 to 1968.

Other outstanding black athletes with Texas ties included Elvin Hayes, an All-American and one of the all time high scorers in college basketball at the University of Houston in the late 1960's. Tommie Smith, whose family moved from Texas to California, became one of the world's best 220 yard dash and 880 yard relay runners in the mid-1960's. Another migrant to California, Lee Elder of Dallas, captured the black United Golf Association championship in 1967. Curtis Cokes of Dallas won the world's welterweight boxing championship in the late 1960's.

Inspiration for the small but growing black middle class came from other sources. When the City University of New York during the fall of 1967 presented an exhibition entitled "The Evolution of Afro-American Artists, 1800-1950," it included the work of John Biggers, head of the art department at Texas Southern University. Most of his early drawings, paintings, and sculpture depicted Negro life in the rural South. But that same year the University of Texas Press published *Ananse: The Web of Life in Africa*, a volume of his drawings from a trip to Ghana and Nigeria. The following fall the Houston Museum of Fine Arts featured his work in a special show.

In the literary world John Mason Brewer achieved acclaim as one of the nation's leading folklorists. After his birth in Goliad he acquired degrees from Wiley College and Indiana University. He taught on the public school and college level in

Texas and other southern states while he wrote two volumes of history, two of poetry, and six of folklore between 1933 and 1965. In recognition of his skill Theta Sigma Phi in 1954 voted him one of the twenty-five best Texas authors. He later became the first black member of the Texas Institute of Letters and vice-president of the American Folklore Society.

Black people in Texas achieved political, educational, and economic progress after emancipation. Yet most advances came in the period 1940-1970 because Negroes placed increased pressure for change on white Texans and because the federal government sustained their assertion of equal rights in several realms. At every step along the way most Anglos opposed change and resisted to differing degrees, as the reaction to real school integration again indicated in the early 1970's.

Some white Texans, especially religious, academic, and literary leaders, lent their support to the cause of black equality. Two writers, John Howard Griffin and Grace Halsell, temporarily darkened their skin color to personally experience and report on racism in the books *Black Like Me* and *Soul Sister*. Larry King, a liberal political aide turned writer, approached the problems of race relations in a novel, *The One Eyed Man*, and a series of autobiographical essays, *Confessions of a White Racist*. Yet other Anglo Texans continued to circulate myths such as the stories that Negroes killed Martin Luther King, Jr., and Medgar Evers to have martyrs for their cause. That continued refusal to accept the realities of race relations, coupled with the deep seated fears of social and sexual contact, which lay behind many fears of school and residential integration, suggested the psychological barriers that remained in the path of real understanding and equality.

Black people, who had expressed both anger and hope more openly in the period 1940-1970, to some extent turned inward again to their own community for security and strength in the early 1970's, out of both a heightened sense of pride and a weariness with white hostility. Their greatest pressure for change continued in the realm of economics. A phrase common in the black community suggested that integration of public accommodations was useless if one could not afford their services. Some writers described events of the late 1950's and early 1960's as a "Second Reconstruction." It was unsettling, to those who in the early 1970's still hoped for complete equality, that the first Reconstruction had ended on the same note, which afterward produced the economic emphasis of Booker T. Washington. His efforts proved to be of limited value because rapid technological changes destroyed many jobs for which he had trained black people. Similar prospects appeared to face many Negroes in the 1970's, especially with the federal government in disarray if not retreat on civil rights questions. Thus complete pessimism was not necessary to produce fears that, while there would be no return to disfranchisement and legal segregation in the 1970's, black status in Texas and the United States might change little in the immediate future and still fall short of full equality.

7

People of Struggle and Progress

Politics and Legal Status

Between 1970 and 1995, African Americans in Texas expanded their role in state and local politics, despite lingering limitations. In 1975 the legislature adopted an act to force voters to reregister, but minority voters successfully opposed that law under the federal Voting Rights Act, which had been expanded to include Texas the same year. After African-American voter registration in the state peaked at 83 percent in 1968, it dropped to about 65 percent in the 1970's and 1980's.

Most African-American voters remained Democrats and helped elect Governors Mark White (in 1982) and Ann Richards (in 1990). Greater conservatism among white voters, however, elected Republican Governors William Clements in 1978 and 1986 and George Bush Jr. in 1994, each of whom reflected less interest in minority concerns. Only a limited number of Republicans came from the developing African-American middle class. Use of derogatory racial comments helped defeat some political figures, such as agriculture commissioner Reagan Brown in 1982. No African-American candidate won a statewide political office, but White appointed Myra McDaniel secretary of state in 1984, and Richards appointed more African Americans to state boards in the 1990's than had previous governors.

As a result of redistricting after the 1970 census and her effectiveness in the Texas senate, Barbara Jordan won election in 1972 as the first black Texan in Congress. There she served as a voice for reform, representing a Houston district where African Americans and Mexican Americans formed the majority. She decided against reelection in 1978 and later was elected to the National Women's Hall of Fame. Another successful legislator, Mickey Leland, took her place, but after his death in a plane crash in 1989, Craig Washington moved up from the legislature to win that district. In 1994 Sheila Jackson Lee defeated Washington but still maintained African-American representation from Houston in Congress.

The reapportionment of congressional districts after the 1980 and 1990 censuses stirred debate and court challenges as minorities struggled to achieve greater representation. In 1992 a second black Texan, Eddie Bernice Johnson, won a seat in Congress from a new Dallas district. Further court cases arose in 1994 as whites sought to have new minority districts rejected by conservative federal judges appointed by Republican presidents.

Black Texans also focused on expanding representation in the state legislature. Working with Mexican Americans, African Americans litigated against at-large elections for the legislature. Federal court decisions in 1972 and 1973 required single-member districts for legislators in Dallas and Bexar (San Antonio) counties. Another decision in 1974 called for single-member districts in eight other major cities in Texas, which led to African Americans winning legislative seats from most major urban areas—a total of fifteen by 1985. Some became leaders, as did Wilhelmina Delco, who spoke for education. Most reflected moderate to liberal views, although a few, such as Clay Smothers of Dallas, took conservative positions. As minority representation in the legislature approached the corresponding population percentage, white Republicans challenged several districts drawn after the 1990 census, and in 1995 the legislature agreed to redraw about half the districts.

Minority attorneys then focused on city council, county commission, and school board elections. Court cases at Nacogdoches and reviews by the Justice Department in the mid-1970's began a trend toward single-member districts, which took place in forty-one cities or counties by 1990. Yet white state government leaders expressed reservations about renewal of the Voting Rights Act in 1981. African-American members of city councils jumped from 59 to 138 in that period. Yet thirty small cities with at least 10 percent minority population retained at-large elections in 1989 and had no African-American council members. Black officeholders in Texas increased from 45 in 1971 to 472 by 1992. With that growth came the creation in 1989 of the Texas Association of Black

City Council Members, which selected T. J. Patterson of Lubbock as its first president. Yet the percentage of African-American officeholders remained well below the percentage of black population in the state.

Among African-American officeholders in 1982 were three small-town mayors; by 1990 the number had grown to twelve. Not until 1995 would a major Texas city, Dallas, elect its first African-American mayor. In a city where minorities were 51 percent of the population, the people chose Ron Kirk, who earlier had been Texas's secretary of state.

As African-American voting increased, other forms of discrimination declined after 1970. Yet some legal problems still existed. Public housing remained segregated in the 1990's, despite a desegregation order in 1982. In all-white Vidor, near Beaumont, the federal housing department struggled in the early 1990's to overcome harassment and move black families into the housing project. Some white residents welcomed the families; others, such as a woman facing a court order to pay for past intimidation, did not. Acts of harassment or discrimination flared in other small towns during the 1990's.

Radical groups continued inciting such acts. In 1979 the Ku Klux Klan paraded in Dallas, and during the early 1980's Klansmen organized camps in East and North Texas. Small Klan marches occurred in Houston, San Antonio, Nacogdoches, and Austin between 1983 and 1986, and again in Houston and Austin in the early 1990's. Neo-Nazi and skinhead groups appeared in the 1980's, especially in Houston and Dallas. Members burned an African-American church in Ellis County in 1989 and killed African Americans in Fort Worth and Lubbock in the 1990's. The same period witnessed the rise of private militia groups with Klan connections. In 1993, responding to the actions of these groups, the legislature adopted an anti-hate crime law that led to convictions, and the Texas Commission on Human Rights brought suit against Klan groups in 1994, seeking compensation for persons they had harassed.

Concern about biased law enforcement continued, especially when a few police officers were identified as Klansmen. A 1995 study indicated that if African Americans ventured into white suburbs, they received double the percentage of traffic tickets received there by whites. Additionally, the Justice Department found that police actions caused more complaints and civil-rights cases in Texas than in any other state during 1984–90. Incidents occurred statewide from Houston and Dallas down to small towns, with some police officers escaping punishment and others being fired or convicted.

In Dallas and Houston, struggles over police actions led to change. A federal judge found discrimination in the hiring of police in Dallas; in a force of 2,000 in 1979, only 106 were African Americans. Protests in Dallas also led to a police review board. In Houston, blacks and Hispanics formed only 8 percent of the force, well below their 45 percent of the city population. In 1982 the city council hired Lee Brown, an African-American police chief, despite opposition from white officers. When Brown left in 1989, African Americans formed better than 13 percent of the police force. In the 1970's, African-American officers began serving in the highway patrol, and the first regional commander was appointed in 1993. The Texas Rangers did not include African Americans until the appointment of Lee Roy Young in 1988. In the early 1990's, the Texas National Guard faced questions about discrimination.

The judicial process also faced continued criticism in Texas. Challenges to all-white juries for trials involving black defendants occurred repeatedly after 1970. On Dallas juries in the 1980's, only one of twelve African Americans (compared to one in three whites) was chosen for murder cases. Black leaders in Lubbock protested in 1994 that bail bonds for persons who attacked African Americans were lower than for those who attacked whites.

Questions also arose regarding the attitudes of judges and the process of their selection. In 1983, three justices of the peace in Tarrant County refused to perform interracial marriages. Judges who used racist language stirred protests at Fort Worth in 1979 and at Richmond and Lubbock in the early 1990's. In 1989 a federal judge ruled that at-large elections of state district judges in Texas cities discriminated against minority candidates—only 17 of 172 judicial seats in the nine most populous counties were held by minority judges. The state legislature finally agreed to a plan for single-member districts, but the Fifth Circuit Court overturned the original ruling in 1994. A few African-American judges and justices of the peace began to appear in Texas city courts in the 1970's. In 1979, Gabrielle McDonald became the first African American to be appointed a federal district judge in Texas, and in 1990, Morris Overstreet became the first African American to win a statewide election as a member of the Texas Court of Criminal Appeals.

Statistics gathered in the early 1990's revealed higher percentages of convictions and sentences of greater length for minority members. The African-American percentage of inmates in Texas prisons grew from 36 percent in 1985 to 46 percent in 1991. Two cases of false conviction attracted national attention. Lenell Geter, an African-American engineer, served fourteen months in jail for robbery before new evidence freed him in 1984. Clarence Brandley spent ten years on death row before a judicial review found bias in the original trial and freed him in 1990.

Because of racial bias in executions, the U.S. Supreme Court ruled against existing state capital-punishment laws—including the Texas law—in 1972. After Texas rewrote its law to eliminate bias, minorities still constituted 50 percent of those executed in the 1980's and 1990's—29 percent of them African Americans. Despite evidence that whites seldom faced the death penalty for violence against a black person, in 1987 the Supreme Court refused to set aside the new capital-punishment laws.

In the late twentieth century, law-enforcement officials noted that the percentage of blacks in prison resulted in part from economic problems. African-American leaders in Dallas and other cities expressed concern over the greater economic profits in illegal activities and the accompanying violence, especially by gangs, within minority neighborhoods. In the 1990's, African-American leaders organized marches against such activities. Cities such as Fort Worth and Dallas strove to reduce violence by creating new recreation programs and curfews and buying guns from the populace, but economic problems limited their success.

Labor and Business

The economic status of African Americans in Texas improved to some extent between 1970 and 1995. In the 1970's, with less discrimination and more job-training programs, the median income for black Texans increased from 50 percent of the white level to 60 percent. But that level did not advance in the 1980's or the 1990's. Black unemployment remained at about twice the white level. The percentage of black Texans with incomes below the poverty level declined from 55 percent in 1959 to 28 percent by 1980, but still remained above the white level of 12 percent. By 1990 the percentage of African Americans in Texas below the poverty level had risen to 30 percent.

Discrimination continued to be a possible cause of economic problems. In 1987 the Dallas office of the U.S. Equal Employment Opportunity Commission received 5,800 complaints. Cities generally increased their hiring of minorities after 1970, but mostly in lower-paying positions. The number of lesser-skilled positions in turn was reduced in the 1990's by privatization of some services in Lubbock and other cities. In the professional world, the *Dallas News* found in 1989 only eleven African Americans among more than a thousand partners in large Dallas law firms—well below the national average of 2 percent or less. During the 1980's, African-American doctors found themselves harassed by excessive supervision and paperwork in some hospitals at Fort Worth and other cities. Finally, African-American farm owners declined from 15,000 in 1960 to 5,000 by 1984, and those who remained usually had farms one-fourth the size of white farms.

Desegregation of retail businesses in the 1960's allowed black consumers new opportunities for purchasing goods. But African-American business people, who usually had small stores, faced tough competition from national corporations. Black retail businesses in Texas grew slowly, from 4,763 in 1972 to 5,690 by 1987. Other African-American businesses profited more from desegregation. The greatest expansion came in service businesses, which tripled from 4,974 to 17,671 in the same fifteen years. African-American businesses involved in public utilities, transportation, and manufacturing doubled in number. In total, from 1972 to 1987, African-American businesses in Texas increased from 15,001 to 35,725, ranking third behind California and New York. In Houston alone, African-American businesses increased from 4,673 to 10,025 in those years, placing them fourth among U.S. cities. Yet African Americans still owned only 6 percent of the businesses in Texas by 1994.

The problem of securing business loans slowed the development of African-American enterprises. In Dallas a private Minority Enterprise Small Business Investment Company provided an alternative to bank loans. In 1995, however, Craig Joseph of Houston was turned down by eight Houston banks before he obtained a loan to expand his family's thirty-year-old restaurant that had twenty employees. A more hopeful development occurred in Lubbock, where a credit union was established in a minority section in the mid-1990's.

In the 1970's, some cities such as Houston set goals for contracting with businesses owned by minorities and women. The state percentage of contracts with such underutilized businesses grew from less than 2 percent in 1991 to almost 16 percent in 1995. The federal Small Business Administration and Minority Business Development Agency also provided assistance. To promote African-American business development, members from several of the fifty black chambers of commerce in Texas met at Lubbock, in 1987, to revive a state association. Yet some of those chambers felt pressure to join with white chambers of commerce in order to secure greater funding.

Several successful African-American business people emerged after 1970. George Smith developed a multimillion dollar company in Houston to distribute and service pipelines during the 1970's. Smith Pipe and Supply counted 135 employees by 1980. In 1988, *Black Enterprise* magazine ranked Pro-Line Corporation of Dallas, owned by Comer Cottrell, as eighteenth among the hundred largest African-

American businesses in the nation. Six black auto dealerships in the state stood among the top hundred in that survey. Percy Creuzot developed twelve Frenchy's restaurants in Houston with more than three hundred employees.

Education

Economic advances and problems from 1970 to 1995 rested in part on changes and limitations in education. Efforts to desegregate public schools continued. African-Americans began to win election to school boards, especially after the federal courts ordered single-member districts in the 1980's. In an effort to integrate schools in the 1970's, the courts ordered larger school districts, such as in Dallas, Houston, and Austin, to bus more students. Still, in 1978, a study found 42 percent of Houston schools and 37 percent of Dallas schools remained virtually one-race schools. Some white neighborhoods in Houston tried to form their own school districts and avoid desegregation in the late 1970's. Tri-ethnic committees, which included Mexican Americans and Anglo Americans, were created to assist several urban school boards.

Movement of whites to suburbs made minorities the majority in cities such as Dallas and Houston by the 1980's. With school desegregation much more difficult in the 1980's, several large districts reduced busing and created more programs to attract white students to minority schools. Even so, some magnet schools remained divided, with black and white students often in different classes. By 1989, only 37 percent of African-American students in Texas attended desegregated schools. Consequently, when federal courts began declaring that school districts had achieved unitary or desegregated status, minority leaders questioned some decisions.

239

African-American teachers expressed concerns about other issues. Some won court cases to retain positions after districts tried to fire them despite sound records. In 1979, African Americans were superintendents in only two of more than a thousand districts in Texas (later, Marvin Edwards, an African-American educator, served as superintendent of the Dallas district from 1988 to 1993). New competency tests for teachers in 1986 raised concerns about bias, but more than 95 percent of African-American teachers passed. The need for more African-American teachers became clear when a 1993 survey showed that only 7 percent of the new teachers in the state were African American, and a 1995 survey showed that 49 percent of the Texas schools employed no African-American instructors.

African-American parents and students raised further issues. Some districts closed black schools or reduced them from high schools to junior highs to promote desegregation. Textbooks that omitted African Americans also caused concern. Schools that retained the Confederate flag and "Dixie" as the school themes offended many African Americans. Some schools, such as in Austin, acknowledged the problem and made changes; others, such as in Grand Prairie, Midland, and Fort Worth, proved reluctant. A few white teachers and school board members still employed racist language in 1995.

More important were concerns about dropout rates and scores on the tests required for graduation in the 1980's and 1990's. By 1980, high school graduates formed 53 percent of African Americans who were over twenty-five years old, although that was still below the overall state percentage of high school graduates. The dropout rate for African-American students declined from 41 percent in 1988 to 23 percent by 1993 as districts focused more on the issue.

The new skills tests found minority students passing at a rate below the state percentage, and educators differed over whether lower family income, fewer experienced teachers, or more segregation was the principal cause.

In 1984, poorer districts, often with more minority students, went to court seeking greater equalization of state funding, and in 1987 a state judge declared the existing system unconstitutional. The legislature in 1991 adopted a new system of County Education Districts that narrowed the gap between rich and poor districts but did not produce complete equity.

African Americans attended Texas colleges in growing numbers after 1970, as most state universities sought to recruit and retain minority students. To attain that goal, colleges created multicultural centers and honored outstanding minority graduates. Texas Tech students elected their first black homecoming queen in 1992. African-American students ranged from 10 to 20 percent of the student body in most community colleges by 1982, with two campuses in Dallas above 40 percent. At most state universities, African-American students formed 10 percent or less, although Lamar counted 20 percent and the downtown campus of the University of Houston registered 30 percent. Former all-white private colleges generally achieved less than 10 percent, but Dallas Baptist enrolled 18 percent African-American students and Lon Morris 16 percent. By 1993, African-American students formed 9 percent of the enrollment in institutions of higher education in Texas, still below their 12 percent of the population. In graduate schools the percentages remained lower, with the eight medical schools in Texas counting African-American students as 3 percent of their enrollment in 1992. The percentage of college graduates among African

Americans more than twenty-five years old in Texas increased to 9 percent by 1980, about half the rate for whites.

Despite enrollment advances, other problems remained in higher education. Most fraternities and sororities continued as exclusively white, with some engaging in theme parties derogatory of minorities. That stimulated African-American protests at Texas Tech, Texas A & M, and the University of Texas at Austin in the 1990's. At several universities, white student opposition to the possibility of a multicultural requirement reflected the reluctance of some to understand diverse racial groups.

Efforts to attract African-American faculty and administrators produced limited results until the 1980's. Minority complaints and growing political influence stimulated the appointment of church leader Zan W. Holmes and astronaut Bernard A. Harris Jr. as regents for the University of Texas and Texas Tech in the 1990's. Marguerite Ross Barnett became the only African-American president of a major Texas university when she led the University of Houston from 1990 until her death in 1992. Other African-American administrators served at Texas colleges in the 1980's and 1990's. In 1993 the University of Texas at Austin could count only 52 African Americans among its faculty of 2,300—about 2 percent—but even that stood above several other large universities. Most pointed to limited numbers of new African-American Ph.D.s, but aggressive hiring efforts at some schools produced more success.

Because of the racial climate at predominantly white colleges, many African-American students continued to attend historically black colleges. Yet some state legislators in the 1980's suggested closing Prairie View and Texas Southern to eliminate duplication, save money, and promote integration.

African Americans generally opposed such action and argued successfully for better financial support of both institutions. In 1988, Prairie View reached an enrollment peak at 5,640 students, while Texas Southern reversed a decline and grew to 8,554. Some traditionally African-American colleges also developed more diverse student bodies, with Huston-Tillotson and Texas Southern about two-thirds black by the 1980's, while Jarvis and Paul Quinn remained at more than 95 percent. Many of those colleges faced financial problems, which led to the closing of Mary Allen in 1977 and Bishop in 1988. Paul Quinn then moved from Waco to the Bishop campus at Dallas in 1990. Other private black colleges survived, but their enrollments remained between 300 and 800 students in the 1980's.

Social Life

As the population of Texas grew between 1970 and 1995, African Americans remained at 12 percent of the total. Thus in 1990 the black population of Texas stood at slightly more than two million, third behind New York and California. Ninety percent lived in towns and cities, a 15 percent increase since 1960. After having reached a peak of 91 percent in 1960, residential segregation fell to 78 percent by 1980. The growing African-American middle class expanded into new neighborhoods, with some remaining integrated (such as Wynnwood Hills in Dallas) and others becoming African American (such as MacGregor Way in Houston). Working-class neighborhoods face different problems. In Austin, expansion of the University of Texas into an African-American community displaced people to more crowded neighborhoods. Most waste disposal sites in Houston were located in African-American communities. A 1992 survey found that Texas banks rejected black home-loan applications from one and a half to five times as often as those of whites. After new evidence of redlining, the legislature in 1995 passed a stronger law requiring fair opportunity to buy home-owners insurance.

One result of continuing economic problems became the growing number of one-parent families. The change included whites and blacks, with greater impact in the larger working class among African Americans. By 1980, two-parent families formed 64 percent of African-American households in Texas, a 12 percent decline since 1970. Yet it remained above the 57 percent nationally for African-American families. By 1990, households headed by women formed 40 percent of the African-American families in Texas. For these families, extended family connections helped in raising children. New groups, such as 100 Black Men and 100 Black Women, appeared in the 1990's and sought to provide positive role models at the local level.

African-American churches continued to support strong family roles and provided summer youth programs and child care for working mothers. Some urban churches maintained their membership after 1970, but others faced a decline, especially in male participation. Muslim as well as Christian congregations continued in larger Texas cities.

Four Baptist conventions and three Methodist denominations continued to be the largest black religious groups in Texas. The Missionary Baptist General Convention of Texas counted 300,000 members in the 1990's. By 1994 the predominantly white Baptist General Convention of Texas had developed connections with about four hundred black congregations, some of which retained ties to black conventions. The predominantly white United Methodist Church also included black congregations, as well as a few that were integrated. African Americans Ernest T. Dixon Jr. in 1980 and Alfred L. Norris in 1992 became bishops, leading Texas Methodist conferences with white membership majorities. At the local level cooperative parishes in integrated neighborhoods and city-wide interdenominational services were created to promote interaction between black and white church groups.

Social life for African Americans included several major events in the period 1970–95. The Juneteenth celebration of emancipation in Texas, which became a state holiday in 1979 under legislation by representative Al Edwards, grew to include parades, picnics, and entertainment. Black history month in February continued in schools and colleges, with exhibits, dramatic presentations, and speakers. Many of the larger Texas cities honored the slain civil rights leader, Martin Luther King Jr., with streets in his name in the 1980's and 1990's, and after celebrations of his birthday increased, the day became a state holiday in 1991. By the 1990's some African-American families in Texas also began to celebrate Kwanzaa, a cultural-awareness week in December. Finally, African Americans throughout Texas joined the million-man march to Washington in 1995 to promote unity and address problems, but many expressed disagreement with the anti-Jewish views of the organizer, Louis Farrakhan, of the Nation of Islam.

African-American cultural activities expanded in several directions after 1970. The Museum of African American Life and Culture in Dallas and the George Washington Carver Museum in Austin provided exhibits on African-American history in Texas, and other museums showcased paintings of black folk artists. David Williams founded the Texas African American Heritage Organization in the 1980's. Buffalo soldier reenactment groups appeared. African-

American sculptor Eddie Dixon, of Lubbock, created a statue of black soldiers at Fort Leavenworth, Kansas, in the 1990's. Famous African-American musicians, such as Clarence "Gatemouth" Brown and Albert Collins, were joined by younger performers in Texas cities. Terry Cook of Plainview and Texas Tech joined the Metropolitan Opera in the 1980's. African-American actors and actresses began in local theater groups, with some, such as Phylicia Rashad, going on to motion pictures or television. To cover such activities in 1991, Gemeral Berry Jr. established the magazine *Our Texas* for African Americans in the state.

As sports increased its entertainment attraction, African-American athletes played expanded roles in Texas. African-American high school football stars attended the colleges where running back Earl Campbell at the University of Texas in 1977, and quarterback Andre Ware at the University of Houston in 1989, each won the Heisman Trophy as the college player of the year. Not until the 1980's did greater concern develop over low graduation rates for black athletes. Campbell later played for the Houston Oilers, and in 1991 he entered the Pro Football Hall of Fame, as did Tony Dorsett for his success with the Dallas Cowboys in the 1970's and 1980's.

African-American players dominated basketball in Texas universities by the 1980's. Nolan Richardson, who played at Texas Western in the 1960's, coached the University of Arkansas to a national championship in the 1990's. Sheryl Swoopes led the Texas Tech Lady Raiders to a national championship in 1993 and became the female amateur athlete of the year. In professional basketball, Hakeem Olajuwon, a University of Houston star in the 1980's, led the Houston Rockets to championships in 1994 and 1995.

In other sports, black Texans continued to make

246

an impact. Ernie Banks was named to the Baseball Hall of Fame in 1977. Don Baylor became one of the few African-American managers in professional baseball during 1992. Boxer George Foreman, of Houston, won the heavyweight title in the 1970's and again in the 1990's. Terry Norris, of Lubbock, became super welterweight boxing champion in 1992. In track, world sprint record holders Carl Lewis and Leroy Burrell trained at the University of Houston. Zina Garrison became the first African-American winner of the Junior Wimbledon tennis title in 1982 and a top professional player who promoted programs for children in Houston.

Yet despite those successes, racial slurs and discrimination directed at players still occurred from 1970 to 1995. An African-American coach won damages for his discriminatory firing in 1977 at Big Spring. At San Angelo Central High, the star African-American quarterback found himself replaced by a white player despite protests in 1995. Some country clubs hosting major golf tournaments still remained all-white in the 1990's.

From 1970 to 1995, black Texans continued to struggle with lingering discrimination while making uneven progress. Problems remained in limited school desegregation, below-average family income levels, and the related areas of higher rates of crime and one-parent families, but progress appeared in the form of more businesses, greater college enrollment, participation in government, and opportunities for select individuals in sports and entertainment.

Bibliographical Essay

These comments are intended to guide the interested reader to more extended discussions of the topics treated in each chapter. Broader studies of black history are not included unless they provided important material on Texas. My interpretations of various periods and events, however, have been influenced by the writings of: David B. Davis, W. E. B. DuBois, John Hope Franklin, Eugene Genovese, Louis R. Harlan, Winthrop Jordan, August Meier, Allan Spear, Kenneth Stampp, Joel Williamson, and C. Vann Woodward.

Chapter I: Explorers and Settlers

Original accounts of Estevan's travels may be found in Frederick W. Hodge, ed., *Spanish Explorers in the Southern United States* (New York, 1907). Recent studies are Jeannette Mirsky's thoughtful "Zeroing In on a Fugative Figure: The First Negro in America," *Midway*, VIII (June, 1967), 1-17; and John Upton Terrell's more detailed *Estevanico the Black* (Los Angeles, 1968).

Though they require additional study, free black people in Spanish Texas receive scattered mention in Carlos E. Castaneda, *Our Catholic Heritage in Texas, 1519-1936* (7 vols.; Austin, 1936-1950); Herbert Eugene Bolton, *Texas in the Middle Eighteenth Century* (Berkeley, 1915); and Jack D. Forbes, "Black Pioneers: The Spanish-Speaking Afroamericans of the Southwest," *Phylon*, XXVII (Fall, 1966), 233-246. Merton L. Dillon, "Benjamin Lundy in Texas," *Southwestern Historical Quarterly*, LXIII (July, 1959), 46-62, discusses plans for a free Negro colony in Texas.

Free black settlers in Texas from the late Spanish period to 1865 are studied in Harold Schoen, "The Free Negro in the Republic of Texas," *Southwestern Historical Quarterly*, XXXIX (April, 1936), 292-308, XL (July, October, 1936, January, April, 1937), 26-34, 85-113, 169-199, 267-289; Andrew Forest Muir, "The Free Negro in Harris County, Texas," *ibid.*, XLVI (January, 1943), 214-238, "The Free Negro in Fort Bend County, Texas," *Journal of Negro History*, XXXIII (January, 1948), 79-85, "The Free Negro in Jefferson and Orange Counties, Texas," *ibid.*, XXXV (April, 1950), 183-206, and "The Free Negro in Galveston County, Texas," *Negro History Bulletin*, XXII (December, 1958), 68-70; George Ruble Woolfolk, "Turner's Safety

Valve and Free Negro Westward Migration," *Pacific Northwest Quarterly*, LVI (July, 1965), 125-130; Earl W. Fornell, "The Abduction of Free Negroes and Slaves in Texas," *Southwestern Historical Quarterly*, LX (January, 1957), 369-380; Alexander T. M. Pratt, "Free Negroes in Texas to 1860" (M. A. thesis: Prairie View Agricultural and Mechanical College, 1963); Diane Elizabeth Prince, "William Goyens, Free Negro on the Texas Frontier" (M. A. thesis: Stephen F. Austin State College, 1967); and Frederick Law Olmsted, *Journey Through Texas* (New York, 1857).

Chapter II: Slaves

There is no major study devoted strictly to slavery in Texas. Slavery in Spanish Texas is mentioned in Castaneda, *Our Catholic Heritage in Texas*, and Rose Mary F. Haynes, "Some Features of Negro Participation in Texas History Through 1879" (M. A. thesis: Texas College of Arts and Industries, 1948). The slave trade into Texas receives discussion in Eugene C. Barker, "The African Slave Trade in Texas," *Southwestern Historical Quarterly*, VI (October, 1902), 145-158; and the Ephriam Douglass Adams, ed., "Correspondence from the British Archives Concerning Texas, 1837-1846," *ibid.*, XVII (October, 1913), 67-92.

Quotations and accounts of individual action by slaves in this chapter are primarily from B. A. Botkin, ed., *Lay My Burden Down: A Folk History of Slavery* (Chicago, 1945), a collection of slave reminiscences. Others are from Olmsted, *Journey Through Texas*; Norman R. Yetman, *Life Under the "Peculiar Institution": Selections From the Slave Narrative Collection* (New York, 1970); and Jeff Hamilton and Lenoir Hunt, *My Master*

(Dallas, 1940). The best general account of slavery in Texas, though somewhat dated in racial viewpoint and limited to slaves on large plantations, is contained in Abigail Curlee, "A Study of Texas Slave Plantations, 1822-1865" (Ph.D. dissertation: University of Texas, 1932). Similar though more restricted studies are: Curlee, "The History of a Texas Slave Plantation," *Southwestern Historical Quarterly*, XXVI (October, 1922), 79-127; Dorman H. Winfrey, *Julien Sidney Devereux and his Monte Verdi Plantation* (Waco, 1962); and Johanna Rosa Engelking, "Slavery in Texas" (M. A. thesis: Baylor University, 1933). Brief comments on the treatment and varied reactions of slaves may be found in Phillip Durham and Everett L. Jones, *The Negro Cowboys* (New York, 1965); Francis Richard Lubbock, *Six Decades in Texas, or Memoirs* (Austin, 1900); Frances Jane Leathers, ed., "Christopher Columbus Goodman: Soldier, Indian Fighter, Farmer, 1818-1861," *Southwestern Historical Quarterly*, LXIX (January, 1966), 353-376; Alleine Howren, "Causes and Origin of the Decree of April 6, 1830," *ibid.*, XVI (April, 1913), 378-422; Castaneda, trans., "A Trip to Texas in 1828: José María Sanchez," *ibid.*, XXIX (April, 1926), 249-288; Harriet Smither, ed., "Dairy of Adolphus Sterne," *ibid.*, XXXII (October, 1928), 165-179; John Mason Brewer, *Dog Ghosts and Other Texas Negro Folk Tales* (Austin, 1958), *An Historical Outline of the Negro in Travis County* (Austin, 1940), "Juneteenth," in J. Frank Dobie, ed., *Tone the Bell Easy* (Austin, 1932), and "John Tales," in Mody C. Boatright, ed., *Mexican Border Ballads* (Austin, 1946); John Q. Anderson, "Old John and the Master," *Southern Folklore Quarterly*, XXV (September,

1961), 195-197; Mrs. David Winningham, "Sam Houston and Slavery," *Texana*, III (Summer, 1965), 93-104; William Ransom Hogan, *The Texas Republic: A Social and Economic History* (Norman, 1946); F. Lotto, *Fayette County* (Schulenburg, 1902); Leonie R. Weyland and Houston Wade, *An Early History of Fayette County* (LaGrange, 1936); Walter F. Cotton, *History of Negroes of Limestone County From 1860-1939* (Mexia, 1939); Doyal T. Loyd, *A History of Upshur County, Texas* (Gilmer, 1966); Gustave Dresel, *Houston Journal: Adventures in North America and Texas, 1837-1841* (Austin, 1954); Macum Phelan, *A History of Early Methodism in Texas, 1817-1866* (Dallas, 1924); Walter N. Vernon, *Methodism Moves Across North Texas* (Dallas, 1967); Carter E. Boren, *Religion on the Texas Frontier* (San Antonio, 1968); A. E. Keir Nash, "The Texas Supreme Court and Trial Rights of Blacks, 1845-1860," *Journal of American History*, LVIII (December, 1971), 622-642; and John Lee Eighmy, "The Baptists and Slavery: An Examination of the Origins and Benefits of Segregation," *Social Science Quarterly*, XLIX (December, 1968), 666-673. This lengthy list of books and articles which mention slavery is misleading, for most devote little space to the topic and some are written with an anti-Negro bias. Many county histories offer little or no comment on black people regardless of the percentage of Negro population.

My account of urban slavery in Texas primarily rests on Paul Lack, "Slavery on the Southwestern Urban Frontier: Austin, Texas, 1845-1860" (Seminar paper: Texas Tech University, 1970); and Carland Elaine Crook, "San Antonio, Texas, 1846-1861" (M. A. thesis: Rice

University, 1964). Other volumes which add some information are: Kenneth W. Wheeler, *To Wear a City's Crown; The Beginnings of Urban Growth in Texas, 1836-1865* (Cambridge, 1968); David G. McComb, *Houston, The Bayou City* (Austin, 1969); Annie Carpenter Love, *History of Navarro County* (Dallas, 1933); and Ferdinand Roemer, *Texas* (San Antonio, 1935). Lack is pursuing his study of urban slavery in the Southwest in a dissertation which will involve Austin and Galveston.

Escaped slaves are treated in Marjorie Browne Hawkins, "Runaway Slaves in Texas From 1830 to 1860" (M. A. thesis: Prairie View Agricultural and Mechanical College, 1952); Ronnie Curtis Tyler, "Slave Owners and Runaway Slaves in Texas" (M. A. thesis: Texas Christian University, 1966); and Tyler, "The Callahan Expedition of 1855: Indians or Negroes?" *Southwestern Historical Quarterly*, LXX (April, 1967), 574-585. Runaways also receive some mention in Eugene Barriffe, Jr., "Some Aspects of Slavery and Anti-Slavery Movements in Texas, 1830-1860" (M. A. thesis: University of Southwestern Louisiana, 1968); Kenneth W. Porter, "Negroes and Indians on the Texas Frontier, 1831-1876," *Journal of Negro History*, XLI (July, October, 1956), 185-214, 285-310; and Henry Allen Bullock, "A Hidden Passage in the Slave Regime," in James C. Curtis and Lewis L. Gould, eds., *The Black Experience in America* (Austin, 1970).

Texas slave revolts are discussed by Wendell G. Addington, "Slave Insurrections in Texas," *Journal of Negro History*, XXXV (October, 1950), 408-434; William W. White, "The Texas Slave Insurrection of 1860," *Southwestern Historical Quarterly*, LII (January, 1949), 259-285; and

Herbert Aptheker, *American Negro Slave Revolts* (New York, 1943). These authors believe well developed plans for rebellion existed on several occasions. Wesley Norton, "The Methodist Episcopal Church and the Civil Disturbances in North Texas in 1859 and 1860," *Southwestern Historical Quarterly*, LXVIII (January, 1965), 317-341, raises doubts about elaborate plots in 1860.

Anti-slavery thought in Texas is explored in Harriet Smither, "English Abolitionism and the Annexation of Texas," *Southwestern Historical Quarterly*, XXXII (January, 1929), 193-205; Madeleine B. Stern, "Stephen Pearl Andrews, Abolitionist, and the Annexation of Texas," *ibid.*, LXVII (April, 1964), 491-523; Zoie Odom Newsome, "Anti-slavery Sentiment in Texas, 1821-1861" (M. A. thesis: Texas Technological College, 1968); Hogan, *The Texas Republic*; Barriffe, "Some Aspects of Slavery and Anti-Slavery Movements in Texas"; and Frank Smyrl, "Unionism, Abolitionism, and Vigilantism in Texas, 1856-1865" (M. A. thesis: University of Texas, 1961). Pro-slavery attitudes are discussed in Marilyn McAdams Sibley, *Travelers in Texas, 1761-1860* (Austin, 1967), and Olmsted, *A Journey Through Texas*.

Texas slaves during the Civil War are mentioned in Frank Smyrl, "Texans in the Union Army, 1861-1865," *Southwestern Historical Quarterly*, LXV (October, 1961), 234-250; Albert Castel, "Civil War Kansas and the Negro," *Journal of Negro History*, LI (April, 1966), 125-138; John Ramsey Gordon, "The Negro in McLennan County, Texas" (M. A. thesis: Baylor University, 1932); Hattie Joplin Roach, *A History of Cherokee County, Texas* (Dallas, 1934); J. Lee Stanbaugh and Lillian J. Stanbaugh, *A History of Collin County, Texas* (Austin, 1958); Walter Lord, *The Fremantle Diary* (New York, 1954); and Bell Irvin Wiley, *Southern Negroes, 1861-1865* (New Haven, 1938).

Chapter III: Freedmen

No single study now exists of black Texans during Reconstruction. The only general accounts of that period in Texas history exhibit a clear anti-Negro bias: Charles William Ramsdell, *Reconstruction in Texas* (New York, 1910); and W. C. Nunn, *Texas Under the Carpetbaggers* (Austin, 1962). Paul Casdorph, *The Republican Party in Texas, 1865-1965* (Austin, 1965) is better balanced. The most sympathetic brief summary is in W. E. B. DuBois, *Black Reconstruction in America, 1860-1880* (New York, 1935).

Accounts and quotations about slave reactions to emancipation are primarily from Botkin, *Lay My Burden Down*. White attitudes are described in Barry A. Crouch and L. J. Schultz, "Crisis in Color: Racial Separation in Texas During Reconstruction," *Civil War History*, XVI (March, 1970), 37-49. The best discussions of Negro political activities are: Romey Fennell, Jr., "The Negro in Texas Politics, 1865-1874" (M. A. thesis: North Texas State University, 1963); and John Mason Brewer, *Negro Legislators of Texas* (Dallas, 1935). Dan F. Rankin, "The Role of the Negro Office Holders in the Reconstruction of the Southwest" (M. A. thesis: North Texas State College, 1954), is also helpful.

Violence and law enforcement are described in Hans L. Trefousse, ed., *Background for Radical Reconstruction* (Boston, 1970); Allen W. Trelease, *White Terror: The Ku Klux Klan Conspiracy and*

Southern Reconstruction (New York, 1971); D. L. Vest, *Watterson Folk of Bastrop County, Texas* (Waco, 1963); Ann Patton Baenziger, "The Texas State Police During Reconstruction: A Reconsideration," *Southwestern Historical Quarterly*, LXXII (April, 1969), 470-491; Otis A. Singletary, "The Texas Militia During Reconstruction," *ibid.*, LX (July, 1956), 23-35; Robert W. Shook, "The Federal Military in Texas, 1865-1870," *Texas Military History*, VI (Spring, 1967), 3-53; John A. Carpenter, *Sword and Olive Branch: Oliver Otis Howard* (Pittsburgh, 1964); and Kenneth W. Porter, "Negroes and Indians on the Texas Frontier, 1834-1874," *Southwestern Historical Quarterly*, LIII (October, 1949), 151-163. Arlen L. Fowler, *The Black Infantry in the West, 1869-1891* (Westport, Conn., 1971), recounts the service of the 24th and 25th United States Infantry. The campaigns of the 9th and 10th United States Cavalry are discussed in detail in William H. Leckie, *The Buffalo Soldiers: A Narrative of the Negro Cavalry in the West* (Norman, 1967).

The evolution of Negro laborers from slaves to sharecroppers and urban workers is presented in detail by Winston Lee Kinsey, "Negro Labor in Texas, 1865-1876" (M. A. thesis: Baylor University, 1965); and in John Thomas Hill, "The Negro in Texas During Reconstruction" (M. A. thesis: Texas Christian University, 1965). Other studies which touch on the topic are Claude Elliott, "The Freedmen's Bureau in Texas," *Southwestern Historical Quarterly*, LVI (July, 1952), 1-24; and Forest Garrett Hill, "The Negro in the Texas Labor Supply" (M. A. thesis: University of Texas, 1946). Another aspect of black rural labor is described in Durham and Jones,

Negro Cowboys; and Kenneth W. Porter, "Negro Labor in the Western Cattle Industry, 1866-1900," *Labor History*, X (Summer, 1969), 346-374. The urban economic condition of black people is considered in Alwyn Barr, "Occupational and Geographic Mobility in San Antonio, 1870-1900," *Social Science Quarterly*, LI (September, 1970), 396-403. James V. Reese mentions Negro union members in "The Early History of Labor Organizations in Texas, 1838-1876," *Southwestern Historical Quarterly*, LXXII (July, 1968), 1-20.

The development of education for freedmen is best described by Hill, "The Negro in Texas During Reconstruction"; and Esther Lane Thompson, "The Influence of the Freedmen's Bureau on the Education of the Negro in Texas" (M. A. thesis: Texas Southern University, 1956). Also useful are Frederick Eby, *The Development of Education in Texas* (New York, 1925); William R. Davis, *The Development and Present Status of Negro Education in East Texas* (New York, 1934); Prentis W. Chunn, Jr., "Education and Politics, A Study of the Negro in Reconstruction Texas" (M. A. thesis: Southwest Texas State Teachers College, 1957); and McComb, *Houston*.

There are no adequate accounts of Negro social life in Texas during Reconstruction. Some information is included in McComb, *Houston*; Crouch and Schultz, "Crisis in Color: Racial Separation in Texas During Reconstruction," *Civil War History*, XVI, 37-49; A. C. Greene, "The Durable Society: Austin in the Reconstruction," *Southwestern Historical Quarterly*, LXXII (April, 1969), 492-518; and Brewer, *An Historical Outline of the Negro in Travis County*. Urban population figures are from *The Statistics of the Population Census: 1870* (Washington, 1872).

No study of separate black towns in Texas has been made. Limited information on some may be found in: Hattie Joplin Roach, *The Hills of Cherokee* (n. p. 1952); Cotton, *History of Negroes of Limestone County*; Dorman H. Winfrey, *A History of Rusk County, Texas* (Waco, 1961); Loyd, *A History of Upshur County, Texas*; Julia Jones, *Lee County: Historical and Descriptive* (Houston, 1945); Martha Emmons, *Deep Like the Rivers: Stories of My Negro Friends* (Austin, 1969); Bettie Hayman, "A Short History of the Negro of Walker County, 1860-1942" (M. A. thesis: Sam Houston State College, 1942); Monroe Work, ed., *The Negro Year Book, 1931-1932* (Tuskegee, 1931); University of Texas, Texas Institute of Culture, San Antonio, "Negro Histo-wall" (mimeographed paper).

Negro religious developments of the Reconstruction period are mentioned in Boren, *Religion on the Texas Frontier*; Phelan, *A History of Early Methodism in Texas*; R. Douglas Brackenridge, *Voice in the Wilderness: A History of the Cumberland Presbyterian Church in Texas* (San Antonio, 1968); H. T. Kealing, *History of African Methodism in Texas* (Waco, 1885); I. B. Loud, "Methodism and the Negroes," in Olin W. Nail, *History of Texas Methodism, 1900-1960* (Austin, 1961), 87-111; J. M. Carroll, *A History of Texas Baptists* (Dallas, 1923); L. R. Elliott, ed., *Centennial Story of Texas Baptists* (Dallas, 1936); Lawrence L. Brown, *The Episcopal Church in Texas, 1838-1874* (Austin, 1963); Stephen Daniel Eckstein, *History of the Churches of Christ in Texas, 1824-1950* (Austin, 1963); and Alwyn Barr and others, "The History of First Methodist Church," *First Church Beacon*, XXVII (Austin, April 22-September 2, 1966).

Chapter IV: Voters and Laborers

The most important study of black Texans in the late nineteenth century is Lawrence Rice, *The Negro in Texas, 1874-1900* (Baton Rouge, 1971). It includes chapters on state and local politics, disfranchisement and segregation, crime, rural and urban labor, education, and social life. I shall not mention a number of unpublished theses because he notes them in his lengthy bibliography.

On Negroes in Texas politics one also should see Alwyn Barr, *Reconstruction to Reform: Texas Politics, 1876-1906* (Austin, 1971); Brewer, *Negro Legislators of Texas*; Casdorph, *Republican Party in Texas*; Maud Cuney Hare, *Norris Wright Cuney: A Tribune of the Black People* (New York, 1913); William Oliver Bundy, *Life of William Madison McDonald* (Fort Worth, 1925); Jack Abramowitz, "John B. Rayner—A Grass-Roots Leader," *Journal of Negro History*, XXXVI (April, 1951), 160-193; Lawrence C. Goodwyn, "Populist Dreams and Negro Rights: East Texas as a Case Study," *American Historical Review*, LXXVI (December, 1971), 1435-1456; J. A. R. Moseley, "The Citizens White Primary of Marion County," *Southwestern Historical Quarterly*, LXIX (April, 1946), 524-531; and Robert Saunders, "Southern Populists and the Negro, 1893-1895," *Journal of Negro History*, LIV (July, 1969), 240-261. The views of the State Convention of Colored Men of Texas in 1883 have been reprinted most recently in Thomas R. Frazier, ed., *Afro-American History Primary Sources* (New York, 1970). Significant events in Houston and San Antonio are described in August Meier and Elliott Rudwick, "The Boycott Movement Against Jim Crow Streetcars in the South, 1900-1906," *Journal of American History*, LV (March, 1969), 756-775.

The fate of black militia units may be traced through Texas Adjutant General, *Reports*, 1882-1906. Negro troops on the Texas frontier are discussed in Leckie, *Buffalo Soldiers*; Fowler, *Black Infantry in the West*; Theodore D. Harris, ed., *Negro Frontiersman: The Western Memoirs of Henry O. Flipper* (El Paso, 1963); Donald R. McClung, "Henry O. Flipper: The First Negro Officer in the United States Army, 1878-1882" (M. A. thesis: East Texas State University, 1970); Ervin N. Thompson, "The Negro Soldiers on the Frontier: A Fort Davis Case Study," *Journal of the West*, VII (April, 1968), 217-235; H. Bailey Carroll, "Nolan's 'Lost Nigger' Expedition," *Southwestern Historical Quarterly*, XLIV (July, 1940), 55-75; and M. L. Crimmins, "Captain Nolan's Lost Troop on the Staked Plains," *West Texas Historical Association Year Book*, X (1934), 68-73. The controversial dismissal of black troops in 1906 is discussed in John D. Weaver, *The Brownsville Raid* (New York, 1970); Ann J. Lane, *The Brownsville Affair* (Port Washington, N. Y., 1971); and James A. Tinsley, "Roosevelt, Foraker, and the Brownsville Affray," *Journal of Negro History*, XLI (January, 1956), 43-65.

Accounts of blacks in the cattle industry are Durham and Jones, *Negro Cowboys*; Kenneth W. Porter, "Negro Labor in the Western Cattle Industry, 1866-1900," *Labor History*, X, 346-374; W. S. Savage, "The Negro Cowboy on the Texas Plains," *Negro History Bulletin*, XXIV (April, 1961), 157-158, 163; Hettye Wallace Branch, *The Story of "80 John"* (New York, 1960); R. C. Crane, "D. W. Wallace ('80 John'): A Negro Cattleman on the Texas Frontier," *West Texas Historical Association Year Book*, XXVIII (1952), 113-118; and Brewer, *Dog Ghosts and*

Other Texas Negro Folk Tales. Barr, "Occcupational and Geographic Mobility in San Antonio, 1870-1900," *Social Science Quarterly*, LI, suggests the limited possibilities of labor advancement for Negroes. B. B. Lightfoot, "The Negro Exodus from Comanche County, Texas," *Southwestern Historical Quarterly*, LVI (January, 1953), 407-416, describes opposition to any black settlers in some counties. J. Vance Lewis mentions his early medical career in *Out of the Ditch: A True Story of an Ex-Slave* (Houston, 1910). Marilyn T. Bryan discusses a Negro businessman of this period in "The Economic, Political and Social Status of the Negro in El Paso," *Password*, XIII (Fall, 1968), 74-86. The early newspaper career of Emmett J. Scott is described in Arna Bontemps, *100 Years of Negro Freedom* (New York, 1961). Black emigration movements are analyzed by Edwin S. Redkey, *Black Exodus: Black Nationalist and Back-to-Africa Movements, 1890-1910* (New Haven, 1969).

James M. McPherson, "White Liberals and Black Power in Negro Education **1865-1915**," *American Historical Review,* LXXV (June, 1970), 1357-1386, touches on internal problems of some denominational colleges in Texas. George Ruble Woolfolk explores the connections between education and politics in *Prairie View: A Study in Public Conscience, 1878-1946* (New York, 1962). Sketches of David Abner, Jr., and Richard Harvey Cain may be found in William J. Simmons, *Men of Mark* (Cleveland, 1887).

Statistics on residential segregation and church membership are from the reports of the eleventh census in 1890. Figures on marriage and divorce rates are in Mattie Lloyd Wooten, "The

261

Marital Condition of the Population of Texas: 1890-1930," *Southwestern Social Science Quarterly*, XVI (June, 1935), 69-85. The writings of Sutton Griggs are analyzed in Robert A. Bone, *The Negro Novel in America* (New Haven, 1958); and Melvin James Banks, "The Pursuit of Equality: The Movement for First Class Citizenship Among Negroes in Texas, 1920-1950" (D.S.S. dissertation: Syracuse University, 1962). For black religion one should also see Loud, "Methodism and the Negroes," in Nail, *History of Texas Methodism, 1900-1960*, pp. 87-111; Brackenridge, *Voice in the Wilderness*; DeBose Murphy, *A Short History of the Protestant Episcopal Church in Texas* (Dallas, 1935); Eckstein, *History of the Churches of Christ in Texas*; Castaneda, *Our Catholic Heritage in Texas*, VII; Sister Mary Immaculata Turley, *Mother Margaret Mary Healy-Murphy: A Biography* (San Antonio, 1969); Shell Barth, Jr., "A History of the Negro Presbyterian Church U.S. in Texas" (M. A. thesis: University of Texas, 1965); and John Mason Brewer, *The Word on the Brazos: Negro Preacher Tales from the Brazos Bottoms of Texas* (Austin, 1953). From this book come the quotations in dialect which appear in the sections on education and social life.

Chapter V: Outsiders

The basic study for the early twentieth century is Bruce Alden Glasrud, "Black Texans, 1900-1930: A History" (Ph.D. dissertation: Texas Technological College, 1969), which includes chapters on politics, anti-black violence, segregation and discrimination, economics, education, culture, and black responses to their status. Bill Chambers, "The History of the Texas Negro and His Development Since 1900" (M. A.

thesis: North Texas State College, 1940), also covers the 1930's, although his account is more superficial and dated in viewpoint.

For political events the most important study is Banks, "Pursuit of Equality." See also Casdorph, *The Republican Party in Texas*; Paul Lewinson, *Race, Class, and Party* (New York, 1932); McComb, *Houston*; Audrey Granneberg, "Maury Maverick's San Antonio," *Survey Graphic*, XXVIII (July, 1939), 421-426; and Robert W. Hainsworth, "The Negro and the Texas Primaries," *Journal of Negro History*, XVIII (October, 1933), 426-450. Accounts of anti-black violence in Texas may be found in Arthur I. Waskow, *From Race Riot to Sit In: 1919 and the 1960's* (New York, 1966), and Ely Green, *Ely: Too Black, Too White* (Amherst, 1970). Edgar A. Schuler describes "The Houston Race Riot, 1917," *Journal of Negro History*, XXIX (July, 1944), 301-338. Jim Crow practices are discussed in Charles S. Johnson, *Patterns of Negro Segregation* (New York, 1943); McComb, *Houston;* and Leonard B. Murphy, "A History of Negro Segregation Practices in Texas, 1865-1958" (M.A. thesis: Southern Methodist University, 1958). For his views on race relations see Maury Maverick, *A Maverick American* (New York, 1937); and Richard Henderson, *Maury Maverick* (Austin, 1970). Some additional information is provided on black responses by an attorney in Lewis, *Out of the Ditch;* and about migrants in Benjamin Brawley, *The Negro Genius* (New York, 1940); Richard Bardolph, *The Negro Vanguard* (New York, 1959); *The Red Book* (Houston, 1915); and Ira B. Bryant, "The Need for Negro History in the Schools of Texas," *Negro History Bulletin,* XX (January, 1957), 77-78. Quotations about reasons for moving North are from "Letters of Negro Migrants, 1916-1918," *Journal of Negro History,* IV (July, October, 1919), 291-340, 412-465; and Emmett J. Scott, *Negro Migration During the War* (New York, 1920). The subtle rejoinder quotation is from Emmons, *Deep Like the Rivers;* while quotations of white racial views are from Green, *Ely.*

For information on economic status Glasrud may be supplemented with Branch, *The Story of "80 John"* [Wallace], the black rancher. Illegal liquor production during prohibition is mentioned in Girlene Marie Wilson, "Negro Stories from the Colorado Valley," in Mody C. Boatright and others, eds., *And Horns on the Toads* (Dallas, 1959). Labor and business are mentioned in McComb, *Houston*; Gordon, "The Negro in McLennan County"; Brewer, *Austin*; and "A Negro Millionaire's Advice to His Race," *U. S. News & World Report* (September 4, 1967). Some aspects of the depression period in the 1930's are described in Hill, "Negro Labor in Texas"; Hayman, "The Negro in Walker County"; Donald Wayne Whisenhunt, "Texas in the Depression, 1929-1933" (Ph. D. dissertation: Texas Technological College, 1966); C. C. Yancy, "Negro Participation in the Agricultural Adjustment Agency Program in Texas" (M. E. thesis: Colorado A & M College, 1946); Ora Emma Ulrich, "A Study of the Expenditure of Urban Negro Work Relief Families in Travis County, Texas, as compared to an Adequate Diet" (M. A. thesis: University of Texas, 1935); Monroe N. Work, *The Negro Yearbook . . . 1937-1938* (Tuskegee, 1937); Mary Everett, "A Texas Plantation: Then and Now," *Sewanee Review,* XLIV (October-December, 1936), 386-404; and George B.

Tindall, *The Emergence of the New South, 1913-1945* (Baton Rouge, 1967).

Studies of education which offer additional information on the 1930's, are: Woolfolk, *Prairie View*; Hayman, "The Negro in Walker County"; Gordon, "The Negro in McLennan County"; Davis, *The Development and Present Status of Negro Education in East Texas*; William Pickens, *Bursting Bonds* (Boston, 1923); and Frederick Brownlee, *Heritage of Freedom* (Philadelphia, 1963). Emmons, *Deep Like the Rivers*, discusses the creative uses by black people of the English language. The biographical sketch of James Farmer is based on Phillip T. Drotning and Wesley W. South, *Up From the Ghetto* (New York, 1970).

On Negro housing conditions Glasrud may be supplemented by Hill, "Negro Labor," and Drotning and South, *Up From the Ghetto*. The statistics in U. S. Bureau of the Census, *Negro Population, 1790-1915* (Washington, 1918); *Fifteenth Census of the United States: 1930, Population* (Washington, 1932), vol. III, pt. 2; and *Sixteenth Census of the United States: 1940, Population* (Washington, 1943), vol. II, pt. 6, suggest residential racial patterns. Family life is considered in Wooten, "The Marital Condition of the Population of Texas: 1890-1930," *Southwestern Social Science Quarterly*, XVI, 69-85; C. C. White and **Ada M. Holland**, *No Quittin' Sense* (**Austin**, 1969); and Green, *Ely*. Folksongs expressing black views are from J. Frank Dobie, ed., *Follow de Drinkin' Gou'd* (Austin, 1928). Additional material on Negro religion is contained in Benjamin E. Mays and Joseph W. Nicholson, *The Negro's Church* (New York, 1933); and Murphy, "Segregation Practices in Texas." Social life and recreation are considered in Green,

Ely; Edwin B. Henderson, *The Black Athlete* (New York, 1968); McComb, *Houston*; Brewer, *Dog Ghosts*; Bill C. Malone, *Country Music U. S. A.: A Fifty-Year History* (Austin, 1968); John A. Lomax and Alan Lomax, eds., *Negro Folk Songs as Sung by Lead Belly* (New York, 1936); Ross Russell, *Jazz Style in Kansas City and the Southwest* (Berkeley, 1971); Marvin Kimbrough, "Our Notable Blacks," *Austin*, X (October, 1968), 24-25, 40; Marguerita Cartwright, "Etta Moten: Glamorous Grandmother," *Negro History Bulletin*, XVIII (March, 1955), 137-138; Monroe N. Work, ed., *Negro Year Book* for 1931-1932 and for 1937-1938 (Tuskegee, 1931, 1937); Murphy, "Segregation Practices in Texas"; John Mason Brewer, *Heralding Dawn: An Anthology of Verse* (Dallas, 1936); and Jesse O. Thomas, *Negro Participation in the Texas Centennial Exposition* (Boston, 1938).

Chapter VI: People of Anger and Hope

There is no broad study of black Texans for the period after 1940, though Neil Sapper is preparing a dissertation at Texas Tech University on the period 1930-1954.

For Negro activity in state and national politics one should see Banks, "Pursuit of Equality"; Donald S. Strong, "The Rise of Negro Voting in Texas," *American Political Science Review*, XLII (June, 1948), 510-522; Doris T. Asbury, "Negro Participation in the Primary and General Elections in Texas" (M. A. thesis: Boston University, 1951); Alan Scott, "Twenty-five Years of Opinion on Integration in Texas," *Southwestern Social Science Quarterly*, XLVIII (September, 1967), 155-163; Mildred H. Meltzer, "Chapters in the Struggle for Negro Rights in Houston.

1944-1962" (M. A. thesis: University of Houston, 1963); O. Douglas Weeks, *Texas One-Party Politics in 1956* (Austin, 1957), *Texas in the 1960 Presidential Election* (Austin, 1961), and *Texas in 1964: A One-Party State Again?* (Austin, 1965); Chuck Stone, *Black Political Power in America* (New York, 1970); Murphy, "Segregation Practices in Texas"; Harry Holloway, "The Negro and the Vote: The Case of Texas," *Journal of Politics*, XXIII (August, 1961), 526-556, and "The Texas Negro as a Voter," *Phylon*, XXIV (Summer, 1963), 135-145; James R. Soukup, Clifton McCeskey, and Harry Holloway, *Party and Factional Division in Texas* (Austin, 1964); Clifton McCleskey, *The Government and Politics of Texas* (Boston, 1969); Dan Nimmo and Clifton McCleskey, "Impact of the Poll Tax System on Voter Participation: The Houston Metropolitan Area in 1966," *Journal of Politics*, XXXI (August, 1969), 682-699; Pat Watters and Reese Cleghorn, *Climbing Jacob's Ladder: The Arrival of Negroes in Southern Politics* (New York, 1967); the Addenda to the 1970 reprint of Brewer, *Negro Legislators of Texas*; the *Texas Observer* (Austin), October 28, 1966, July 18, 1969; and daily newspapers.

Local political situations are discussed in Harry Holloway, *The Politics of the Southern Negro from Exclusion to Big City Organization* (New York, 1969), which includes chapters on Houston and Marion County; Herbert H. Werlin, "The Victory in Slaton," *Negro History Bulletin*, XXV (February, 1962), 112-113; Wilhelmina Elaine Perry, "The Urban Negro. . ." (Ph. D. dissertation: University of Texas, 1967), a sociological study of Houston Negroes in the early 1960's; Sarah Beal Watley, "The Power Structure in the Negro Sub-community in Lubbock, Texas "

(M. A. thesis: Texas Tech University, 1970); Stone, *Black Political Power in America;* United States Commission on Civil Rights, *Political Participation* (Washington, 1968); U. S. Departments of Commerce and Labor, *The Social and Economic Status of Negroes in the United States, 1970* (Washington, 1971); *New South* (Spring, 1968, Fall 1969); and the *Texas Observer*, December 19, 1969.

The problems of desegregating public and private facilities are described in Murphy, "Segregation Practices in Texas"; Meltzer, "Struggle for Negro Rights in Houston"; McComb, *Houston*; Perry, "Urban Negro"; Scott, "Twenty-five Years of Opinion on Integration in Texas," *Southwestern Social Science Quarterly*, XLVIII, 155-163; Margaret L. Hartley, "Black Boundaries in Big Texas," *Southwest Review*, XXXVII (Winter, 1952), 68-71; and the *Texas Observer*, April 8, 1960, March 6, 1964, and August 6, 1965.

Violence and law enforcement receive passing mention in several sources. The service of Doris Miller is described in Langston Hughes, *Famous Negro Heroes of America* (New York, 1958). Material on black soldiers in Texas is from Ulysses Lee, *The Employment of Negro Troops* (Washington, 1966). The poem about wartime segregation is from Witter Bynner, *Take Away the Darkness* (New York, 1947). A brief account of the Beaumont riot is contained in Florence Murray, ed., *The Negro Handbook – 1944* (New York, 1944). The Felton Turner case is described in Perry, "Urban Negro." Anti-black police action is mentioned in White and Holland, *No Quittin' Sense*; the *Texas Observer*, November 14, 1958, May 13, 1966; *Civil Liberties in Texas* (Austin),

268

Spring, 1970; and daily newspapers. Information on black policemen and calls for police review boards are from the *Texas Observer*, May 13, October 28, 1966; and *Newsweek*, August 16, 1971. Houston Negroes' image of the police is noted in William McCord and others, *Life Styles in the Black Ghetto* (New York, 1969); and *Newsweek*, May 3, 1971. Henry Allen Bullock discusses the "Significance of the Racial Factor in the Length of Prison Sentences," *Journal of Criminal Law, Criminology, and Police Science*, LII (November-December, 1961), 411-417. Harsh sentences for protest leaders are mentioned in *New South*, (Fall, 1968), and the *Texas Observer*, June 12, September 4, 1970, and daily newspapers. The Texas Southern University "riot" is considered in McCord, *Life Styles in the Black Ghetto*, and in the *Texas Observer*, June 9-23, 1967, July 24, 1970, and daily newspapers. The Carl Hampton affair is described in *Motive*, XXXI (November, 1970); the *Texas Observer*, August 21, 1970, July 30, 1971, and daily newspapers.

The basic study of black economic problems for this period is Jo Ann P. Stiles, "The Changing Economic and Educational Status of Texas Negroes, 1940-1960" (M. A. thesis: University of Texas at Austin, 1966). On agriculture it may be supplemented with Frederic O. Sargent, "Economic Adjustment of Negro Farmers in East Texas," *Southwestern Social Science Quarterly*, XLII (June, 1961), 32-39; and United States Commission on Civil Rights, *Equal Opportunity in Farm Programs* (Washington, 1965). Urban and industrial labor is considered in Carolyn Cott Webber, "The Negro in the Texas Industrial Labor Market, 1940-1947" (M. A. thesis: University of Texas, 1948); Henry Allen Bullock, "Racial

Attitudes and the Employment of Negroes,"
American Journal of Sociology, LVI (March,
1951), 448-457; Murphy, "Segregation Practices in
Texas"; and Ray Marshall, *The Negro Worker* (New
York, 1967). Patrick B. Mullen offers a glimpse of
a new black occupational field in "The Function of
Folk Belief Among Negro Fishermen of the Texas
Coast," *Southern Folklore Quarterly*, XXXIII
(June, 1969), 80-91. The limited black professional
class in 1940 is outlined by Henry Allen Bullock in
"Negro Higher and Professional Education in
Texas," *Journal of Negro Education*, XVII
(Summer, 1948), 373-381. Public employment
problems are discussed in Robert Eli Teel,
"Discrimination Against Negro Workers in Texas:
Extent and Effect" (M. A. thesis: University of
Texas, 1947); United States Commission on Civil
Rights, *For All the People By All the People: A
Report on Equal Opportunity in State and Local
Government Employment* (Washington, 1969); and
the *Texas Observer*, June 28, November 15, 1963,
October 28, 1966. Income and unemployment
figures are contained in James S. Hollingsworth,
"An Analysis of Selected Demographic
Characteristics of the Texas Nonwhite Population"
(M. A. thesis: Texas A & M University, 1964);
McCord, *Life Styles in the Black Ghetto*; United
States Department of Labor, *Manpower Report of
the President* (Washington, 1971); and the *Texas
Observer*, November 15, 1963. The C. C. White
quotation is from *No Quittin' Sense*.

White views on economic discrimination are
described in Henry Allen Bullock, "Some
Readjustments of the Texas Negro Family to the
Emergency of War," *Southwestern Social Science
Quarterly*, XXV (September, 1944), 100-117.
Efforts to overcome black economic problems are

mentioned by Banks, "Pursuit of Equality"; Murphy, "Segregation Practices in Texas"; the *Texas Observer*, June 28, 1963, May 13, 1966, August 9, 1968, September 26, 1969, November 27, 1970; *Together*, XIII (January, 1969); Erbin Crowell, Jr., "HOPE in Houston," *Civil Rights Digest*, I (Fall, 1968), 16-23; and Opportunities Industrialization Center brochures.

Black business problems and developments are discussed in Jacob Thomas Stewart, "Characteristics of Negro-owned and Operated Business Establishments in Houston" (Ph. D. dissertation: University of Texas, 1956); William J. Slaton, "Negro Businesses in Texas," *Texas Business Review*, XLIII (July, 1969), 194-198; Florence Murray, *The Negro Handbook, 1946-1947* (New York, 1947); Jesse P. Guzman, ed., *1952 Negro Year Book* (New York, 1952); Editors of Ebony, *The Negro Handbook* (Chicago, 1966); "A Negro Millionaire's Advice to his Race," *U.S. News and World Report*, September 4, 1967; and daily newspapers.

The drive for equal and integrated education is discussed at length in Banks, "Pursuit of Equality"; Murphy, "Segregation Practices in Texas"; and Stiles, "Economic and Educational Status of Texas Negroes." For information on black schools in the 1940's and 1950's see Henry Allen Bullock, "The Availability of Education in the Texas Negro Separate School," *Journal of Negro Education*, XVI (Summer, 1947), 425-432; Ira B. Bryant, "Vocational Education in Negro High Schools in Texas," *ibid.*, XVIII (Winter, 1949), 9-15; Charles W. Schupack, "A Comparative Study of White and Negro Schools in Fayette and Eight Adjoining Counties" (M. A. thesis: University of Texas, 1953); William M. Pender,

271

"Curriculum and Instructional Problems of the Smaller Secondary Schools for Negroes in East Texas" (Ed. D. dissertation: University of Texas, 1960); and Harry E. Ashmore, *The Negro and the Schools* (Chapel Hill, 1954). Attitudes on school desegregation are described in Scott, "Twenty-five Years of Opinion on Integration in Texas," *Southwestern Social Science Quarterly*, XLVIII, 155-163.

Further information on the pace and process of school integration may be found in William Peters, "Houston's Quiet Victory," *Negro History Bulletin*, XXIII (January, 1960), 75-79; McComb, *Houston*; Urban J. D. Leavitt, "Desegregation and Attendance Zoning in Austin" (M. A. thesis: University of Texas, 1956); Werner F. Grunbaum, "Desegregation in Texas: Voting and Action Patterns," *Public Opinion Quarterly*, XXVIII (Winter, 1964), 604-614; United States Commission on Civil Rights, *Reports* (Washington, 1959, 1961, 1963), *Public Schools: Southern States: Texas* (Washington, 1963), *Staff Report: Public Education* (Washington, 1964), *Title VI One Year After: A Survey of Desegregation of Health and Welfare Services in the South* (Washington, 1966), *Southern School Desegregation, 1966-1967* (Washington, 1967), *Political Participation* (Washington, 1968), *Federal Enforcement of School Desegregation* (Washington, 1969); National Education Association, *Beyond Desegregation: The Problem of Power; A Special Study in East Texas* (Washington, 1970); *New South*, (Winter, Spring, Summer, Fall, 1967); *Texas Observer*, October 28, 1966, March 28, 1969; June 4, July 2, 16, August 13, September 10, 1971; and daily newspapers. Genevieve T. Alexander presents "An Historical

Analysis of Catholic Educational Integration in Texas" (M. A. thesis: University of Texas, 1959).

Desegregation of higher education in Texas is described by Banks, "Pursuit of Equality"; Murphy, "Segregation Practices in Texas"; Marilyn B. Davis, "Local Approach to the Sweatt Case," *Negro History Bulletin*, XXIII (March, 1960), 133-137; Charles H. Thompson, "Separate But Not Equal: The Sweatt Case," *Southwest Review*, XXXIII (Spring, 1948), 105-112; United States Commission on Civil Rights, *Equal Protection of the Law in Public Higher Education* (Washington, 1960); W. Astor Kirk and John Q. Taylor King, "Desegregation of Higher Education in Texas," *Journal of Negro Education*, XXVII (Summer, 1958), 318-323; Earl J. McGrath, *The Predominantly Negro Colleges and Universities in Transition* (New York, 1965); and the *Texas Observer*, March 6, 1964, June 18, 1971. Information on black colleges is presented by Stiles "Economic and Educational Status of Texas Negroes"; Vernon McDaniel, "Negro Publicly-Supported Higher Institutions in Texas," *Journal of Negro Education*, XXXI (Summer, 1962), 349-353; Ronald J. Rousseve, "Teachers of Culturally Disadvantaged American Youth," *ibid.*, XXXII (Spring, 1963), 114-121; *ibid.*, (Summer, 1967), 334; *Civil Rights Digest*, III (Spring, 1970), 16; *Daedalus*, C (Summer, 1971); *New South*, (Summer, 1969); the *Texas Observer,* May 10, 1968, April 9, 1971; and the *Texas Almanac, 1970-1971.* For black students and studies on predominantly white campuses see the *Texas Observer,* May 23, 1969, and black studies or ethnic studies program brochures from the various universities. Efforts to promote minority studies in the public schools are discussed by J.

Reuben Sheeler, "Negro History Week in the Houston Area," *Negro History Bulletin,* XIX (October, 1955), 2; and in the *Texas Observer,* March 28, 1969 . The statistics on black high school and college graduates in Houston are from U.S. Departments of Commerce and Labor, *The Social and Economic Status of Negroes in the United States, 1970.*

Black migration into Texas cities and out of the state is mentioned in James D. Tarver, "Migration Differentials in Southern Cities and Suburbs," *Social Science Quarterly*, L (September, 1969), 298-324; Audie L. Blevins, Jr., "Migration Rates in Twelve Southern Metropolitan Areas: A 'Push-Pull' Analysis," *ibid.*, 337-353; John P. Davis, ed., *The American Negro Reference Book* (Englewood Cliffs, N.J., 1966); and U.S. Departments of Commerce and Labor, *The Social and Economic Status of Negroes in the United States, 1970.* Henry Allen Bullock describes "Some Readjustments of the Texas Negro Family to the Emergency of War," *Southwestern Social Science Quarterly*, XXV (September, 1944), 100-117; and comments on "Spatial Aspect of the Differential Birth Rate," *American Journal of Sociology*, XLIX (September, 1943), 149-155. Negro population concentrations can be seen in United States Bureau of the Census, *U.S. Censuses of Population and Housing: 1960; Census Tracts* (Washington, 1962); Karl E. Taeuber and Alma F. Taeuber, *Negroes in Cities: Residential Segregation and Neighborhood Change* (New York, 1965); the *Texas Observer*, August 27, 1971; and daily newspaper articles.

Jack Dodson discusses "Minority Group Housing in Two Texas Cities," in Nathan Glazer and Davis McEntire, *Studies in Housing and Minority Groups* (Berkeley and Los Angeles,

1960). Ghetto housing problems are also mentioned in U.S. Bureau of the Census, *1970 Census of Population: Texas: General Housing Characteristics* (Washington, 1971); Murphy, "Segregation Practices in Texas"; McComb, *Houston*; and the *Texas Observer*, December 25, 1970. The public housing situation is noted in the United States Commission on Civil Rights, *Report* (Washington, 1959). J. Allen Williams, Jr., described "The Effects of Urban Renewal Upon a Black Community: Evolution and Recommendations," *Social Science Quarterly*, L (December, 1969), 703-712. For information on "Pig City" see Barbara Bryan Taylor, "Voluntary Metropolitan Councils: Lubbock's Adaptation to Changing Urban Needs" (M.A. thesis: Texas Technological College, 1969).

Social attitudes of Houston Negroes are explored in McCord, *Life Styles in the Black Ghetto*; and the *Texas Observer*, June 9, 1967. Henry Allen Bullock used Houston to study race as related to "Urban Homicide in Theory and Fact," *Journal of Criminal Law, Criminology, and Police Science*, XLV (January-February, 1955), 565-575. Bobby Seale describes his Texas youth briefly in *Seize the Time* (New York, 1968). Figures on female heads of households are from U.S. Bureau of the Census, *1970 Census of Population: Texas: General Population Characteristics* (Washington, 1971). James E. Stafford, Keith K. Cox, and James B. Higginbotham interviewed Houston housewives to determine "Some Consumption Pattern Differences Between Urban Whites and Negroes," *Social Science Quarterly*, XLIX (December, 1968), 619-630. The urban folklore of black Texans sheds additional light on their social conditions and thought as described in Roger D.

275

Abrahams, *Positively Black* (Englewood Cliffs, N.J., 1970). Negro leadership is discussed in Perry, "The Urban Negro"; and Gary Cartwright, "The Tin Star State," *Esquire*, LXXV (February, 1971), 95-99, 130-134. The relationship of black and white churches to Negro needs is mentioned in Murphy, "Segregation Practices in Texas"; Watley, "The Power Structure in the Negro Sub-community in Lubbock, Texas"; Boren, *Religion on the Texas Frontier*; Barth, "Negro Presbyterians"; Eckstein, *History of the Churches of Christ in Texas*; Loud, "Methodism and the Negroes," in Nail, *History of Texas Methodism, 1900-1960*, pp. 87-111; and the *Texas Observer*, March 6, 1964, May 13, 1966.

Black newspapers in Texas are noted in Murray, *Negro Handbook--1944* Guzman, *1952 Negro Handbook*; and Editors of Ebony, *Negro Handbook* [1966]. Negro problems with white newspapers are mentioned in the *Texas Observer*, May 23, 1969.

Black athletic participation in Texas and Negro athletes from Texas are mentioned in Murphy, "Segregation Practices in Texas"; Drotning and South, *Up From the Ghetto; The Baseball Encyclopedia* (New York, 1969); Henderson, *The Black Athlete*; and daily newspapers. John Biggers presents some of his works of art in *Ananse: The Web of Life in Africa* (Austin, 1967). Others are mentioned in Lindsay Patterson, ed., *The Negro in Music and Art* (New York, 1967). The leading black literary figure from Texas is the subject of James W. Byrd, *J. Mason Brewer: Negro Folklorist* (Austin, 1967).

A variety of white racial views of the 1950's and 1960's in Texas are described by John Howard Griffin, *Black Like Me* (New York, 1960); Grace

Halsell, *Soul Sister* (New York, 1969); Larry L. King, *Confessions of a White Racist* (New York, 1971); and William Brink and Louis Harris, *Black and White: A Study of U.S. Racial Attitudes Today* (New York, 1967).

Chapter VII: People of Struggle and Progress

For the period 1970–1995, newspapers in Austin, Dallas, Houston, and Lubbock provided much information on topics not yet discussed by historians. Also helpful were articles in magazines such as *Texas Monthly, Texas Outlook,* and *Texas Observer.*

The most important studies of politics are Chandler Davidson, *Race and Class in Texas Politics* (Princeton, 1990); and the chapter on Texas in Chandler Davidson and Bernard Grofman, eds., *Quiet Revolution in the South: The Impact of the Voting Rights Act, 1965–1990* (Princeton, 1994). Ruthe Winegarten, *Black Texas Women: 150 Years of Trial and Triumph,* clarifies women's roles in government. The later chapters in Jim Schutze, *The Accommodation: The Politics of Race in an American City* (Secaucus, 1986), offer insights into Dallas politics.

For legal problems, one should see James W. Marquart, Sheldon Ekland-Olson and Jonathan R. Sorensen, *The Rope, the Chair, and the Needle: Capital Punishment in Texas, 1923–1990* (Austin, 1994); Robert D. Bullard, *Invisible Houston: The Black Experience in Boom and Bust* (College Station, 1987); Nick Davies, *White Lies: Rape, Murder, and Justice, Texas Style* (New York, 1991), on the Brandley case; Frank R. Kemerer, *William Wayne Justice: A Judicial Biography* (Austin, 1991); and Andrew Hacker, *Two Nations: Black and White, Separate, Hostile, Unequal* (New York, 1992).

Information on economic changes and problems may be found in U.S. Bureau of the Census, *1980 Census of Population, Detailed Population Characteristics, Texas* (Washington, 1983); U.S. Bureau of the Census, *1980 Census of Population, Detailed Population Characteristics, U.S.*

Summary (Washington, 1984); U.S. Bureau of the Census, *Poverty in the United States: 1987* (Washington, 1989); and Bullard, *Invisible Houston.* Business developments may be seen by comparing U.S. Bureau of the Census, *Minority-Owned Businesses, Black: 1972 Survey of Minority-Owned Business Enterprises* (Washington, 1974); with U.S. Bureau of the Census, *1987 Economic Census: Survey of Minority-Owned Business Enterprises, Black* (Washington, 1990).

For public schools, one should begin with Glenn M. Linden, *Desegregating Schools in Dallas: Four Decades in the Federal Courts* (Dallas, 1995). See also U.S. Bureau of the Census, *1980 Census of Population, Detailed Population Characteristics, Texas;* and Hacker, *Two Nations.* Additional information on colleges is from the *Chronicle of Higher Education* (December 15, 1982); and *Utmost Magazine* (Fall 1985).

Housing patterns are considered in Dudley L. Poston and Jeffrey Passel, "Texas Population in 1970: Racial Residential Segregation in Cities," *Texas Business Review* 46 (July 1972): 142–47; Sean-Shong Hwang and Steve H. Murdock, "Residential Segregation in Texas 1980," *Social Science Quarterly* 63 (December 1982): 737–48; and *Utmost Magazine* (October 1986). Information on family patterns may be found in U.S. Bureau of the Census, *1980 Census of Population, Detailed Population Characteristics, Texas;* U.S. Bureau of the Census, *1980 Census of Population, Detailed Characteristics, U.S. Summary;* and U.S. Bureau of the Census, *1990 Census of Population, General Population Characteristics* (Washington, 1992).

For religion, see Marvin C. Griffin, *Texas African-American Baptists: The Story of the Missionary Baptist General Convention of Texas* (Austin, 1994); and the *United Methodist Reporter* (June 1980). Some social and cultural activities are discussed in Alan Govenar, *Meeting the Blues* (Dallas, 1988); and *Texas Monthly* (July 1978 and October 1980). Comments on Texas athletes appeared in *Sports Illustrated* (March 7, 1988; June 28, 1991; and July 4, 1994).

Index

Harrison, Benjamin, 74
Harrison County, 67, 77, 78, 136, 155, 176, 201
Harrison County Flag, 54
Harvey, I. H. "Sporty," 226
Haskell, Tex., 137
Hastie, William, 174
Hate crimes, law against, 234
Hawkins, Tex., 161
Hayes, Elvin, 227
Hayes, Rutherford B., administration of, 72
Haynes, Abner, 226
Haywood, Felix, 40, 58
Head start programs, 209
Health conditions, 19, 105
Health facilities, 142
Hearne, Tex., 183
Hearne Academy, 103
Heisman Trophy winners, 246
Hempstead, Tex., 43, 101, 187
Heralding Dawn: An Anthology of Verse, 171
Hill County, 49
Hobby, W. P., 144
Hofheinz, Roy, 182, 185
Hogg, James, 75, 85
Holiness churches, 166
Holmes, Zan Wesley, Jr., 179, 180, 242
Holy Rosary Parish, 108
Homes: loans, 244; ownership, 163, 221. *See also* Housing
Hondo Field, 188
Hooks, Matthew "Bones," 91
Hoover, Herbert, 133
HOPE Development, Inc., 202
Hoskins, Dave, 226
Hospitals, 142, 185
Household of Ruth, 167
Housing, 104, 163, 221, 222, 224, 233
Houston, Sam, 7, 9, 32
Houston, Tex., 8–11, 16, 24, 35, 47, 60, 62, 65, 67, 72, 74, 80, 82, 86, 89, 90, 95, 96, 104, 105, 108, 115, 133–36, 140–42, 144–46, 150, 152, 155, 164, 166, 168, 170, 174, 176–79, 182–95, 199–203, 205, 208, 210, 211, 214, 215, 218–21,

223, 225, 231, 233, 234, 237–39, 243
Houston and Texas Central Railroad, 151
Houston College (Baptist), 103, 160
Houston College for Negroes, 161, 214
Houston County, 90
Houston *Informer,* 139, 145, 170, 186, 214
Houston Museum of Fine Arts, 227
Houston *Observer,* 146
Houston Oilers, 246
Houston Rockets, 246
Humphrey, Hubert, 180
Humphreys, R. M., 90
Huntsville, Tex., 115, 183, 187
Huston-Tillotson College, 217, 243. *See also* Samuel Huston College, Tillotson College

Ikard, Bose, 58
Immigration, 3–5, 7, 8, 12
Impacted area funds, 209
Imperium in Imperio, 106
Independence, Tex., 68
Independent candidates, 73
Independent Voters League, 134, 136
India, ambassador from, 185
Indians, American, 2, 3, 7, 13, 14, 20, 28, 29, 31, 32, 49, 50, 86, 87
Industrial labor. *See* Labor, urban
Insane asylums, 105, 141
Insurance, 244
Inter-denominational Ministers Alliance, 147
Intermarriage, 5, 10, 180, 181; prohibited, 8, 42, 82, 83, 207
International Longshoremen's Association, 93
International Migration Society, 97
International Workingmen's Association, 59
Interracial Congress of 1920, 139

Interscholastic League of
Negro Schools, 159
Interstate Commerce Commis-
sion, 186

Jackson, A. S., 145
Jackson, Maynard H., 136
Jackson, Silas, 91
Jacksonville, Tex., 189, 190, 199
Jarvis Christian College, 161,
217, 243
Jaybird-Woodpecker war, 78
Jeanes Fund, 158
Jefferson, Blind Lemon, 169
Jefferson, Ruth, 224
Jefferson, Tex., 68
Jester, Beauford, 175, 214
Job corps training centers, 201
Joe (slave at Alamo), 6
John (escaped slave), 29
John (slave at Alamo), 6
Johnson, Andrew, 43–45, 56
Johnson, Brit, 49
Johnson, Budd, 169
Johnson, Daniel E., 97
Johnson, Eddie Bernice, 231
Johnson, Jack, 137, 169
Johnson, James S., 103, 104
Johnson, Lee Otis, 191, 192
Johnson, Lyndon, 178, 179, 187
Johnson, Martin, 37
Johnson, Matthew, 192
Jones, Al, 91
Jones, Samuel, 138, 139
Joplin, Scott, 97
Jordan, Barbara, 179, 231
Joseph, Craig, 238
Josephite Fathers, 109
Juneteenth, 39, 65, 106, 167,
168, 245
Justice Department. *See* United
States Justice Department

Kansas, 96
Kavanaugh, Nelson, 4, 10
Kealing urban renewal project,
222
Kelly, James, 91
Kendleton, Tex., 65
Kennedy, John F., 178
Kiddoo, J. B., 56, 57, 62
King, Larry, 228

King, Martin Luther, Jr., 178,
245
King, W. E., 144
Kiowa Indians, 50
Kirk, Ron, 233
Kirk, W. Astor, 215
Knights of Labor, 92, 93
Knights of Pythias, 107, 167
Korean War, 188, 189
Ku Klux Klan, 45, 46, 52, 57,
66, 116, 139, 148, 189, 233,
234
Kuba, Louis, 193
Kwanzaa, 245

Labor, urban, 4, 10, 11, 24, 53,
58–60, 69, 92–96, 149–51,
154, 197–202
Labor unions, 59, 60, 79,
92–94, 149–51, 200
Laborers Union Association, 60
Ladonia, Tex., 160
Laffite, Jean, 14
LaFollette, Robert, 116
Lamar County, 43
Lamar State College, 241
Landownership, 40, 54, 58, 69,
88–90, 147, 148, 153, 155,
156, 196
Language, 100, 101, 156
Lavaca County, 33
Law and order leagues, 143
League of United Latin Ameri-
can Citizens, 183
Ledbetter, Huddie "Leadbelly,"
169
Lee, Sheila Jackson, 231
Legislature, blacks in, 48, 51,
57, 67, 72, 73, 77, 179, 180,
230, 232–34
Leland, Mickey, 231
Lemmons, Bob, 91
Leon County, 78
LeVias, Jerry, 227
Lewis, Carl, 247
Lewis, J. Vance, 144
Liberia, 96, 97
Liberty County, 159
Libraries, 141, 185
Lightner, L. H., 167
"Lily white" Republicans,
74–76, 80

288

290

San Antonio *Advance,* 95
San Antonio *Express,* 138
San Antonio *Zeitung,* 35
San Augustine, Tex., 32, 187
San Jacinto, battle of, 6
San Jacinto County, 181
San Marcos, Tex., 201
Sands, Harriett Newell, 4
Santiago Mountains, 50
School boards, 239, 240
Scott, Emmett J., 95, 96
Screwmen's Benevolent Association, 59, 60
Seale, Bobby, 223
Second Cavalry, 188
Segregation, 42, 63, 81–83, 94, 98, 104–6, 140–42, 163, 164, 184–91, 220, 233, 239–43. *See also* Education
Seguin, Tex., 103
Seminole Indians, 29
Separate state, 106
"Separate but equal," 145
Sepia, 225, 226
Shafter, William R., 88
Share-cropping. *See* Tenant farming
Shenandoah, 16
Sheridan, Philip, 45
Sherman, Tex., 137
Shillady, John R., 144
Shiner, Tex., 190
Shivers, Allan, 176, 177, 206, 207
Shuffer, J. J., 90
Sigler, Henry, 10
Silsbee, Tex., 137
Simpson, Ben, 15
Simpson, L. H., 182
Sisters of the Holy Ghost, 109
Skinheads, 233
Slater Fund, 100, 158
Slaton, Tex., 183
Slaveholders, 17
Slave revolts, 7, 32–34
Slavery, "natural limits" of, 20
Slaves, 13–38; labor, 17–22, 24; legal status, 21, 25, 36; living conditions, 18, 19, 26; punishment, 20, 21; resistance, 27–34; urban, 24–26
Slave trade, 14–17

Small Business Administration, 203
Smith, Al, 133
Smith, Antonio Maceo, 136, 147, 174
Smith, Bubba, 226
Smith, George, 23
Smith, H. C., 37
Smith, Henry, 85
Smith, Henry "Buster," 169
Smith, James, 37
Smith, Lonnie, 174
Smith, Mark, 6
Smith, Preston, 180, 222
Smith, R. L., 90, 148, 149, 153
Smith, Tommie, 227
Smith County, 29
Smith-Hughes Act, 158
Smith Pipe and Supply, 238
Smothers, Clay, 232
Snyder, James, 103
Social life, 21, 25, 65–69, 104–11, 163–72, 219–29, 243–47
Soldiers. *See* United States Army, Militia, Texas National Guard
Sororities, 242
Soul Sister, 228
Southern Association of Colleges and Secondary Schools, 162, 217
Southern Methodist University, 157, 216, 218, 227
Southern Pacific Railroad, 151
South Texas, 207
Southwest Baptist Theological Seminary, 216
Southwest Conference, 216, 226, 227
Spain, and Texas, 1–3, 5, 13, 14
Spiritualist churches, 166
Sports, 106, 168, 169, 210, 216, 226, 227, 246, 247
Stance, Emanuel, 50
Standard Savings and Loan Association, 203
State Board of Control. *See* Texas State Board of Control
State Convention of Colored Men, 1883, 83

291

293